T0305053

Law and Corporate Finance

ELGAR FINANCIAL LAW

Series editor: Takis Tridimas, *Queen Mary, University of London, UK*

This important new series comprises of high quality monographs on a wide range of topics in the field of financial law, hosting work by established authors of international reputation, alongside younger and more emerging authors. The series is synonymous with original thinking and new, challenging research. The subjects under consideration range from financial services law, through securities regulation, to banking law and from financial fraud, through legal aspects of European Monetary Union and the single currency, to the legal workings of international financial institutions.

Law and Corporate Finance

Frank B. Cross and Robert A. Prentice

University of Texas at Austin, USA

ELGAR FINANCIAL LAW

Edward Elgar

Cheltenham, UK • Northampton, MA, USA

Published by
Edward Elgar Publishing Limited
The Lypiatts
15 Lansdown Road
Cheltenham
Glos GL50 2JA
UK

Edward Elgar Publishing, Inc.
William Pratt House
9 Dewey Court
Northampton
Massachusetts 01060
USA

Reprinted 2016

A catalogue record for this book is available from the British Library

Library of Congress Cataloguing in Publication Data

Cross, Frank B.
    Law and corporate finance/Frank B. Cross and Robert A. Prentice.
        p. cm. — (Elgar financial law)
    Includes bibliographical references and index.
        1. Corporations—Finance—Law and legislation—United States.
    2. Corporations—Finance—Law and legislation. I. Prentice,
    Robert A., 1950– . II. Title.
    KF1428.C76   2007
    346.73'0664—dc22

                                                        2006034556

ISBN 978 1 84720 107 2

Printed and bound in Great Britain by the CPI Group (UK) Ltd

Contents

Figures and tables

FIGURES

TABLES

To Indy and Kira

1. The role of the law in corporate finance

This book examines the role of legal regulation in the growth and success of corporations and other business firms. Many companies chafe at the everyday operation of the law, which may seem to frustrate their business plans. Many economists complain that excessive legal regulation and litigation is compromising our economy's competitiveness. While individual instances of unwise and inefficient law doubtless abound, the legal system governing business is vital to economic development, and many of those legal demands to which many businesspersons object are in fact quite beneficial to the economic system. The book examines the theoretical and empirical association of legal regulation and economic welfare, focusing on the basic foundational law, corporate law and securities law. This chapter provides the background for that discussion, reviewing the significance of the financial system to our economy and the nature of legal regulation of that financial system.

The law and its requirements pervade contemporary society. While the scope of the term "law" is not perfectly unambiguous, we use the commonplace understanding of the term. The law represents the rules created and enforced by a nation's governmental authority. The law implies the use of this government authority and power to impose and enforce certain rules. By its nature, this is a constraint on the purely voluntary transactions of a laissez faire market. The legal restrictions placed on the firm are inevitably controversial in a fundamentally capitalist society.

The requirements of the law are of substantial importance to business enterprises. The law regulates the behavior of business in countless ways, ranging from employment law requirements, to environmental law requirements, to antitrust rules, and so on. As this chapter will explore in more detail presently, it is important to remember that the law not only constrains and regulates, it also enables. Nothing is more important to modern business than property law,[1] which ensures investors and enterprises that they will be able to exploit, retain and enjoy the fruits of their labors, and contract law, which ensures that they will have a remedy if the entities that they buy from and sell to every day fail to live up to their promises.

Central to this book are two more specialized bodies of law—corporate law and securities law. In America corporate law is primarily state law. It governs, among other matters, the internal structure of corporate enterprises themselves, dictating how corporate officers and directors must deal with their shareholders and govern the corporation. In the securities law field, there is state, federal and international law, but that emanating from the federal Securities Exchange Commission (SEC) is most important. Generally speaking, securities law not only regulates the major players in the securities industry (brokers, dealers, investment advisers, mutual funds, stock exchanges, and so on), it also regulates transactions in securities issued by business. Over time federal securities statutes and SEC rules regarding mandated corporate disclosure, fraud prevention, and, more recently, corporate governance have imposed a heavy burden upon American companies and foreign companies who access American capital markets. Being a public company fully exposed to SEC regulation requires audit fees, registration fees, directors' and officers' insurance premiums and other costs that have averaged roughly US$2.5 million per year for public companies (much more for the biggest companies, less for the smallest), and those numbers are rising rapidly in light of the requirements of a recent federal law, the Sarbanes-Oxley Act of 2002, that companies pay particular attention to their internal controls. Every company must consider whether the benefits that the enabling aspects of federal securities law allow them to garner justify the added costs. This book will, in part, attempt to make that calculus with a focus not on individual companies but on the economy as a whole.

This examination is particularly timely, for the law of corporate governance and securities regulation has been quite prominent on the business pages of recent newspapers. The multibillion dollar collapse of Enron produced considerable litigation against and liability for its officers, directors and advisers, both civil and criminal. Although Enron is the poster child for an era of corporate fraud, the financial scandals at WorldCom, Global Crossing, Adelphia, Tyco, Rite-Aid, Lucent Technologies, Nortel, HealthSouth and others indicate that problems have been more widespread than a few bad apples at one Houston energy company. The fact that fully 10 percent of New York Stock Exchange (NYSE)-listed companies materially restated previously published financial statements between 1997 and 2002 sends the same signal.[2] Accounting firms and investment banks judged complicitous in the corporate scandals suffered severe consequences. Perhaps the most prestigious accounting firm in the world, Arthur Andersen, blinked out of existence in the wake of the Enron scandal. Investment bank Citigroup paid US$2.65 billion to investors' claims that it helped disguise WorldCom's accounting fraud and the Department of

Justice filed criminal charges against Merrill Lynch for assisting Enron in manipulating its financial reports. Martha Stewart was convicted for obstruction of justice associated with her alleged insider trading. The New York Stock Exchange's chairman and chief executive officer, Richard Grasso, was charged with taking excessive remuneration for his position. Richard Scrushy, CEO of HealthSouth, has been sued for blatantly making up the numbers in financial reports for that company. The CEO of Rite Aid was sentenced to eight years in jail for his part in a long-standing securities fraud. Enron executives have pled guilty or are on trial as the book is sent to press.

The corporate scandals of the past decade illustrate the relevance of the law to our market economy in corporate governance. Clearly, the law is not a panacea, for it failed to prevent the scandals. Some suggest that the law is even counterproductive, creating more economic harm than it forestalls by, for example, leading investors to assume that the law will protect them from fraud, causing them to fail to be fully vigilant in making investment decisions. Of course, the frequency and severity of such dishonest corporate behavior might have been far greater in the absence of such laws. Finding proof of such counterfactuals (what would have happened in the absence of the law) is impossible, but the net economic effect of corporate and securities law can be analyzed and measured to some extent.

LAW, FINANCIAL DEVELOPMENT AND ECONOMIC GROWTH

The basic rationale for any law is typically grounded in notions of justice and fairness, and the law historically has reflected a sense of corrective justice. The law may enforce contracts among parties simply because it is unfair or unjust for one party to guarantee some action, thereby induce some favor from another party, and then renege on its own promise. Similarly, the branch of law known as torts operates to correct behavior that is regarded by society as unjust, such as the theft of property or the use of physical violence against another's person. The law of both contracts and torts recognizes exemptions to these general rules, though, when justice so dictates, for example, the right to use physical force in self-defense. The law reflects other values as well, such as the classic liberal value of individual freedom of choice.

While the law at least seems to be grounded in notions of fairness, these questions are not the central concern of this book. We are concerned with the role of the law in advancing the economic wellbeing of a society, with its associated benefits. Some argue that this is the true essence both of the law and of fairness itself. Louis Kaplow and Steven Shavell of Harvard Law School have argued prominently and at length that the general welfare and not questions of distributional fairness provide the philosophical justification for the law.[3] This is a well-ventilated philosophical debate that is beyond the scope of our book. Instead, we simply analyze the extent to which the law advances the general welfare of a society by facilitating economic growth, which is surely of some value even if it is not the only relevant value.

Some might challenge the value of national economic development, arguing that distributional fairness (whether as corrective justice or egalitarian distribution) should trump overall societal economic wellbeing. The two objectives are not instrinsically in conflict, though. Most would prefer a fairly distributed large economic pie to a fairly distributed small economic pie. Others might argue that greater material wellbeing has no intrinsic philosophical value and may not even enhance utilitarian goals such as human happiness.[4] Those who make this argument, though, are typically those who enjoy a world of substantial material wellbeing. Those suffering the conditions of poverty seldom demean the value of greater material wealth. Moreover, there is considerable evidence that, in general, greater material wellbeing does have a payoff in human happiness.[5] In any event, it seems clear that people generally place value on their material welfare, so this is our primary concern when analyzing the impact of law, especially corporate law and securities law, upon the economy.

Although economists commonly emphasize the efficiency value of private ordering in advancing society's welfare, they have increasingly emphasized the role of the law in creating societal wealth. For example, Douglass North helped create the "New Institutional Economics" and won a Nobel Prize for his historical investigation of the importance of legal institutions in promoting economic growth.[6] He declared that the effectiveness of enforcement of property rights and contracts is . . . "the single most crucial determinant of economic performance . . ."[7] This economic theory is centrally grounded in analysis of transaction costs, which this book will discuss extensively. The availability of reasonably reliable enforcement of appropriate legal rights, by a government with power and economies of scale, is of considerable benefit for enhancing economic development. This economic analysis is now widely, if not universally, accepted. The law can serve to facilitate capitalism, which in turn facilitates economic growth.

One crucial aspect of capitalism's facilitation of economic growth is found in the ability of individuals to invest their resources productively, profiting the individuals while simultaneously benefiting others by creating employment opportunities and societal wealth. Companies need cash or other financial resources in order to grow, to purchase new production equipment and raw materials or hire workers. New companies, without profits to reinvest, have a particular need for this outside source of financing. Well developed markets help ensure the efficient allocation of financing. They direct resources to uses where the return is greatest and permit greater specialization. They also facilitate the diversification of investment and consequent reduction of investor risk. Additionally, financial markets contribute to the development of innovations and new technologies.

Bank lending is one possible source of outside cash for companies needing investment resources. Another common source is equity markets, with individuals or organizations buying stock in the companies. The two systems of financing are very different, with banks receiving more assurance of repayment with interest while equity investors take an ownership interest, with its associated greater level of risk and reward. While the two sources of finance should be complementary and mutually reinforcing, different nations have different patterns of reliance on bank vs equity investment and different degrees of participation in equity markets. The value of stock market financing was disputed for some time, when East Asian countries' success was fueled by bank lending and cross-ownership arrangements for investment, without much in the way of freely traded national equity markets. Some even suggested that the developed equity markets of countries such as the United States could be counterproductive, by creating demands for short-term performance at the expense of long-run economic success. Time has not been supportive of these theories, though, and empirical research generally bears out the importance of developed and free equity markets, although the incentive for short-term focus by American companies remains a concern.

Considerable research indicates that greater national financial development produces greater national economic welfare. Various scales are available for measuring financial development and its economic effect, and studies have used different measures but fairly consistently found a significant positive association. Much of this research has compared different countries. A 1993 study by Robert King and Ross Levine considered the development of 80 countries over a 30-year period in the second half of the twentieth century. Their research found that certain measures of countries' general financial development were closely associated with the subsequent economic growth rates of those countries.[8]

A subsequent study by Levine and Zervos went further and investigated the effects of factors such as stock market liquidity, size, volatility and integration with world capital markets.[9] They used the measures for 47 countries to examine the effect of markets on economic growth, productivity and other factors, after controlling for other political and economic factors.

They found that stock market liquidity and development of the banking system were significantly associated with contemporaneous and future rates of economic growth, productivity growth and capital accumulation. Other measures, such as market volatility, showed no countervailing negative effect on economic growth.

The World Bank and other organizations have also investigated the importance of financial markets for social welfare, using other methods. A study examined firm-level data in 30 countries to test the number of firms with high growth rates that could be attributed to the availability of long-term financing. The proportion of successful companies was higher in countries with a more liquid stock market (and better legal systems).[10] Another study looked at the size of a country's credit and equity markets relative to its overall GDP and its allocation of capital.[11] Efficient capital allocation was significantly correlated with more developed financial sectors. Countries with relatively advanced financial systems better channeled investment to growing industries and away from declining industries. Other research found that the government opening up financial markets in emerging nations was associated with significant increases in real economic growth.[12] There is substantial empirical support for the intuitively obvious claim that better developed financial markets providing capital to business are associated with greater economic growth.

While the association between a nation's financial development and its economic growth is strong, some have questioned the direction of the causality. They note that financial development may just be a leading indicator of economic growth, rather than its underlying cause.[13] While this is possible, research has sought to establish directionality by considering legal origins and other instrumental variables to demonstrate that certain legal rules are associated with financial development, which in turn translates into substantial economic growth.[14]

The directional causality is further confirmed by historical research. The earliest decades of the United States saw remarkable growth, both in the general economy and in the financial markets. The financial development meant that capital from Europe flowed into the United States, providing entrepreneurs and more established businesses with access to financing. When this history was subjected to statistical testing, the results clearly indicated that the financial development was a contributing cause to the nation's great economic growth of the time.[15] Studies of the historical evidence from other countries further confirm the association, finding that financial development was a causal determinant of the industrial development of the United States, United Kingdom, Canada, Sweden and Norway.[16] Other historical analyses ascribe the eighteenth-century success of Scotland and Belgium to the remarkable efficiency of their capital markets at the time. The linkage between financial markets and economic growth has been demonstrated theoretically and empirically. Consequently, strategies for enhancing financial markets have become an important part of plans to further economic growth for the benefit of the society as a whole.

Much of the research in this area compares countries with different financial markets, but some research examines financial development within particular countries. One study found that the better a country's level of financial development, the more rapid was the growth of those industries that were typically dependent on external financing.[17] Financial markets are linked, to some degree, with corporate governance. The quality of corporate governance among a nation's companies contributes to their economic success. Some empirical research found that European companies with better corporate governance had better earnings-based performance ratios than did those with poorer governance.[18] A study in Russia found a strong correlation between corporate governance quality and firm valuation.[19] A broader McKinsey study found that OECD-based companies with better corporate governance had a higher valuation by 10 percent or more.[20] It is well-established that thriving financial markets contribute to national economic success and that quality corporate governance contributes to thriving financial markets. The key policy question involves the degree to which the law can facilitate quality corporate governance and financial markets.

Today financial markets in the United States operate subject to extensive legal regulation and control. The connection between some measure of legal protection and development of financial systems is increasingly recognized. The legal protection of property rights enables financial development, even in the absence of external sources of finance.[21] Basic legal protection of property and contract enforcement facilitates the use of more external finance. Laws governing corporations and securities transactions can sometimes do likewise. These effects are a primary focus of this book. Before analyzing the possible association of such categories of law with financial development and economic growth, it is important to summarize the nature of the basic, corporate and securities laws that govern American firms.

THE STRUCTURAL LAW OF THE FIRM AND THE SECURITIES MARKETS

As discussed above, American firms are subject to a plethora of laws of all types. Our focus is on laws that relate directly to equity investment. Bank lending of course is another source of investment capital that can substitute for equity investment, albeit sometimes with less efficiency. Consequently, we will consider the role of banks at only a secondary level. Our primary concern is the legal regulation of business enterprises and of equity markets.

The role of law and its effect on the firm can be analyzed at three distinct levels, which have developed chronologically. At the most basic level is the simple existence of some sort of legal system. This involves the existence of some adjudicatory authority, such as courts, who apply some basic garden variety law, such as that of property, contract and tort. The second level is the more complex law of corporations (or other forms of business enterprise). Corporate law establishes the authority for incorporated entities and typically provides regulatory rules for their operation. The third level is that known as securities law. While corporate law generally governs the relationship between the corporation and its existing shareholders, securities law, at least an important branch of it, goes further and creates additional rules for the sale of securities to outsiders. These corporate and securities laws overlap in various ways but also supplement one another in their coverage and demands. They seldom conflict, though when they do the federal statutory provisions (generally securities law) generally take precedence under our Constitution. This became particularly salient recently when some provisions of the Sarbanes-Oxley Act of 2002 federalized aspects of corporate governance that had previously been largely within the bailiwick of the states.

Legal rules may be separated between categories of the "empowering" and the "restrictive." While this distinction is simplistic, it provides a useful framework for analyzing particular rules. Empowering legal rules are those that facilitate voluntary private ordering and wealth creation. Thus, the recognition of legal rights in private property provides some assurances that better enable individuals to use that property productively and create wealth and later transfer rights in the property. Such laws are not empowering for the property thief, but they empower property owners. Similarly, the law of contracts can be considered empowering, insofar as its assurances of government enforcement facilitate additional voluntary transactions among individuals. The basic law also contains restrictive rules, however. Restrictive rules seem to interfere with the voluntary private ordering of transactions. A restrictive rule will prevent certain types of transactions, such as contracts made by minors or those otherwise considered incapable of binding themselves. The common law of fraud is a restrictive rule that rejects enforcement of some privately negotiated agreements.

While economists are generally skeptical of restrictive rules, it is possible that they actually empower private transactions and thereby facilitate economic growth. A key question this book will address is whether securities fraud rules ultimately diminish economic growth by restricting freedom of contract between sellers of securities and investors, or actually encourage economic growth by encouraging investors to "play the game" because they are confident it is a fair one. In some circumstances, even restrictive rules may be empowering. Ulysses restrictively lashed himself to the mast in order to empower himself to safely hear the Sirens sing. Financially, firms may accept restrictions on their freedom in order to access the benefits that those restrictions bring in the market.

Affiliated with the debate between empowering and restrictive legal rules are disputes over the source of law. Within the English tradition, the basic law is judge-made common law, developed on a case-by-case basis, using past decisions as guiding precedents to be adapted to particular case facts. Most of the relevant corporate and securities law, by contrast, is legislative in origin. Some economists are more skeptical of such statutory rules, believing that the case-by-case development of common law is likely to be more efficient and enable more individual choice, while legislative creations are more likely the product of rent-seeking interest groups. This belief has found some empirical support in research comparing nations that use the common law with nations from the civil law tradition, where all law is of legislative origin.[22] Nations relying upon the common law tend to have greater economic success. The distinction made in this research is a questionable one, though, because the practical difference between the application of common and civil law is not so great as often portrayed.

Although the American law of securities fraud has its genesis in statutes, those statutes are largely patterned after the common law of fraud and the details of that law are almost entirely developed by judges, in the fashion of the common law. Nevertheless, there remains a significant academic dispute over the wisdom of the relative apportionment of lawmaking authority between the judiciary, the legislature and executive branch administrators who may establish rules interpreting legislation. Judge-made law is often considered to be empowering and relatively efficient, in contrast to the more restrictive rules found in statutes. On the other hand, the judges who make common law typically do not view efficiency as an important value to advance.[23] This dispute, like the question of restrictive legal rules, will be a recurring theme in the book.

Still another related issue is the level of government applying the law. The basic law and corporation law are for the most part state law, while securities law is largely federal, New York Attorney General Eliot Spitzer's recent activism notwithstanding. Some economists tend to favor state laws as more efficient. Laws at the state level provide some additional choice for firms, who may select the states whose laws they prefer. This distinction may also be exaggerated. On the one hand, the globalization of business enables some choice between national rules, and on the other the ability to choose among states is limited somewhat by the extraterritorial application of those rules. Conflicting state laws may also interfere with the efficient operation of a national economic market, as evidenced by the conservative assault on state product liability laws, and their case for national tort reform. More centrally, the creation of some overriding universal laws, which seem to limit choice, may be efficient for reasons discussed further in Chapter 2. Before entering into the contested disputes over the substance of the law and the manner of its implementation, it is important to address in somewhat more detail the fundamental structure of the basic, corporate and securities laws of this country.

Basic Law

The American basic law has a lineage of centuries and English common law dates back as far as 1066. The central elements of this traditional English common law are those of property, contract, and tort. These legal rules developed as empowering structures that liberalized the feudal system of the time and provided individual rights against even the King. Other nations, even those that do not have common law, have a very similar structure of basic legal rules. Civil law nations rely on a statutory code, not case-by-case judicial evolution of the law. The civil law codes also create systems of property, contract and tort law and, in practice, permit considerable judicial implementing discretion, as in the common law. The basic law creates or at least recognizes certain interests in property as legal rights which the government will protect. It recognizes certain negotiated transactions as contracts which the government will enforce.

The basic background law is procedural as well as substantive and the procedures are arguably as important as the substance of the law. A legal system requires defined decisionmakers, such as judges, the structural power to enforce the decisions of those adjudicators, and some sort of procedure for the adjudication. These structures and procedures are essential to give effect to the substantive requirements of the law. Without them, the substantive rules are just words. The Soviet Constitution, for example, explicitly granted many rights that were unavailable in practice, because the courts did not enforce them against the government.

It is not enough for a nation to have appropriate substantive legal requirements; it must also possess institutions such as a judicial system that can effectively implement those requirements. Legal systems may fail for many reasons. If the courts are not independent, they will do the self-interested bidding of their master (usually the executive branch) and fail to apply the law in any reasonably objective manner. If the courts are corrupt and can be bribed, they cannot be counted on to enforce the legal rules and provide essentially no law to society. If the courts are starved for resources, they may be unable to resolve legal disputes, no matter how well-intentioned the judges are. In India, for example, the judicial system is enormously backlogged. There is a clear correlation between limits on India's national wealth and the time required for its judicial system to enforce a judgment.[24] One-third of the pending Indian cases began over ten years earlier; one famous dispute among neighbors took 39 years to resolve and outsurvived both the parties. If it is inordinately costly for a party to invoke legal protections, their value will be correspondingly reduced. Creating a law or even a legal system does not guarantee its effective functioning.

While numerous things may go wrong with the operation of the law, the legal system functions well in many nations. No national system is flawless but many legal structures operate successfully, given the inherent limits of humans and institutions. Those who enter contracts, in developed nations at least, have a reasonable expectation that they can effectively exercise their legal rights should the contract be breached. Numerous property, contract, and tort cases are filed and typically promptly resolved. Although most cases are voluntarily settled and not tried, this settlement takes place "in the shadow of the law" and is therefore somewhat contingent upon the function of the legal system. In countries such as the United States, the functioning basic law is largely taken for granted.

The existence of the basic law is generally presumed, at least in our modern society. All nation-states have some legal adjudicatory system to resolve disputes. A true state of anarchy is unknown in the world today. However, the basic law is not universal in scope and should not be presumed to be a necessary situation for all human dealings. Some transactions are by nature held to be illegal (for example, extortion or dealing in illegal substances), and the law typically refuses to govern them. The world of these transactions is often called the "underground economy", which operates alongside but outside the reach of the law. Every nation in the world has a substantial underground economy, though its size varies considerably among countries.[25] Moreover, some actors voluntarily place their legal transactions outside the rule of the law. Robert Ellickson has demonstrated how cattle ranchers in California have chosen to resolve various disputes, such as trespassing cattle, by private norms rather than using the available legal system.[26] Lisa Bernstein has documented how diamond merchants have opted out of the legal system for resolution of their transactional disputes.[27] Even parties that use the law in transactions may not use it completely. Many agreements provide for some private dispute resolution mechanism, such as arbitration, rather than courts. Many contracts are intentionally left incomplete with open-ended terms that the parties intend to work out voluntarily. Thus, the reach of the law is not universal even in contemporary America. The most significant fact, though, may be that the vast majority of businesses voluntarily choose to subject themselves and their transactions to legal governance, even when they have the choice of opting out of the legal system.

The legal system appears to offer some value for private transactions. Basic law is generally considered to be empowering in its recognition of property rights and its enforcement of contracts, and such law is typically embraced by even conservative economists. The fundamental law of torts is generally restrictive in nature, but this nature is limited, to at least some degree, by the parties' ability to "contract around" the law of torts. This ability to opt out of various tort law provisions is not universal and is the source of some economic controversy regarding the tort/contract boundary. While there is an ongoing debate over the intrinsic efficiency of common law rules, the basic law, at least the common law heritage, is generally considered to be, on balance, efficient and empowering.

Corporate Law

Corporate law presents a somewhat more complex case. The basic law of corporations is generally applauded by even conservative economists as essentially empowering.[28] The establishment of limited liability entities such as corporations enables individuals to invest their resources productively, while simultaneously limiting the magnitude of the economic risk faced by those individuals. A corporate investor places his or her invested funds at risk but is generally free from liability with respect to his or her other resources. The issuance of corporate shares also facilitates the free and efficient transferability of ownership interests. This structure offers a considerable benefit, both to the individual and to society as a whole. Corporate law is primarily created by states, not the federal government. It is legislative in origin but provides a considerable judicial role, especially when, as in Delaware (which is far and away the most important jurisdiction), it is largely implemented by the courts of equity rather than those of law. However, some aspects of corporate law receive criticism as unduly restrictive, and some economists have argued that companies be given greater ability to choose among corporations laws or to contract around their terms.

Corporate law is sometimes conceived as contractarian in nature, as a deal between the individual and the government. There is no natural right to the limited liability protections offered by corporate law. From a fairness perspective, the law may be presented as the government's bestowal of the benefit of limited liability in exchange for an agreement to abide by certain rules of corporate governance, laid down in the details of the corporate code. The contractarian justification cannot truly explain the law of limited liability, however. Some limited liability entities, such as limited partnerships, are governed by a law that is much less restrictive than the law of corporations. More centrally, the authorization of limited liability entities is justified by the benefits they provide society, not the private benefits to investors. Limited liability encourages investment, which encourages the development of new production, with new employment opportunities and overall economic growth to the benefit of society. Consequently, corporate law's requirements should be determined by their effect on the overall societal welfare not as some sort of payback in exchange for liability protection. Corporate law, thus, should stand or fall on its benefits to society.

The essence of corporate law is the limited liability it provides and the rules for corporate governance that it establishes. To obtain the benefits of limited liability for investors, corporations must abide by the rules of corporate governance law. Entities choose to incorporate within a particular state and thereby become subject to that jurisdiction's distinct corporation law. In the United States, virtually all companies incorporate either in Delaware or in their own home state. The incorporation process requires the development of articles of incorporation (sometimes called the corporate charter or certificate), which is publicly available and becomes something like the constitution that governs the corporation. The law places some requirements on the contents of these articles but allows considerable discretion.

The key aspect of corporate law is the allocation of power in the company among the shareholders, the board of directors, and corporate officers. Basic authority rests with the owner/shareholders, who can elect or remove directors and make certain very fundamental decisions for the company. The directors supervise the corporation's business, though, and shareholders are not authorized to tinker with the day-to-day managerial decisions (except indirectly through changes on the board). The directors hire the officers who generally manage the company on a day-to-day basis.

Much of corporate law is directed at the potential agency problems that arise between the shareholders who own the corporation and the directors and officers who manage it. The directors and officers are the agents of the shareholders and should operate it in their principals' best interest. Like all individuals, though, directors and officers have their own self-interests that they may advance at the expense of the shareholders' interests. Corporate law aims to restrain the self-interested actions of directors and officers through the imposition of certain fiduciary duties that are owed to shareholders. Unconstrained, directors and officers might act selfishly or foolishly. The duty of loyalty is to ensure that officers do not enrich themselves at the expense of shareholders, by self-dealing or usurping the business opportunities of the corporation. The duty of care is to ensure that officers work to benefit the company and its shareholders and are not lazy or cavalier. These duties are defined and to some degree limited by corporate law, and doctrines such as the business judgment rule can limit the role of the law in corporate governance. Nevertheless, the law of fiduciary duties is of central importance in corporate law.

In some circumstances, the self-interest of officers and directors may directly interfere with efficient, voluntary transactions. Occasionally, large investors seek to acquire entire companies and are willing to pay shareholders a substantial premium to obtain a controlling interest in those companies. The target company's officers, realizing that their lucrative employment is at stake, may design an elaborate system of "poison pill" defensive measures that functionally prevent their shareholders from engaging in a voluntary transaction with the acquirer. Corporate law has responded to such situations with legal rules subjecting the officers' anti-takeover decisions to a higher than normal level of scrutiny, in order to protect the interests of the shareholders from the desire of insiders to entrench their positions at the expense of the shareholders.

Corporation law typically contains a series of specific requirements. Although the law grants substantial discretion to the directors to decide to pay or not pay dividends, it does insist that dividends not be paid when the corporation will be rendered insolvent and creditors necessarily harmed. To protect voting rights, corporation law has comprehensive rules governing the process and substance of shareholders' voting for director candidates and major structural changes in the company. The law sets out certain minimum requirements for the composition and processes of corporate boards. Companies must hold regular meetings of their shareholders for the election of directors and certain major corporate decisions. Shareholders are given some legal right to inspect the corporate books and records. If the shareholders are forced to divest their ownership interests, such as in a merger, there is a right to a judicial appraisal of share value to ensure that the shareholders receive fair compensation. Corporate laws also provide for the end of the corporation's life and dissolution. For the most part, these specific rules also address potential agency problems and serve to assure shareholders that they will be treated fairly, consonant with the more general fiduciary requirements.

State corporations law is not the only authorization for business enterprises. States also authorize sole proprietorships, general partnerships and limited liability entities such as limited partnerships, limited liability partnerships (LLPs) and limited liability companies (LLCs). These organization forms tend to have fewer legal restrictions than the corporation. Partnerships are governed by a partnership agreement and the law allows for more private ordering in this context. Corporate law, like partnership law, provides a basic set of default rules that can be substantially altered by the owners so long as third parties are not prejudiced. Partnership law provides somewhat more scope for entities to opt out of the legal rules, though. For corporations, many of the default rules are also binding rules.

For example, in Delaware, individual directors may be exculpated from personal liability for breach of the duty of care, though not for breach of the duty of loyalty. Corporations also may buy insurance to protect their directors and officers from the risk of great personal liability. Companies may issue preferred shares, which are largely ruled by their certificate of designations, even when its terms conflict with some aspects of the general corporate law. Thus, corporate law, while it contains multiple restrictive components, allows considerable space for private ordering of investment contracts.

Securities Law

Securities law is even more controversial from the perspective of economists. Much of securities law, and certainly its more controversial elements, is fundamentally restrictive. Securities law, for example, often prohibits corporate officers from profiting from their positions by trading in securities based on their nonpublic information about their companies, a practice known as insider trading, and securities law also creates liability for material misrepresentations of fact made by companies and their officers and directors. The restrictive provision of securities law relating to fraud claims has been considered excessive by some and their potency was reduced by legislative action in the 1990s, under the Private Securities Litigation Reform Act of 1995 (PSLRA) and the subsequent Securities Litigation Uniform Standards Act of 1998 (SLUSA). Perhaps ironically, these were federal level legislative actions directed in part at judicial interpretations regarded as excessively restrictive. The fundamental disclosure, fraud prevention and governance requirements of securities remained intact following PSLRA and SLUSA, however, notwithstanding significant academic and political criticism.

US federal securities law developed during the Great Depression, following the stock market crash of 1929, as is described further in Chapter 4 (though various state regulations of securities preceded this federal legislation). The initial major federal law in the area was the Securities Act of 1933. This law basically governs the initial issuance of securities, rather than transactions in already-issued shares. To issue such shares, a company must either file an extensive registration statement with the SEC and transmit to potential investors a prospectus, or must find an exemption in the statute. The 1933 Act and SEC rules promulgated pursuant to it have detailed and extensive disclosure requirements, including provision of audited financial statements. The Securities Act also created a system of liability when the registration statement and prospectus contain materially false information. Like most other federal securities laws, the 1933 Act's provisions are enforced both by the government and by private parties. The SEC can bring civil proceedings to punish violations. The Department of Justice can file criminal charges against intentional violators. And often investors who have suffered economic injury as a consequence of violations of the Act may bring civil damage actions against various wrongdoers.

Securities law was soon expanded with the passage of the Securities Exchange Act of 1934, which created the Securities Exchange Commission. While the Securities Act focused on the initial sale of securities to the public, the Exchange Act focused on the secondary securities markets. Realizing that companies sell new securities only infrequently and therefore would seldom be required to file 1933 Act registration statements, Congress provided that major public corporations would have to file periodic reports to keep investors updated as to their financial status. As those requirements have evolved, they now require public companies to file annual, quarterly, and periodic statements with the SEC as well as to transmit annual reports to shareholders. Again, the 1934 Act and attendant SEC rules contain comprehensive and detailed disclosure requirements. One of the major controversies of securities law, and one that we shall address in this book, is whether the disclosure requirements of the 1933 Securities Act and the 1934 Exchange Act are necessary. Many argue that issuers and investors would voluntarily bargain to an optimal level of disclosure in the absence of these disclosure requirements. Another relevant question is whether the rules require too much disclosure and disclosure of the right kind.

The 1934 Exchange Act does much more than require periodic reporting by public companies. It contains a broad antifraud provision, section 10(b), now supplemented by SEC Rule 10b-5, that punishes false statements and misleading omissions made in those periodic reports and in other communications by issuers, their officers and directors, and other buyers and sellers of securities. As with the 1933 Act, violations of section 10(b)/Rule 10b-5 can be punished by SEC administrative and civil actions, by criminal charges brought by the SEC and by investors' civil damage actions, often brought as class actions. These lawsuits are quite controversial. Many believe that they represent a terrible abuse of the legal process and profit primarily plaintiffs' attorneys at a tremendous cost to public companies and their officers, directors, auditors, attorneys and investment bankers who are often defendants in such lawsuits. As noted earlier, the PSLRA of 1995 and SLUSA of 1998 were passed to make it harder for plaintiff

investors to win such suits and for plaintiffs' attorneys to profit from bring-
ing them. The controversial nature of the suits is highlighted by the fact that
some observers have concluded that the PSLRA and SLUSA sent a
message to officers, directors, auditors, and others that they did not need to
take securities fraud liability seriously and indirectly created the atmosphere of abuse that spawned the Enron debacle and related scandals. Such
suits may be considered either a destructive abuse of the law or a necessary
supplement to enforcement by an often undermanned SEC.

The Exchange Act also registers and regulates stock brokers and dealers.
It regulates stock exchanges and authorizes self-regulation of securities
professionals by organizations such as the New York Stock Exchange
(NYSE) and the National Association of Securities Dealers (NASD). The
Exchange Act also includes provisions that affect corporate governance by
creating disclosure requirements for proxy solicitations when shareholders
are asked to vote for directors at annual meetings and for extraordinary
corporate transactions such as mergers at special meetings. False statements made in proxy solicitations, whether by incumbent directors, insur-
gent shareholders, or others, can be punished under section 10(b), if
intentional, and under section 14(a) even if only negligently made.

The Exchange Act was amended by the Williams Act in 1968 to regulate
tender offers, in which a corporate acquirer makes a public offer to all corporate shareholders of a target company to buy their shares, usually in
order to take control of the company. An unregulated tender offer provides
opportunities for abuse, including coercion by the offering party, manipulation and self-dealing by management of the target company, and undue
secrecy and fraud by all parties involved. As in so many other areas, federal
regulation of tender offers requires full disclosure of relevant information,
punishes fraud, and adds various substantive and procedural provisions
designed to rationalize the process and give target shareholders an opportunity to digest the disclosed information.

The insider trading provisions of the Exchange Act are particular controversial. Corporate directors, officers and other insiders will be privy to
some nonpublic information about the company that could significantly
affect the value of its stock. This information might involve imminent
events such as a lucrative merger offer, positive or negative government
action, or a major technological breakthrough that will likely result in a
valuable patent being granted. Buying or selling shares on this inside information can enable the insider to reap large gains after the information
becomes public and the market price reacts to disclosure of the information. In most cases, this practice was not illegal under the basic law or corporate law but under the Exchange Act, such trading by insiders on
nonpublic information is usually unlawful.

Section 16 of the Exchange Act presumes that officers, directors, and holders of 10 percent of a public company's stock will use inside information in their trades. Therefore, actual use of inside information is not an element of liability. Nor is an intent to violate the law. Section 16 forces these company insiders to report their trades in their company's stock and to forfeit to the company "short-swing" profits that occur when a sale at a higher price follows within six months of a purchase at a lower price (profit gained) or a sale at a lower price follows within six months of a sale at a higher price (loss avoided). Six months is presumed to be the limit of the useful life of inside information. The Sarbanes-Oxley Act accelerated the filing of section 16 reports by insiders.

The broader and more controversial form of insider trading regulation derives from section 10(b)'s general antifraud provisions. Its coverage is broader in that one need not be an officer, director, or 10 percent shareholder in order to be potentially liable. However, in contrast to section 16, one must be conscious of material, nonpublic information at the time of the trade. Liability under this form of insider trading is extended to four categories of defendants. First are company insiders who work for the company whose shares are traded; they need not be top officers or directors. Second are temporary insiders who receive material, nonpublic information from the company for a business purpose, such as investment bankers who are hired by an acquirer to raise money in an as yet unannounced tender offer for the stock of a target company. Third are misappropriators, who essentially convert the material, nonpublic information to their own use in breach of a fiduciary duty owed to the source of that information. Finally are tippees who receive information from a tipper (a company insider, temporary insider, misappropriator or other tippee) who is passing the information along in breach of a duty not to trade. Tippee liability is imposed to ensure that tippers cannot profit indirectly by trading through friends, relatives, and others.

Securities law does not typically concentrate so much on the agency problems and fiduciary duties that are the focus of much corporate law. Instead, it focuses on transactions and protects individuals who are not yet shareholders and therefore not yet entitled to fiduciary protection. This generalization is not universally true—insider trading securities law, for example, hinges on the violation of some fiduciary duty by an insider. Furthermore, and as noted earlier, the Sarbanes-Oxley Act federalizes a substantial part of corporate governance law in an attempt to blunt corporate fraud. To minimize abuse of the agency relationship, Sarbanes-Oxley accelerates section 16 filings, prohibits companies' loans to their officers, prevents officers and directors from selling their company's shares during pension black-out periods that keep lower-level employees from selling, and forces officers to forfeit performance-based bonuses and profits from sales of stock that occur because of inflated securities prices that later fall when the company must restate its financial statements due to misconduct. In addition, the Sarbanes-Oxley Act seeks to require directors to obtain reliable information upon which to make their decisions and to deny top officers "plausible deniability" when frauds occur by requiring companies to install, document, and test internal control procedures. Via the stock exchanges, the SEC has required listed companies to have a majority of their directors be independent, and all directors on crucial board committees—audit, compensation, and nomination—to be independent. Sarbanes-Oxley requires that the audit committee, not the CEO or CFO, choose, monitor, and compensate their public company's outside auditor.

OVERLAP

The Sarbanes-Oxley Act's incursions into the realm of corporate governance demonstrate that the basic law, corporate law, and securities law overlap and intersect, as is most clearly illustrated by the law of fraud. The basic law has long recognized fraud claims which have the following basic elements: (1) a false statement of fact (or sometimes an omission); (2) made with knowledge of its falsity, or *scienter*; (3) reasonable reliance on the false statement by the plaintiff; and (4) consequent damages. This law is general and applies in numerous contexts, including corporate investments. Many common law fraud cases are brought in the United States and many succeed, but proof of *scienter* may be quite difficult, and proof of reasonable reliance may also prove troublesome. In some contexts, false factual statements may be actionable with a lower standard, such as negligent misrepresentation, but these contexts are limited ones.

Corporate law generally does not have a distinct law of fraud, but its law of fiduciary duties overlaps the law of fraud. Fraudulent behavior directed toward a company's shareholders will typically violate the fiduciary duties of loyalty, due care or disclosure. Fiduciary law has various advantages over the law of fraud for the prospective plaintiff. It has a much relaxed standard for *scienter*, extends to actions that are not misrepresentations and therefore require no reliance, and in some circumstances even shifts the burden of proof to the defendant to justify his or her actions. Corporate fiduciary law also allows large groups of shareholder plaintiffs to join together in a single lawsuit, which provides efficiency benefits and may strengthen the chance of success. This law does have one major procedural obstacle, however. In general, these breaches harm the corporation and, in general, shareholders can recover only derivatively for the reduced value of the corporation. Unless the board is clearly biased or displayed no reasonable business judgment, such a derivative action requires that the potential plaintiff shareholder first make a demand on the board, which may choose not to pursue even a legitimate legal claim, as not being in the corporation's best interests. Fiduciary law is also limited to the existing shareholders of a company (and not necessarily all of them), so a number of injured parties may be unable to sue. A purchaser of stock generally has no corporate law remedy for fraud that occurred prior to the purchase.

Securities law has its own laws of fraud, the elements of which, as noted above, roughly trace those of the common law. The key fraud provision is found in section 10(b) of the Exchange Act, and it adds some additional requirements to the common law elements of fraud, such as the necessity that the fraudulent statement be made in the context of the purchase or sale of securities (such that those who fail to buy or sell due to fraud cannot sue). Section 10(b) also adds a more rigorous requirement that the false statement be material. The law of securities fraud has relaxed other common law elements, though. Under the traditional common law, a plaintiff must have seen or heard the statement and directly relied on it. Under contemporary securities law, a plaintiff can sue for fraud without having read or directly relied on the statement, because the fraud presumably was read and relied on by others and incorporated in the market price of the stock under the efficient market theory. This presumption of reliance enables vast numbers of investors who have never relied upon, read, nor even seen corporate misstatements to proceed via a class action which may produce extremely large total damages. Such class actions are less available under the common law because of the individualized reliance requirement. With the reliance presumptions of securities law, the common questions of falsity and *scienter* predominate, so the class action device may be available. Securities law also functionally strengthens the law of fraud because the securities laws have such extensive disclosure requirements. The many disclosures create more opportunities to sue for false statements or for omissions, when the disclosures contained only "half truths." Securities law also provides potential liability for fraud through market manipulation that may not directly involve a misrepresentation of fact. The Securities Act of 1933 also contains some provisions that are relevant to securities fraud, which have much more relaxed standards of proof but are also much more limited in their scope.

The common law, corporate law and securities law of fraud thus overlap in part but have distinguishing attributes as well. These alternative paths generally strengthen legal protections, because a plaintiff may avail himself or herself of whatever legal regime offers the best chance of success and may usually sue on any or all theories simultaneously. The various approaches are aimed at combating different problems and, for plaintiffs, the more laws mean the more potential paths for litigation success. Critics may argue that these different legal theories are too much, more than necessary to prevent objectionable fraudulent practices. If so, the laws could waste resources in litigation and deter reasonable corporate practices that offer economic benefits. This issue is at the heart of the book. There is some inevitable tradeoff between legal restrictions and free choice, but it is not necessarily the case that freer choice is inevitably the economically superior option.

The economics of basic, corporate and securities law are explored in much greater detail in the remaining chapters of this book. We will analyze, both theoretically and descriptively, how those laws operate. In the process, we will suggest that the distinction between empowering and restrictive rules is not so discrete as it might facially appear. Many of the same economic justifications for the most basic legal rules of property and contract law can be extended to justify restrictive corporate and securities laws. Legal rules that seem superficially restrictive may in fact have a substantial empowering effect, which furthers voluntary private transactions, even though they simultaneously preclude some such voluntary deals. In many cases, such restrictive rules may have a net empowering effect that promotes transactions, even as they may obstruct some voluntary contracts. This book examines that effect, first theoretically and through the lens of the history of legal regulation of firms. Following this analysis, we perform an empirical analysis of the effects of this legal regulation, which builds on the existing studies of this effect. Finally, we evaluate numerous prominent proposals for legal reform in the US law of corporate governance and securities regulation. The fact that law may enhance financial development and economic growth does not imply that every particular legal requirement has this effect, and some laws may be counterproductive. The last chapter of the book examines whether these proposals for law reform have merit.

So, in general, we will be asking whether corporate law and securities law have, on balance, a beneficial economic effect. We will also explore whether those laws are best administered primarily at the state, national, or even international level. One aspect of that exploration will be whether regulatory competition is a better approach than regulatory cooperation.

OUTLINE OF CHAPTERS

The second chapter of this book examines the economics of these legal rules from a classical economic perspective. The economic justification for legal institutions revolves around transaction costs. In the absence of the law, private parties may face considerable risk in transactions, which require some measure of trust in contracting parties. In order to ameliorate the level of this risk, parties may incur considerable transaction costs. These individuals must identify exchange partners, define the terms of the exchange, monitor the partner's compliance with those terms, and enforce the terms if compliance fails. The costs affiliated with this process may be considerable. When the amount of these costs surpasses the net benefits of the exchange itself, those benefits must be forgone. Without state enforcement of economic rights, "high transaction costs will paralyze complex production systems, and specific investments in long-term exchange will not be forthcoming."[29] Hence, reducing transaction costs is central to promoting mutually beneficial economic exchanges.

Although legal systems are typically justified by reference to justice or fairness, for economists it is the reduction of transaction costs that justifies the costs of legal institutions and rules. Leading economists, such as Ronald Coase and Oliver Williamson, have explained how the relative costs of undertaking transactions can explain why businesses organize themselves into firms rather than simply being a web of contracts and why the law can facilitate the efficient transactions of individuals and firms. When a business trades goods for money, it obviously has production costs associated with those goods but it also has transaction-related costs. These transaction costs may be great, exceeding the actual production cost of the goods. Indeed, as society has become more complex, it has been estimated that the transaction cost sector has grown to represent more than 50 percent of the entire US economy.[30] In this circumstance, the minimization of those transaction costs can be of great importance.

One primary virtue of the law, including the basic law, corporate law, and securities law, is in its ability to reduce transaction costs. By providing a reasonably predictable and effective system for the enforcement of transactional commitments, plus a set of relatively uniform default rules, the law can considerably reduce the costs for investors for each individualized transaction. Information disclosure requirements, such as those found in securities law, can have a similar effect in controlling investigatory costs for particular investments. Governmental legal regulation can also increase costs, though, and may increase transaction costs, so one cannot automatically presume the economic benefit of any and all government action. This chapter analyzes why the US law governing the firm and investments are often efficient.

The third chapter goes beyond the classical economic perspective to draw upon the findings of human psychology. The classical model relies on human "rational choice," which suggests that individuals will choose wisely the action that is in their best interest. In the economic context, the model suggests that individuals will make the choice (such as the investment) that offers the most lucrative benefits, after calculating probable risks, prospects, and associated costs of action. The rational choice paradigm is convenient for modeling and surely contains some element of truth. People generally prefer more money to less, all other things being equal, and will make the choice that provides more money. However, the rational choice model may fail to account for human frailties. Investors are not calculating robots and they may be influenced by various irrational factors in their choice. A mountain of experimental psychological research has identified some of these irrational factors, which may produce a systematic distortion of random decisionmaking, not just random mistakes.

Our knowledge of these psychological influences on human decision-making can help inform our choice of efficient legal and financial systems. To the extent that people have systematic psychological biases or use potentially unreliable psychological shortcuts called heuristics, the law can help offset these features and nudge markets toward more efficient, fair outcomes. In the absence of any such effect, market participants will enter into unwise, inefficient transactions that benefit neither themselves nor society more broadly. While all humans, including government regulators and judges, are subject to these cognitive limitations, it may be possible to design structures that minimize their effects, and the corporate and securities laws can represent just such structures.

The fourth chapter of the book examines in more detail the history of legal regulation of the firm in the United States. The basic legal system of property, contract, and tort predates the American Revolution, as the United States employed the traditional practices and precedents of English common law, and these laws provided some governance for business of the era, including the development of fiduciary law. State corporate law traces its origins to the earliest days of our nation, and much of the early law restricted the activities that corporations could undertake. Delaware passed an empowering corporate law in 1899 that allowed companies much greater freedom in designing their certificates and provoked a wave of reincorporation in that state. Since that time, Delaware has sought a balance of empowering and restrictive rules and maintained its status as the preeminent state of major incorporations in the United States.

The story of the development of federal securities law forms a central part of the history in this chapter. For most of American history, the nation had successful markets in corporate securities without any governing federal securities law. The Securities Act and Exchange Act were promulgated in the 1930s, to respond to particular patterns of behavior that were considered abusive. The requirements of securities law have developed considerably since that time, though, under the implementing actions of the SEC and the development of the law in court decisions. Two constant themes of federal securities regulation have been that fraud is bad and that greater disclosure is good. A focus of this book will be upon whether those two guidelines have produced good or ill for America's financial markets and economic wellbeing. The recognition of a private right of action over and above government enforcement, enabling investors to bring their own suits, considerably enhanced the impact of securities law, though these private actions have been quite controversial and allegedly contrary to the welfare of securities markets.

The fifth chapter of the book embarks on an empirical study of the effect of the law on financial markets and economic wellbeing. This association has now been the subject of various economic cross-country studies, using many different dependent and independent variables, which has generally shown a positive effect for the legal system and particular legal rules. While these studies make a persuasive case for the value of the law, they have been conducted by economists and have not successfully captured legal variables. In many cases, they have used overly simplistic binary variables for the law, or have ignored legal procedure for legal substance, or vice versa.

We do not replicate this considerable and impressive past research but seek to build upon it. Our empirical analysis uses some of the same variables as in prior studies but adds variables to better capture the substantive and procedural features of national legal systems. The chapter seeks to integrate the findings of the prior research by incorporating its various independent variables (the different measures of legal governance of the firm) and dependent variables (the different measures of financial and broader economic outcomes). The chapter demonstrates how various legal requirements, including some of the restrictive requirements, have a positive impact on various measures of economic wellbeing.

The sixth chapter of the book turns to contemporary academic and political controversies regarding the proper legal regulation of firms. In the wake of the financial scandals discussed above, the public has often demanded greater legal regulation of companies, as reflected in legislation such as the Sarbanes-Oxley Act. By contrast, a number of conservative academics have made more rigorous economic arguments for the value of less regulation of corporations and securities markets, in the interest of enhancing financial markets. We analyze these recommendations, based on the theory and empirical findings of the prior chapters.

Most of the proposals involve greater market choice for companies or investors, based on the presumption that restrictive statutory requirements limit valuable exchanges. These proposals include:

- the legalization of insider trading on nonpublic information, so that companies can contract with their officers and directors and allow such trading, if they choose, as a form of compensation for their insiders;
- the ability to contract around fraud or other restrictive laws, so that a contracting party may voluntarily choose to forego the right to sue over being defrauded in the transaction;
- the deregulation of corporate issuers and others associated with selling shares in securities markets, in favor of some minimal threshold regulation of investors;[31]
- the creation of competition among states in the requirements of securities laws, supplanting federal securities law;[32]
- the ongoing vigorous debate over the effect of the recently adopted federal Sarbanes-Oxley Act, strengthening internal protections against opportunism.

We can offer no conclusive answers to these controversies. Our final chapter does explain how the case for these reforms is not so clear, from an economic and behavioral perspective, as is sometimes presented. Because even restrictive laws can facilitate contracting and economic growth, one cannot presume that the elimination of such legal restrictions is economically beneficial. We analyze these proposals from the theoretical and empirical perspective of the preceding chapters.

The laws governing the firm have seen considerable academic investigation, especially in recent years. One interesting and ironic development can be seen from this investigation. The theoretical economic analysis has generally questioned the current state of the law as too extensive and restrictive and argued that the law's role should be limited. By contrast, the empirical economic analysis has fairly consistently demonstrated a beneficial role for greater involvement for the law, including some of the particular provisions that have been criticized by the theoreticians. The latter findings must call some of the theoretical prescriptions into question. The remainder of this book reexamines those theoretical claims, as well as the empirical analyses, in hopes of producing a more coherent analysis of legal regulation of the firm and its relative benefits or detriments for societal welfare.

NOTES

1. *See* Hernando de Soto, THE MYSTERY OF CAPITAL (2000).
2. Eugene Spector, *Fraud Made Easy*, NAT'L L.J., September 25, 2002, at A17.

3. *See* Louis Kaplow & Steven Shavell, FAIRNESS VERSUS WELFARE (2002).
4. *See e.g.*, Gregg Easterbrook, THE PROGRESS PARADOX (2003). Easterbrook emphasized that Americans were steadily growing much richer in material terms, but this trend was accompanied by increased dissatisfaction with their lives.
5. *See* Michael R. Hagerty & Ruut Veenhoven, *Wealth and Happiness Revisited: Growing National Income* Does *Go with Greater Happiness*, 64 SOC. INDICATORS RES. 1 (2003).
6. *See e.g.*, Douglass C. North, INSTITUTIONS, INSTITUTIONAL CHANGE AND ECONOMIC PERFORMANCE (1990).
7. Douglass C. North, *Institutions and Economic Performance*, in RATIONALITY, INSTI-TUTIONS AND ECONOMIC METHODOLOGY 245 (Uskali Maki, Bo Gustafsson, & Christian Knudsen eds. 1993).
8. *See* Robert G. King & Ross Levine, *Finance and Growth: Schumpeter Might Be Right*, 108 Q. J. ECON. 717 (1993).
9. *See* Ross Levine & Sara Zervos, *Stock Markets, Banks, and Economic Growth*, AM. ECON. REV. 537 (1998).
10. *See* Asli Demirguc-Kunt & Vojislav Maksimovic, *Law, Finance, and Firm Growth*, 53 J. FIN. 2107 (1998).
11. *See* Jeffrey Wurgler, *Financial Markets and the Allocation of Capital*, 58 J. FIN. ECON. 187 (2000).
12. *See* Geert Bekaert, Campbell R. Harvey, & Christian Lundblad, *Emerging Equity Markets and Economic Development*, NBER Working Paper #7763 (June 2000).
13. *See* R.G. Rajan & Luigi Zingales, *Financial Dependence and Growth*, 88 AM. ECON. REV. 559 (1998).
14. *See* Ross Levine, *Law, Finance, and Economic Growth*, 8 J. FIN. INTERMED. 8 (1999).
15. *See* Peter L. Rousseau & Richard Sylla, *Emerging Financial Markets and Early U.S. Growth*, NBER Working Paper #7448 (December 1999).
16. *See* Peter L. Rousseau & Paul Wachtel, *Financial Intermediation and Economic Performance: Historical Evidence from Five Industrialized Countries*, 30 J. MONEY, CREDIT & BANKING 657 (1998).
17. *See* R.G. Rajan & Luigi Zingales, *Financial Dependence and Growth*, 88 AM. ECON. REV. 559 (1998).
18. *See* Rob Bauer, Nadja Guenster, & Roger Otten, *Empirical Evidence on Corporate Governance in Europe: The Effect on Stock Returns, Firm Value and Performance* (October 23, 2003).
19. *See* Bernard Black, *Does Corporate Governance Matter? A Crude Test Using Russian Data*, 149 U. PENN. L. REV. 1231 (2001).
20. Carlos E. Campos, Roberto E. Newell, & Gregory Wilson, *Corporate Governance Develops in Emerging Markets*, MCKINSEY ON FINANCE 19 (Winter 2002).
21. *See* Simon Johnson, John McMillan, & Christopher Woodruff, *Property Rights, Finance and Entrepreneurship*, Stanford Law and Economics Olin Working Paper No. 231 (March 2002) (studying Eastern European countries after the fall of communism and finding that property rights were sufficient to support necessary investment from retained earnings).
22. *See e.g.*, Rafael La Porta, Florencio Lopez-de-Silanes, Andrei Shleifer, & Robert W. Vishny, *Legal Determinants of External Finance*, 52 J. FIN. 1131 (1997).
23. Jonathan Baron & Ilana Ritov, *Intuitions About Penalties and Compensation in the Context of Tort Law*, 7 J. RISK & UNCERTAINTY 17, 32 (1993).
24. *See* World Bank, WORLD DEVELOPMENT REPORT 2002: BUILDING INSTI-TUTIONS FOR MARKETS 123 (2002).
25. *See* Friedrich Schneider & Dominik Enste, *Shadow Economies: Size, Causes, and Consequences*, 38 J. ECON LIT. 77 (2000).
26. Robert C. Ellickson, ORDER WITHOUT LAW (1991).
27. Lisa Bernstein, *Opting Out of the Legal System: Extralegal Contractual Relations in the Diamond Industry*, J. LEGAL STUD. 21 (January 1992).
28. *See* Frank H. Easterbrook & Daniel R. Fischel, THE ECONOMIC STRUCTURE OF CORPORATE LAW 2 (1991).

29. Thrainn Eggertsson, ECONOMIC BEHAVIOR AND INSTITUTIONS 317 (1990).
30. *See* John Wallis & Douglass C. North, *Measuring the Transactions Sector in the American Economy*, in LONG TERM FACTORS IN AMERICAN ECONOMIC GROWTH 121 (S. Engerman & R. Gallman eds. 1986).
31. *See e.g.*, Stephen Choi, *Regulating Investors Not Issuers: A Market-Based Proposal*, 88 CAL. L. REV. 279 (2000).
32. *See e.g.*, Roberta Romano, *Empowering Investors: A Market Approach to Securities Regulation*, 107 YALE L.J. 2359 (1998).

2. The economics of the law and corporate finance

Legal regulation is always subject to economic questions, because laws typically interfere in some manner with private choice and potentially beneficial private transactions. When the law prohibits certain behaviors, or requires certain behaviors, or penalizes certain behaviors, it can prevent private parties from employing (or eschewing) those behaviors, even when both parties to a transaction believe the behaviors to be to their benefit. In addition, legal compliance adds its own costs to market transactions, as private parties must investigate the law and take sometimes costly steps to comply with the law and bear costs associated with the enforcement of that law. Consequently, free market economists are commonly dubious of the law's value. However, in many cases there is a strong case for the economic value of the law, including the corporate and securities laws, which will be discussed in this chapter.

Understanding the economic value of law begins with the concept of trust. Every business deal requires some element of trust in the transaction's other party. Some transactions, such as hiring a babysitter to look after one's children, involve a great deal of trust. Even a straightforward exchange of goods for money, though, involves some measure of trust. The person acquiring the goods typically trusts the seller's assurances that the goods are as represented—functioning as expected and not unreasonably hazardous, among other concerns. Even the seller paid in cash must have some trust that the currency is not counterfeit. Parties trust their transactional partners not to take unfair advantage of their circumstances. Oliver Williamson called taking advantage of a business partner "opportunism."

Trust is fundamental to commercial transactions. The extent of the necessary trust will vary, of course, by the nature of the deal. An immediate exchange of goods for money requires less trust than other types of transactions. A person lending his money to be repaid over time must repose a great deal of trust in the borrower, as must an investor. Various circumstances affect the amount of trust entailed by a deal. A buyer may place more trust in a seller who is well known to the buyer. The risks of trust may also be mitigated by investigation. Research into the seller's background and reputation and goods can all reduce the risk of trusting. This research is a form of transaction cost, though, which adds to the cost of the bargain and will be discussed below in greater detail. Absent blind trust, a party must undertake the costs of investigating the trustworthiness of a potential partner. Market transaction costs include "costs of information, bargaining/negotiation over transactions, contracting (formal or informal), monitoring and enforcement of agreements, and search and information costs."[1] The virtue of legal regulation comes largely from a reduction in these costs.

THE BASIC LAW AND TRUST

One potentially positive function of the basic foundational law of property, contracts, and torts is the facilitation of transactions that rely on trust. While the law cannot guarantee that a business partner is trustworthy, it can penalize him for being untrustworthy. If a party breaches a contract, by failing to perform or providing inferior goods, the other party may sue for the breach and recover damages. If a party engages in fraud to induce a transaction, the other party may sue for damages, perhaps including punitive damages, or may sue to rescind the contract altogether (and in many courts still receive punitive damages). While litigation is costly and unpleasant, the important feature of the law is its deterrent effect. If individuals know that they will be liable for untrustworthy behavior, and therefore cannot benefit from untrustworthy behavior, they are less likely to be untrustworthy.

While the story of legal reinforcement of trust is a standard one, some have argued that this benefit of the law is mythical and that the law instead destroys the trust necessary for private transactions, interfering with the economy. Robert Putnam's well-known work, *Bowling Alone*, argues that the growth of law in America and the pressure to "get it in writing" have undermined the basic level of interpersonal trust in our society.[2] Lawyers are said to induce mistrust and suspicion in their clients. The law also enables unwarranted lawsuits against even trustworthy parties, as the law may be a tool for opportunistic behavior. Outside the litigation context, some businesspersons "accuse lawyers of impairing the trust and cooperation needed for a successful alliance" and therefore "often admit lawyers to negotiations as late as possible and even then minimize their role."[3] The law and lawyers are said to undermine the nation's "social capital," the degree to which citizens are both trusting and trustworthy in their dealings.

Social scientists have fueled the claim that the law interferes with the trust-facilitating business relationships. A political economist, Michael Taylor, argued that apparently altruistic cooperation could develop without the law and would decay in the presence of the law.[4] He claims that it is anarchy that engenders trust and effective government that destroys trust. Management researchers have studied the association of legalization of trust and found some evidence that legal formalization of relationships may erode trust.[5] Some scholars have contended that use of the law signals to parties that "they are neither trusted nor trustworthy to behave appropriately without such controls," thus leading to a spiral of legalization and mistrust.[6] Researchers from other fields, including law, political science, and sociology, have suggested that legal restrictions could crowd out trusting behavior.

The case against the basic law of contracts has been made by reference to relational contracts, which are exchanges where parties have declined to rely on legal contract protections. Rather than working out detailed terms, the parties to these relational contracts choose to work out any disagreements that arise through some conciliatory process, in order to maintain their relationship. Sociologists have argued that this relational contract process is really the essence of most business dealings.[7] They have argued that trustworthiness can only be demonstrated in the absence of binding agreements. In these contracts, mutual trust supplants the need for legal governance of the transaction. In the United States, even relational contracts exist in the shadow of the law, where the parties could still sue for at least gross breaches of contract, but some argue that voluntary cooperation can eliminate the need for any legal intervention. They may even argue that the law interferes with the relational trust of such contracts, contrary to the interests of the parties.[8]

One can easily see some benefits to relational contracts, as rushing to the courts over every minor breach is surely inefficient. In some countries, such extralegal contracts are commonplace. Groups ranging from very small traders in Mexico to bankers in Japan contract informally without any legal formalities.[9] Some business categories, such as diamond merchants, have essentially removed themselves from legal governance in favor of their own private system.[10] These examples might seem to demonstrate that the law is not necessary to create the trust necessary for business transactions and may even be counterproductive. Evolutionary psychologist Matt Ridley maintains that the government's legal regulation of trade has had "mostly disastrous results."[11]

At face value, however, the theoretical criticism of the law seems implausible. Consider that airlines are closely regulated for safety and additionally face basic tort liability for negligence. It seems very unlikely that people would place more trust in flying if planes were utterly deregulated and the airline industry had no liability risk for accidents. The value of the law's protections can be plainly seen in the commonality of contracts that are not purely relational. Parties typically choose to reduce their significant agreements to formal legal terms, oftentimes detailed and voluminous. The law does not compel them to take this action. This is a voluntary choice, presumably taken because it is more efficient and enables transactions that might otherwise be foregone. At this level, the law merely provides market participants with another choice for arranging their deals.

Long-term contracts, such as investment contracts, are very trust-intensive. Investors are highly vulnerable to opportunism, placing their funds in the hands of others. Consequently, such investors are unlikely to take the risks of investment absent a great deal of trust. If the investor were extremely famil-iar with a manager of his or her money, perhaps as a relative, such trust may be innate. In other circumstances, the investor would have to establish this level of familiarity by researching the manager's character. Such research would involve an examination of the nature of the business and the manager's past business history, an investigation that could be quite extensive and difficult, demanding considerable transaction costs. We explore the value of the law in enhancing trust and reducing these transaction costs, examining in sequence the effects of the basic foundational law, corporate law, and securi-ties law.

THE SIMPLE ECONOMICS OF LAW AND TRUST

The above critique of the effect of law on trust should be considered very naïve. It assumes that individuals will be openly trusting of others, without any self-protection, and that others will inevitably prove trustworthy. Investments are transactions where performance is not simultaneous but may be greatly delayed. Absent simultaneity, the first performer runs the risk that the second performer will fail to perform.[12] In this situation, without legal protections, the first performer can rely only upon trust.

It is simply not realistic for a person to be so trusting, automatically and without evidence. If individuals are rational, they will not be blindly trust-ing of others but will take care to protect their own interests. Taken from a conventional economic perspective, the trust associated with business transactions involves a one-sided form of the famous Prisoner's Dilemma. If both sides of a deal are honest and carry out their promises, both profit to some degree. However, if one side of the deal is dishonest and steals the consideration from the transaction, providing nothing in return, the dis-honest party may profit greatly, while the trusting party loses.

Figure 2.1 illustrates the problem with a simple matrix. In this scenario, one party has the choice of whether to enter some form of investment con-tract or not. The other player has the choice of whether to honestly perform or to opportunistically steal from the investor. No legal restrictions

	Honesty	Opportunism
Invest	2,2	–2,4
Don't Invest	0,0	0,0

Figure 2.1   Prisoner's dilemma of investment

influence either decision. In this figure, the first number represents the gain or loss for the investor, the second figure the gain or loss for the other party. In this simplified model, the investor has no opportunity to cheat and the estimated payoffs are artificially set (though the exact numbers do not dictate the results, so long as the relative relationship is not altered).

If there is no contract, neither party sustains any economic effect, hence the result of 0,0. If the contract is performed successfully, each gains from the exchange in the amount 2,2. If the investor invests and the other party is opportunistic, the investor is a net loser of its investment (−2), while the opportunistic party is a big gainer (4). The best strategy for the non-investor party, in this single play scenario, is to be opportunistic. Of course, the investor realizes that the preferred strategy for the other party is to be opportunistic, which causes a loss to the investor, so the investor, in antic-ipation of this opportunism, has a dominant strategy of not investing in the first place. Of course, people do sometimes invest even in the absence of any legal protection and others are honest, by nature, even though oppor-tunism might offer them greater returns. However, if honesty is not rewarded by an economic system, opportunism will be more common and investment will be risky and less frequent. Consequently, the greatest soci-etal loss from uncontrolled or undeterred opportunism is not in the costs of the opportunism itself, the greatest loss lies in the transactions that do not occur, because of fear of rational opportunism that prevents the risk of transactions.

The possible escape from this Prisoner's Dilemma involves the prospect of repeated interactions. In the above figure, the opportunistic party gets a one-shot gain of 4 but presumably no future investments from the investor, as he will be shunned as an untrustworthy business partner. An honest party, by contrast, may gain a series of repeated investments, yielding benefits of the gains from trade (2) times the frequency of these repeated investments, which might seem to be a more lucrative strategy than that of one-shot opportunism. Consequently, the investor would see that the better strategy for the other party was honesty, to induce a string of repeated investments, and would therefore risk the investment.

The effect of repeated transactions does not truly cure the Prisoner's Dilemma, however. At a formal level, economists have demonstrated that the repeat transactions theory depends on infinite repetition of these transactions. Otherwise, "cooperation will unravel from the end."[13] There would always be an incentive for opportunism in the final transaction, which would deter investment in the final transaction, which would in turn create the incentive for opportunism in the penultimate transaction, which would in turn deter investment in that transaction, and so on back to the original transaction. Thus, rational game theory calls the reliance on repeat transactions into question.

There are other problems with the repeated transaction solution as well. The first problem is the artificial presumption that the opportunistic party cannot engage in repeated transactions with even higher payoffs. Even if the opportunist is shunned by the first investor, he or she may find other "suckers." In a very small community, one or two instances of gross opportunism might prevent a party from doing any future business. However, in a larger, more anonymous, community, the individual might succeed in a series of multiple lucrative opportunistic transactions, reaping the benefit of 4, every time the honest party would reap a benefit of only 2. For example, consider the serial con-men who have flourished over time, selling everything from snake oil to shares in uranium mines and other penny stocks.

Nobel Laureate George Akerlof analyzed this point in his famous article, *The Market for Lemons*.[14] He shows how in purely private ordering bad products, such as used cars, can drive out good products, in cases where sellers have more information on product quality than do buyers. Likewise "dishonest dealings tend to drive honest dealings out of the market."[15] The consequences of this phenomenon are not limited to the dishonest dealings themselves. In a dishonest market, there will be far fewer transactions and those that occur will be at a higher cost.

Inevitable detection problems also undermine the repeated transactions answer to the Prisoner's Dilemma. Opportunism need not be gross and immediately obvious. A party might engage in more subtle opportunism that took some time to discover, which would enable the party to reap the benefits of a good reputation and consequent repeat transactions and also some benefits of opportunism. A manager might "cook the books" and make it appear as if he was honest, when he was not. Even with honest accounting, if a corporation suffers adverse results, it may be unclear for some time whether they were simply the consequence of random chance or opportunism and whether the results are likely to continue in the future. In addition, an opportunistic party might succeed in maintaining anonymity, behind a corporate shell or other entity, so that investors are unaware that they may be dealing with a party who has a track record of dishonest, opportunistic behavior. The parties who are best able and most likely to engage in opportunism may be precisely the same ones who are best able and most likely to cover up this behavior, in order to continue profiting from it.

These detection problems are greater than they might first appear. The above discussion has presumed that the existence of opportunism was clear, and parties only had to take the time to discover which parties had behaved opportunistically. In practice, though, the opportunistic party can try to cover its tracks, and it may even try to shift the blame to the other party, claiming that the innocent party was truly the opportunistic one. If the party succeeds, it will accrue the benefits of both opportunism and reputational benefits. The claims of a lawsuit are commonly met with counter-claims alleging that the plaintiff was the party who truly breached the contract. A key benefit of an effective legal system is the sorting out of the claims and the identification of the true opportunistic party. In this manner, the legal system does not replace but can significantly enhance the effectiveness of reputational sanctions. Without such a system, parties would have to bear the considerable expense of conducting their own private mini-trials to identify untrustworthy parties before the fact. This investigation itself would seem to evidence suspicion and mistrust, before the relationship even began.

The claim that the law undermines or crowds out trust is naïve about the inherent goodness of human nature and relies on largely undemonstrated assumptions. The discussion of the nature of business trust is also too sim-plistic, as if the issue were only "trust" or "not trust." In real business rela-tionships, the more relevant question is "To what degree should I trust?" Entities may make sensitive proprietary information available to others, evidencing trust, while simultaneously retaining various protections for their rights, evidencing some measure of distrust. Business research indi-cates that typical relationships contain a blend of trust and distrust.[16] The law enables parties to trust, without trusting absolutely and retaining some protection against opportunism. In addition, businesses have various potential partners and must decide not just to trust but also whom to trust, among the alternatives. The law can facilitate both these decisions involv-ing how much to trust and whom to trust.

Without the law, investors have to rely upon their own private investiga-tion of investment quality and negotiate protection for their future inter-est. Investment contracts are particularly ill-suited to such efforts. It is more difficult for investors to inspect a business than a physical good. The costs of the investigation may be considerable and the efficiency of securities markets may depend on the ability of investors to be passive. Investors benefit from diversifying their portfolios but with added transaction costs for each additional potential investment, such diversification can become quite expensive. To the extent that the law can reduce the need for such investigation or facilitate inexpensive investigation, it can enhance capital markets.

The development of capitalist economies in post-communist states offers a valuable test case for the role of law in market transactions. Research in the relatively new economies of Eastern Europe has demonstrated that law and trust are complementary rather than antagonistic. The researchers surveyed the effect of the law and legal institutions on the success of commercial transactions and considered the effect of relational contracting and various legal measures.[17] For commercial transactions, it found that "the variables capturing the possibilities for forming long-term relationships do not appear to be as important as the law-related variables."[18] A separate study of Eastern Europe found that effective courts perceptibly increased the level of trust in business transactions.[19] Reliance on reputation and repeat transactions apparently does not promote business trust as well as does legal protection.

Despite the inherent limitations of exclusively private ordering, the nature of the repeat play scenario of the Prisoner's Dilemma, where parties can benefit from establishing a reputation for honesty, undoubtedly can have some positive economic effect, especially in relatively small communities. It is distinctly possible that in small societies, where individuals know one another well, legal restrictions simply add unnecessary fixed costs to the trusting equation. Drafting detailed contracts and complying with legal rules and enforcing litigation certainly have their costs. In small, relatively homogenous societies these costs may be unnecessary because private dealings can provide sufficient incentive for honest business behavior.

Even some larger societies may rely on relationship-based systems. The East Asian countries that had such economic success in the late twentieth century relied heavily on relationship investing. These nations were not pure cases of relational trust, because they had powerful governments that directed the relational business. Nevertheless, they relied on interlocking relational investments among business partners rather than more anonymous stock markets.[20] Even in these nations, relational governance can only go so far and as economies grow, relational governance can become much more costly than rule-based governance.[21] As economies grow, relational systems are also more vulnerable to crises. Because they are much less transparent, serious problems in the relationship remain secret until they have reached enormous proportions. Consequently, investors "may not be able to observe the change in the relation until the advent of a crisis, and then panic erupts," as in fact occurred in the East Asian economies.[22]

Under the circumstances of modern society, opportunities for future anonymous transactions still leave opportunism as the preferred strategy. Absent governmental legal protection, "the quality of information and the credibility of punishment both degrade as the size of a group increases."[23] The law may be unnecessary in a very small, homogenous group, such as the diamond merchants mentioned earlier, with few anonymous transactions. However, as the group size grows, private monitoring is far less effective. In this context, the net benefit of opportunism, even with repeated transactions and reputational concern, increases with the distance between the parties. Milgrom and Roberts note that "the reputational mechanism cannot operate effectively in fluid, impersonal, anonymous market settings."[24] As this distance grows (both geographically and otherwise) and additional business partners exist, the investor has a more difficult time determining whom to trust and to what degree. The investor may either invest the transaction costs necessary to ascertain the reliability of more remote business partners or choose to stick with his or her own small community, whose reliability is already well known.

Indeed, the nature of relational trust raises another economic inefficiency associated with private ordering—business xenophobia. Trust is readily extended to family members and then to an "extended family," which may be those of the same ethnicity that form a relational network. People "who are 'black like me' or 'white like me' may be more trusted than others."[25] It is well known that various ethnic groups have succeeded, in America and elsewhere, through relational community-based dealings. Exclusion may also be based upon class commonalities or those of gender. Relational governance thus divides business communities among trusted insiders and outsiders who are not trusted. "Cultural outsiders" are globally branded as "untrustworthy."[26] High levels of relational trust within a group can perversely lower the level of overall societal trust. Affective relational trust thus has a racist, sexist and generally xenophobic consequence. Robert Putnam himself recognized this tendency as the "dark side of social capital."[27] In the place of bearing high transaction costs associated with the investigation of outsiders, investors may simply rely on the heuristic of trusting insiders. This has the additional detriment of making the investors particularly susceptible to affinity fraud, which has flourished in recent years.

The xenophobic effect of purely private systems may well show up in forms such as literal racism. While this outcome is objectionable on moral grounds, it is also economically inefficient. When investment capital is limited by clan or geography or some other proxy for reliability, it cannot flow freely to the most productive use. Investment will be affected by the artificial constructs of social division rather than efficiency, which in turn will preclude the efficient allocation of resources and result in lessened returns to capital. Expanding the number of participants in markets will increase competition which will enhance the efficiency of markets. The relational, even family-oriented, nature of British business has been cited as an explanation for that nation's failure to fully exploit the opportunities offered by the second industrial revolution in chemicals and electrical equipment.[28] Economies can grow when investors can choose among many alternatives and invest their capital where it will be the most productive. However, with more alternatives come greater private transaction costs necessary to avoid opportunism. Given this tradeoff, some will choose to stay close to home in their investment decisions.

The inefficiencies of this relational xenophobia of trust go beyond racism. Parties who transact in a relational system have great sunk costs in one another. Their information about trustworthiness is person-specific and not readily transferable. Switching to a new partner has great transaction costs in establishing trustworthiness and creates a substantial barrier to exit from the business relationship. This effect prevents full competition for future transactions and must undermine entrepreneurialism. The entrepreneur is a new market participant, more likely to lack the reputational track record required for relational trust. The high exit costs of the private relational system also facilitate some affirmative measure of opportunism. The rational business partner knows that it can engage in some measure of even openly opportunistic behavior and still preserve the business relationship, so long as the costs of the opportunism to the other party are less than the exit cost of identifying more reliable alternative business partners. All the above factors, ranging from transaction costs to business xenophobia, operate to confound the efficiency of a purely private system. Introducing the law helps to ameliorate these problems.

To consider the effect of the law on transactions, first return to the one-sided Prisoner's Dilemma problem of Figure 2.1. The situation in that figure changes when there is a future cost to a party's taking an opportunistic benefit, especially if that benefit is rescinded due to opportunism. Introduce the law into the basic single play scenario, and assume that the law permits the investor to sue and rescind a transaction in which the other party takes opportunistic advantage. Figure 2.2 modifies Figure 2.1, with a legal effect. None of the "honesty" or "don't invest" outcomes would change under the law. However, the "invest/opportunism" scenario results in a lawsuit. In this suit, the investor prevails in response to the illegal opportunism and escapes the deal, but still loses something because of the presence of litigation costs necessary to prevail at law. The other party also loses, because it must give up its opportunistic gains from the transaction and also must bear its own litigation costs, resulting in the $-1, -1$ outcome. If the opportunistic party does not contest the lawsuit, the outcome in this

	Honesty	Opportunism
Invest	2,2	–1,–1
Don't Invest	0,0	0,0

Figure 2.2   Investment decision with legal constraint

cell would be 0,0, as there would be no litigation costs but the rescission would restore the parties to the "don't invest" scenario.

This figure illustrates the value of the law for encouraging transactions. Now the dominant strategy for both parties is investment and honest performance of the contract. Both are better off than they would be with any other combination of opportunism or failure to invest. Of course, the cells of this figure assume that the law works perfectly. If this were so, one would never actually see opportunism, which is an inevitably inferior strategy. It is obvious that fraudulent opportunistic behavior continues to exist in our world, even in the presence of legal constraints. The law does not work perfectly and parties may believe that they can get away with some forms of opportunism. Some undoubtedly do, but the existence of legal enforcement and liability awards must materially increase the risk of opportunistic behavior and thereby shift the cost-benefit calculus in the direction of Figure 2.2.

The critics of the law could counter that the above economic model ignores affective trust and basic human trustworthiness. In consequence, the model overstates the need for external law and ignores the risk that the law could "crowd out" extralegal trust among parties. Some defenders of economic models, like Oliver Williamson, essentially claim that there is no such thing as affective trust and might therefore scoff at this answer. Neither approach effectively captures reality. While Williamson's theory, that all decisionmaking is cognitive and rational, might have validity, it does not capture the reality of trust. Individuals often choose to trust others without making a conscious cognitive assessment, based on some shorthand heuristic of trustworthiness (for example, he is a family member) that may or may not have cognitive validity. This is what passes for affective trust, but such affective trust may be easily exaggerated. There are untrustworthy people throughout the world and the person who easily gives up affective trust is sure to suffer from dealings with the untrustworthy. Such an event might be expected to lower the level of affective trust that person gives in the future.

However, a pattern of dealings in which trust is not betrayed can make affective trust easier to give. To the extent that the law makes it less likely that trust will be abused, it can crowd in trust, rather than crowding it out. People would rationally rather do business with someone they think is honest and can sue if he breaches his promise, than just someone they think is honest.

Absent the law, uncertainties about opportunism and the transaction costs associated with ameliorating those uncertainties will substantially interfere with market development. Those dedicated to private ordering have claimed that private organizations may arise to supplant the need for the law. Private entities can investigate the quality of firms and thus may serve the role of monitoring for opportunism or even enforcing against it. Given the high transaction costs of investor investigation, private groups would naturally arise to take advantage of scale economies and sell valuable information about the reliability of other parties. Even in the presence of legal protections, various private monitoring intermediaries such as credit-rating agencies have arisen in the market. Auditors provide a private intermediary function in their verification of the accuracy of a firm's financial reports. Stockbrokers exist to fill this role as well, advising investors on prudent investments.

Private intermediaries, of course, add costs to the transaction. If the collection of information on the reliability of parties is expensive, this could add significant costs to purely private transactions. Moreover, private intermediaries rely on *ex ante* predictions beforehand and provide no *post facto* relief in the event that opportunistic fraud occurs. While there is some obvious benefit in avoiding a bad transaction beforehand, no service that depends on predicting the future can be perfectly accurate, so parties relying on intermediaries still have some risk that the intermediary's assurances will be wrong and the parties will lose their entire investment to unknown risks or opportunistic behavior. This residual uncertainty will also mean fewer investments. In the context of corporate control transactions and the risk of looting, Easterbrook and Fischel argue for legal penalties on the grounds that the "costs of deterrence are less than the costs of dealing with looting through a system of prior scrutiny that would scotch many valuable control shifts as a by-product."[29]

In this case, the ready availability of *post facto* relief may be much more efficient than *ex ante* monitoring. Suppose that a community is largely trusting by nature and only 20 percent of the population is opportunistic, even though such opportunism could be profitable. The investor does not know which individuals are the opportunistic ones, however. To avoid running a 20 percent risk of losing his or her entire investment requires a thorough *ex ante* investigation into every possible party, including the vast majority of honest parties, to ascertain their honesty. With an effective *post facto* backstop, however, the same degree of extensive *ex ante* monitoring would be unnecessary. Because the relief has some costs and may be imperfect, the investor might still engage in some *ex ante* investigation, but the amount can be proportionally less due to the prospect of some *post facto* relief.

A further basic shortcoming of reliance on private informational intermediaries is their own potential opportunism. Suppose party A is interested in the reliability of party B as a business partner and therefore inquires of an intermediary about B's reliability. The problem with this arrangement is that A's contract with the intermediary is of unknown reliability. The intermediary may be dispensing advice without bothering to spend the resources on research or may even be in cahoots with B, taking payments to testify to a defrauder's reliability. To ensure the intermediary's reliability, A might need to consult an intermediary's intermediary. Of course, to ensure that entity's reliability, A might need an intermediary to assess the intermediary's intermediary, and so on. This is not an efficient system.

The response to this concern about opportunism is often that some demonstrably reliable informational intermediaries will arise, because there will be great profits to be made from this role. By establishing a long track record of impeccable accuracy and the attendant reputation of reliability, an intermediary should be able to charge substantially for its services and maintain such very lucrative contracts for so long as it maintains this reputation. Experience does not bear out these claims, however. Indeed, there is reason for concern that private informational intermediaries may exacerbate, rather than correct, opportunism at the corporate level.

Recent experience demonstrates the potential for conspiratorial opportunism among stock issuers and the intermediaries that purportedly monitor them. Brokerage firms traded stock recommendations for other business, such as investment banking opportunities. The most famous case involved Jack Grubman of Salomon Smith Barney. He became very wealthy and brought much investment banking money to his firm by collaborating in the fraud of the companies he was analyzing. His dealings with WorldCom reflected a "warped symbiosis of corporate executive and Wall Street analyst," in which he attended the company's board meetings and advised the company's managers in carrying out their fraud.[30] Grubman worked with the WorldCom chief executive officer, Bernard Ebbers, to jointly profit at the expense of the company's shareholders. Although such extreme cases of conspiratorial opportunism seem obvious in hindsight, many investors were defrauded at an earlier time, and many such cases surely go undetected. Grubman's experience may be juxtaposed against that of Chung Hu, a Houston stockbroker who warned his clients to get out of Enron stock and was fired by UBS Paine Webber for upsetting the Enron executives.[31] The shortcomings of reliance on intermediaries is expanded in Chapters 3 and 4. It does not appear as if brokerage intermediaries offer a reliable solution to managerial opportunism.

The problems with these entities is not confined to the recent market bubble. Informational intermediaries have had a very mixed historical track record in providing private monitoring. Consider the credit-rating agencies, such as Standard & Poors. Unfortunately, as Frank Partnoy has pointed out, those agencies performed abysmally in the 1990s.[32] He noted that "[t]he last ones to react, in every case, were the credit-rating agencies, which downgraded companies only after all the bad news was in, frequently just days before a bankruptcy filing."[33] Jonathan Macey suggests that credit-rating agencies are essentially "captured" by the firms they rate because their ratings can have such a significant negative impact upon the rated companies that the agencies are extremely reluctant to downgrade credit ratings thus detonating a corporate "nuclear bomb."[34]

Accounting firms represent a particularly crucial informational intermediary in the modern economy through corporate auditing. It might seem as if these firms could serve as valuable and reliable intermediaries. Companies hire auditors in order to demonstrate to investors that their books are accurate and hence have an incentive to hire auditors with a reputation for scrupulous accuracy. Accounting firms consequently would have an incentive to maintain that reputation through honest auditing, even without any government regulation. The case is not so clear, though, once one considers counteracting incentives for opportunism. An auditing firm may have other, more lucrative sources of revenue, such as consulting, and may find it profitable to compromise accurate auditing in order to maintain that revenue stream.[35] Even if the firm as a whole had an incentive to maintain an impeccable reputation, individual partners in the firm may have an incentive to cheat, to preserve their client base and compensation from the firm.[36] Accounting firms may be able to get away with opportunism and still retain reputational benefits, due to detection problems. The Generally Accepted Accounting Principles are rife with room for auditing judgment calls. The actual quality of an audit can be very difficult to ascertain.[37] Thus, an auditor can mask opportunism as a debatable discretionary judgment. Even if the auditors themselves were scrupulously honest, firms have some opportunity to mislead their auditors. They exert substantial control over the information provided to auditors and even the most determined auditor usually cannot detect a well-organized fraudulent scheme. Even when auditors do detect the scheme, the client management often escapes serious reputational damage by blaming the wrongdoing on rogue employees.

The flaws in reliance on reputational incentives for auditing intermediaries are evident from experience. Accountants have violated fundamental ethical principles, including taking bribes from their clients. The recent era of corporate scandals has further exposed the shortcomings of reliance on this private monitoring device. Accountants produced very misleading verified financial reports for firms such as Enron, WorldCom, and HealthSouth. Some of these accounting issues were quite complex and in other cases it appears as though the business managers misled their auditors. The existence and especially the magnitude of the scandals, however, evidences the shortcomings in reliance on *ex ante* monitoring by accounting intermediaries. The limitations of reliance on intermediaries to monitor reputation is further discussed in the following chapter.

Perhaps the most remarkable case of intermediary opportunism involves Institutional Shareholder Services (ISS). This organization is a central clearinghouse for information and adviser to large institutional shareholders on matters of corporate governance. Its existence is attributable almost exclusively to the desire of large institutional shareholders to monitor companies for the presence of managerial opportunism at their expense. ISS makes recommendations for clients on various proxy votes and other corporate governance matters and has become quite prominent in this informational and advisory role. However, ISS has developed a separate business in which they take issuer companies as clients and advise them on structuring corporate governance. This, of course, creates an obvious conflict of interest through which ISS can sell higher ratings to companies that purchase its services (just as in the case of auditors who consult).[38]

The limits of the ability to profit from providing accurate information further complicate the shortcomings of private informational intermediaries. While information may be enormously valuable, its dissemination is difficult to control. A party who purchases the valuable private information can readily disseminate to other non-paying parties, at little or no cost. This easy free-riding on information provision makes it difficult for providers to profit fairly from their information gathering and distribution costs. This feature does not eliminate information provision from markets but suggests that private market forces may underproduce the socially optimal quantities of information, because of the inevitable leakage of their product to those who haven't paid for it. Legal requirements, incidentally, can enhance the private provision of valuable information by reducing the costs of information gathering.

An additional theoretical difficulty with reliance on private intermediaries or other reputational controls will be the lack of competition in the market. Such a system has very high sunk costs. It can take some time to develop the valuable reputation necessary in such a system. With the need for such time-consuming development of reputation comes high entry barriers, whether for the transacting firms themselves or the private monitoring intermediaries. As a consequence, such markets will tend to be highly concentrated or even monopolistic. As a result, use of private systems will have to pay the higher costs of monopoly rents, which may include some opportunistic behavior on the part of the monopolist. The high sunk costs of reputational systems have still another serious economic shortcoming in adapting to change. "If a new technology of a given technical superiority becomes available, a relation-based system will be slower to adopt it than a rule-based system," because the incumbent's sunk stake in the prior technology provides less gain from switching to the newer technology, and barriers to entry prevent new competitors from arising and using the new technology.[39]

Legal systems have some of the same sunk costs as private monitoring and enforcement systems. These costs are only justified if they are not unduly great and if the legal systems are sufficiently effective in practice. It takes some time for legal systems to establish their societal utility. Once they do so, they can produce the benefits offered by the law but legal systems also may be resistant to change and use of new technology. However, the government as monopolist monitoring intermediary has advantages over private monopolist intermediaries, at least when the government is a democratic one. A private monopolist has concern only for the welfare of itself (or its owners) and not the general societal welfare. A government, by contrast, has some concern for the overall societal welfare. Government officials will have some incentive to take some monopoly rents from this process, say in the form of nicer office furnishings. Democratic governance limits the amount of this action, though. A casual glance demonstrates that office appointments of the managers of private industry, not to mention their salaries, considerably exceed those of most high level government officers. The government may also offer efficiency benefits from economies of scale beyond those of even large private monopolies. The government, of course, is susceptible to private rent-seeking, as would be a private intermediary institution, but transparent democratic governance limits this effect.[40]

Government enforcement through general revenues also offers other benefits to economic development. Private institutions cannot minimize transaction costs as readily as can the government.[41] Although reliance on a private monopolist intermediary has lower transaction costs than a system where each party must independently investigate all its partners, those parties will still be required to pay the significant costs of private intermediary enforcement. This system might seem more efficient than that of a government, because it internalizes the transaction costs among the parties to the deal. However, economic development and successful capital markets have enormous societal benefits in the form of positive externalities. The entire society benefits from economic growth, over and above the profits gleaned by the parties. Consequently, to align social welfare with private welfare, it is appropriate that some of the costs of transactions, such as government enforcement, be spread throughout the society.

When *ex ante* intermediation protection against opportunism fails, a *post facto* remedy is valuable, both for particular victims and for future deterrence. Purely private *post facto* enforcement has problems that go beyond private monitoring through intermediaries. Private parties in the United States commonly take disputes out of the court system, to arbitration, for resolution. They do so with the knowledge that such arbitration awards will generally be enforced much as would a court's decree. Without the government enforcement that comes with law, some private enforcement mechanism for private dispute resolution would be necessary. Such private enforcement mechanisms exist today, for contracts outside the law or where the law is ineffective.

Throughout history, organized crime has performed functions such as contract enforcement when the law is absent or ineffective. Indeed, the Mafia itself may have arisen because the collapse of feudalism left Sicily without any state authority to enforce deals.[42] Where legal enforcement is weak, organized crime has often filled the gap.[43] The breakdown of government enforcement in Russia and Eastern Europe led to use of organized crime to enforce contracts. In Latin America, shortcomings in the judicial system have led to the use of *justicieros* to enforce private justice. In Japan, the *yakuza* mobsters are used to enforce contracts and extract payments for torts, when weaknesses in the legal system render it inadequate. Private reliance on organized crime for enforcement would seem clearly inferior to that of government, if only because government has a greater interest in overall public welfare, while the interests of organized crime are merely private.

Under some circumstances, private relational governance may be superior to legal rule-based governance. In small, simple economies, the costs of creating and enforcing legal rules may exceed their benefits. Once economies grow larger and more complex, however, this is no longer the case. In the United States of the nineteenth century, there was a steady evolution from informal to formal legal governance of business contracts and firms. Between 1840 and 1920, the relational trust-based governance was slowly supplanted by institutional trust based on law, as the economy grew and the relational governance became inefficient.[44] The East Asian economies of the latter part of the twentieth century underwent a similar evolution.[45] Developed economies are clearly past the tipping point, where legal regulation adds efficiency. With the increased globalization of the world economy, greater legal regulation of business may enhance the prospects for development of even smaller, less developed nations, by better enabling trust in new business partners.

The legalization of contract relations has another often overlooked benefit, beyond the enabling of business trust, because formal contract terms can help clarify the understanding of the parties. Think of an informal, relational contract, like a mother telling her babysitter to make sure her child "eats her dinner." This leaves open the questions of what the dinner should consist of, and whether the child must eat every last scrap of food, and whether the child might eat additional food, and whether certain foods are unsafe for the particular child, and so on. Misunderstandings and misfortunes might be prevented by a more detailed written set of instructions. The typical business contract contains far more complications than found in this simple babysitter analogy. Contracts can be useful to enable a more precise understanding of the agreed upon obligations of the parties. Survey research shows that this clarifying function can be an important value of business contract drafting.[46] Thanks to this function, contracts are "not just compatible with trust and cooperation," they may affirmatively "enhance and sustain such desirable relational features of transactions."[47]

Of course, the precise definition of obligations in a contract can be quite time-consuming and impose considerable transaction costs on the parties. At the extreme, detailed contract definition involves something like foreseeing the future, anticipating all possible scenarios of opportunism or simply unexpected factual developments that could in some way frustrate the contract's purposes. Contract law, though, does not require this level of detail, it simply allows such detail, should the parties believe the transaction costs of the detail to be worth the expense and effort. Again, the law simply offers another alternative to be employed whenever the parties find it to be efficient. One of the values of corporate and securities law is that it does much of the work for the parties, providing various detailed requirements implicit in all the contracts that the law governs. These rules, as discussed below, save parties some of the transaction costs associated with detailed drafting.

The virtue of the basic foundational law is not limited to the prevention of opportunism. Breaches of contract are commonly innocent actions, which were unavoidable by one of the parties or a product of the parties' misunderstanding about the dimensions of their agreement. While these misunderstandings occur even in the presence of detailed contract language, they surely would be far more frequent in a relational deal in which none of the terms were clearly spelled out. Business studies of company relationships have shown this value of legalization in promoting trust.[48] A study of a new drug development joint venture found that a binding contract had benefit in coordinating the relationship and clarifying the parties' duties and also served a valuable "symbolic function," in signaling the parties' "intentions to be a loyal partner."[49]

The basic foundational law of contracts thus yields economic benefits, beyond those available through complete private ordering. Property rights and contract enforcement empower private ordering, a fact recognized by most economists. The *ur*-text of law and economics, Richard Posner's *Economic Analysis of Law*, argues that a purely private system of agreements is not efficient, because legal enforcement is necessary to deter opportunism.[50] Tort law also helps control opportunism, by creating liability for theft or fraud. Most law and economics scholars recognize the value of the foundational law, but they may argue that this traditional common law legal framework is sufficient to govern the firm and therefore question the value of statutory corporate law and securities law. The remainder of the chapter examines those claims.

ECONOMICS OF CORPORATE LAW

The rationale for corporate law is very similar to that for the basic foundational contract law. The corporate context is somewhat different, however, as is the governing law. The principal concern of corporate law is that the corporate officers and directors act in the interest of the shareholders, as their agents. While the officers and directors have contracts, mere contract law has some limitations here. A company's shareholders may represent an enormous number of individuals, with varying amounts at stake, rather than one single individual. The shareholders with a diversified portfolio may have invested in many different corporations, another circumstance which increases the costs of monitoring. Shareholders do not directly enter the contracts with the officers and directors, the contract of one officer agent is typically drafted by other shareholder agents, the directors, and the shareholder chooses to invest, at best with knowledge of the contract terms but relatively little control over them. Monitoring for opportunism is also more difficult in the corporate governance context. Some suggest that monitoring problems are lessened in the corporate context, due to the presence of large professional investors with the ability to conduct such monitoring. While these parties may indeed have both the resources and expertise to monitor corporate managers, their monitoring has the same high transaction costs, especially with a diversified portfolio. Moreover, even professional investor monitoring is beset by behavioral shortcomings, as discussed in Chapter 3. Posner does not discuss corporate law in great detail but is generally positive about its values, explaining that it "reduces transaction costs by implying in every charter the normal rights that a shareholder could be expected to insist on."[51]

The rationale for many of the rules of corporate law is thus similar to a central rationale for contract law, in restraining opportunism. Corporate managers doubtless have greater opportunities for at least discreet opportunism at the expense of shareholders than do parties to a contract. The one-sided Prisoner's Dilemma analysis applies, perhaps with greater force, in this context, yet this is not fully appreciated. Easterbrook and Fischel, for example, embrace contractual relations but doubt the reality of managerial opportunism, suggesting that managers "may do their best to take advantage of their investors, but they find that the dynamics of the market drive them to act as if they had investors' interests at heart."[52] This is simply the repeat play argument in the context of the one-sided Prisoner's Dilemma, and the claim suffers all the same shortcomings of the repeat play argument in contract. Given the greater monitoring difficulties in the corporate context, the deficiencies of the claim are even greater than they are for contract law and the agency problems may thus require a supplementation of contract law with corporate law. Managerial opportunism may take the form of drafting contracts that permit managers to take advantage of shareholders, who suffer considerable transaction costs in monitoring this behavior. Officers' adoption of corporate poison pills to fend off acquisitions and entrench themselves in office is one obvious example of this sort of opportunistic behavior. The threat of such opportunism should not be minimized. A McKinsey study of Asian companies found that 76 percent of investors worried *more* about governance than they did about financial issues.[53] It is too simplistic to rely on managerial self-interest to constrain managerial opportunism.

The value of the mandatory rules provided by corporate law derives from the reduction in transaction costs in monitoring the threat of managerial opportunism. When discussing the reason for providing corporations with limited liability, Easterbrook and Fischel write:

> First, limited liability decreases the need to monitor agents. To protect themselves, investors could monitor their agents more closely. The more risk they bear, the more they will monitor. But beyond a point extra monitoring is not worth the cost. Moreover, specialized risk bearing implies that many investors will have diversified holdings. Only a portion of their wealth will be invested in one firm. These diversified investors have neither the expertise nor the incentive to monitor the actions of specialized agents. Limited liability makes diversification and passivity a more rational strategy and so potentially reduces the cost of operating the corporation.[54]

This rationale applies well to other mandatory corporate rules, such as those requiring and elaborating the fiduciary duties of officers and directors.

Limited liability reduces the magnitude of investor risk, but investors may still suffer great losses from corporate opportunism, as in the case of Enron. A legal rule can enhance efficiency by reducing the need for investors to engage in costly and continuous monitoring of their managerial agents' actions.

There are valid arguments about the costs associated with compulsory corporate rules. Rule enforcement inevitably has its costs. Different entities have differences in their basic businesses and in the identities of their owners and managers and therefore may have different optimal governance arrangements. Forcing certain commonalities upon these entities means foregoing optimality, in at least some circumstances. But this added cost of uniform legal rules only exists if one presumes that the owners and managers of these entities would find and adopt the optimal governance rules, in the absence of the law, a presumption that is not self-evident in light of the agency problems of the firm. Merely identifying the rules could involve considerable transaction cost that is avoided by the legal structure. The economic value of compulsory corporate rules will depend on the extent of the agency problems in a purely private ordering, transaction costs, and on the quality of the rules themselves, not some *a priori* abstract analysis of a perfectly functioning world without any agency and transaction cost problems.

The development of corporate law has reflected recognition of this tradeoff between the risks of opportunism and the costs of legal intervention into corporate decisionmaking. The widely adopted "business judgment rule" gives great deference to the decisions of corporate officers and directors. It dictates that courts will not intervene in corporate decisionmaking when a plaintiff alleges a breach of the agent's duty of care, unless the breach appears especially egregious. This rule recognizes the costs of legal second-guessing, balanced against the risk of agent misbehavior. The true dangers of opportunism lie not in breaching the duty of care, however. The duty of loyalty is the fiduciary duty at issue in the typical case of opportunism, with agents profiting at the expense of their principals. If the entire board has a conflict of interest, or is dominated by an individual with a conflict of interest, the court will give much stricter scrutiny to the corporate decision. The law thus strikes a balance between the value of controlling opportunism and the costs of excessive oversight. Of course, the optimality of this balance is debatable and some have suggested that corporate law fails because it is *too deferential* to free management choice.[55]

The private voluntary choice of firms to adopt the corporate form provides something of a natural experiment that demonstrates the efficiency of the balance struck by corporate law. The law offers limited liability options for investors, other than the corporation. Limited partnerships and limited liability companies (LLCs) both provide such limited liability. These alternative forms have their own state enabling laws that are typically less restrictive than is corporate law. Consequently, they offer greater opportunity for arranging governance contractually, rather than by law. If such private contractual governance were more efficient, one might expect investors to flood to these alternative limited liability entities. And while LLCs and other such entities have become increasingly popular for small business organizations, corporations retain their preeminent role among large business enterprises.[56]

Another criticism of restrictive corporate laws lies in claims of inefficiency arising from the laws' ineffectiveness. Easterbrook and Fischel argue that the general availability of private contractual ordering means that managerial opportunism is like a balloon that, when constricted in one place, merely expands in another. They thus suggest that "if corporate law should forbid managers to divert corporate opportunities to themselves, they might respond by drawing higher salaries or working less hard to open up new business opportunities."[57] At some level, this claim surely has truth. The law does not extinguish the incentives for opportunism, and corporate officers certainly have been known to take excessive salaries. However, the claim falls far short of invalidating restrictive corporate law, for two reasons. First, the two forms of opportunism are not exclusive, that is, a manager might both usurp corporate opportunities and take a higher salary, absent the legal restrictions. The law might therefore reduce opportunism to some degree by eliminating one channel. Second, different forms of opportunism present very different monitoring problems and associated transaction costs for shareholders. The officer's cash salary is transparent and easy to monitor, whereas the officer's usurpation of corporate opportunities is more difficult for shareholders to observe and hence a more appropriate subject for legal deterrence. The corporate law sensibly restricts the latter opportunism more than the former, because salaries are relatively more amenable to control through private ordering. Prevailing standards of corporate law do not fully displace private ordering; Delaware law is empowering in many cases and, when restrictive, can operate to help overcome market inefficiencies in controlling managerial opportunism.

Corporate law can also play an important clarifying function for business relationships, as in the case of contract formalization. An agent automatically assumes some fiduciary responsibility to the principal, but the precise nature of the relationship may be obscure, absent the defined standards of corporate law. A fiduciary has some duty to disclose facts to shareholders but the reach of the duty may be uncertain. A fiduciary has a duty of loyalty, but whether that duty is breached at the margin may be uncertain. Even in an atmosphere of trust, a misunderstanding about the scope of these duties could prevent efficient investment decisions and interfere with the relationship between investors and managers. The law can facilitate this relationship by clarifying expectations.

Corporate law is not absolutely necessary for legal governance of the principal/agent relationship, as parties may contract the specific details of the relationship. This individual contracting, though, adds to transaction costs, as the parties hammer out the details of their relationship. The parties must decide the terms they desire and the extent to which they can compromise, which involves investigation into the need for particular protections and the appropriate language for those protections. Corporate law can reduce these transaction costs with established uniform rules. Default rules still permit the parties some choice to modify the legal standard, though mandatory rules cannot be evaded through contract. Perhaps a greater benefit of the corporate law is not the particular choice of language governing the relationship but the clarification of what that language means. Words are not determinate and parties can agree on words without agreeing on their meaning, and certainly without appreciating what a future court might deem to be the words' meaning.

The words of corporate law are not intrinsically clearer than those contained in a contract, and the potential scope of a general "fiduciary" duty is quite vague. However, the identical statutory language governs many transactions, so the meaning of these particular words becomes better understood over time. While not every provision of corporate law has been well-ventilated in court, the more significant provisions such as fiduciary duties have been extensively litigated over decades, and their dimensions are now relatively well understood. This understanding provides the parties with understanding and certainty that would not be available under contract language that may never have been interpreted in court. Easterbrook and Fischel recognize some value to corporate law providing a set of terms "off-the-rack so that participants in corporate ventures can save the cost of contracting."[58] While there are many private services that provide such "off-the-rack" contract terms, they cannot supply the interpretation of those terms, as can government courts. When "off-the-rack" terms are mandatory, they can offer still greater advantages in this regard, because investors need not beware opportunistic modification of those terms by self-interested managers.

A remarkable practice is the fact that public corporations very rarely use the legally allowed freedom to draft certificates that are different from the default terms provided by state law.[59] This is a private ordering deference to state choice, which seems unusual. The fact represents a market check indicating that either the state will adopt better corporate procedures than will the corporation itself (perhaps due to agency problems) or that the network effects of belonging to a uniform corporate law system exceed whatever benefits might be achieved by marginally more optimal corporate governance rules.

The benefits of the clarification of understandings and consequent certainty associated with corporate law can be seen in the practice of the states. As discussed in Chapter 1, Delaware is by far the most common situs of corporations, which are governed by the law of that state. Still, many companies, especially smaller ones, are incorporated in their home states. When those states have corporate law controversies, they commonly refer to and sometimes automatically defer to the law of Delaware. They resolve disputes as they determine that Delaware would. This interstate deference is much more common in corporate law than in other fields of law, because the Delaware courts are considered expert and reliable, Delaware's law is well developed and clear, and because corporations value such clarity. The state of Delaware's law is surely imperfect, but its relative certainty offers an advantage to companies which may overcome any substantive imperfections.[60] This advantage goes to the economic benefits associated with network externalities, discussed in greater detail in the section below on securities law.

Corporate law addresses the particular risks associated with opportunism by managers who control the investments of shareholders. By creating a legal regime to govern this opportunism, it has the merit of deterring the behavior and averting the transaction costs that would otherwise be necessary for investors who sought to protect their investment. Corporate law also provides the added economic benefit of producing "off-the-rack" contract terms and an effective, uniform system of enforcement of contracts, which also reduce the transaction costs associated with negotiating particular terms of an agreement.

ECONOMICS OF SECURITIES LAW

The economic rationale for securities law is more controversial. In contrast to Posner's positive portrayal of the economics of the basic foundational law, he is critical of various aspects of the federal securities laws. He contends that the securities law requirements neglect the natural efficiency of large capital markets, with their intermediaries and sophisticated investors, and concludes that the "regulation of new issues does not help investors."[61] As compared with the basic foundational law and traditional corporate law, federal securities law is a relatively new development, dating from the 1930s. Prior to that time, securities markets operated under a largely voluntary, private system, though there was some state regulation in the form of "blue sky" laws. Securities regulation has been more controversial among economists than has foundational basic or corporate law.

There were private market equivalents of legal protection for investors, before the securities laws even existed, some of which are addressed in Chapter 4. Prior to 1933, the New York Stock Exchange cued investors based on the securities that it chose to list and supplied some financial information on those securities. While this experience shows the value of disclosure, it does not demonstrate that private disclosure is sufficient. As discussed above, managerial opportunism can prevent optimal disclosure, and private intermediaries do not resolve this issue. Traditional Coasean theory calls for government intervention when such action can reduce transaction costs below those that would otherwise exist. This is the theory supporting contemporary federal securities regulation.

The economic analysis of the securities laws retraces much of the ground covered above with the basic foundational law and corporate law. The basic law provides rules to prevent opportunism in contractual dealings. The corporate law provides rules to prevent managers from opportunistically taking advantage of their existing contract partners. Much of securities law adds rules to prevent additional categories of opportunistic behavior, in the particular context of securities purchases. The economic need for securities law is not obvious *a priori*, but depends on whether the particular context of securities purchases in capital markets has features that demand different or greater protection than those associated with other contracts.

The debate over securities law also replays the claims that the law crowds out relational affective trust. Larry Ribstein thus contends that securities regulation presumes that "investors lack trust" and precludes "any opportunity for genuine trust and trustworthiness by ensuring that everybody acts under legal coercion."[62] In a complex modern world, though, such simple blind trust seems like a poor system for organizing an economy. Corporate investments, which essentially involve handing over large sums of money to the discretion of others, provide a context where unregulated trust can be a prescription for enormous losses. Given the law's ability to actually enhance even affective trust, the crowding out hypothesis cannot dejustify legal regulation of the corporate form. The presence of private structures of monitoring before the law and beyond the law provides ample evidence that reliance on trust is insufficient to support investment markets.

The economic case for mandatory disclosures of securities law lies first in the private underprovision of this information. As discussed above in the context of private informational intermediaries, the difficulty of excluding non-payer free-riders from benefiting from the information means that the free market may not provide the optimal amount of information. Market mechanisms have other shortcomings as well. Buyers may have difficulty ascertaining the reliability of the private intermediary that is auditing the veracity of the issuer's information, which may require the use of intermediary's intermediaries of their own uncertain reliability, and so on.

For some economists, a regime of mandatory disclosure (or even reliance on intermediaries) is unnecessary, because firms will voluntarily disclose that information that shareholders wish to know in order to invest and bid up share prices. There is accumulating evidence about the financial value to firms of providing greater corporate disclosure. In countries with relatively weak legal governance of the firm, companies voluntarily disclose more and adopt higher quality internal governance systems than is legally required, in order to attract equity capital.[63] By regularly disclosing information, these firms assure investors that they can better monitor their investments, which encourages investments in the first place, which gives firms an internal incentive to disclose.

These demonstrated benefits of information disclosure do not necessarily persuade economists to believe in the virtue of mandatory disclosure. If disclosure benefits the firm, no mandate should be necessary. Critics may argue that each firm chooses the optimum amount of disclosure for its own particular circumstances. The existence of voluntary private disclosures, thus, would be considered evidence that the law is unnecessary and possibly inefficient. Private companies will go beyond legal requirements in disclosing in order to attract capital, and they would presumably do so at the optimal level without making unnecessary disclosures, which inevitably add cost for the company.

The presence of some valuable private disclosure may not be optimal, though, and does not defeat the value of mandatory disclosure rules. While there may be some alignment of interest between issuers and investors in disclosure, it is imperfect. A firm that discloses bad news may enhance its credibility, but investors still may not choose a company with credibly bad results. For a company in serious trouble, such as incipient insolvency, there is no incentive to disclose this truth. A shareholder wants to know if a company's managers are performing badly, but a manager would not want to disclose this fact. It is unrealistic to assume that managers will always make voluntary disclosures that shareholders want, even when those disclosures make the managers look bad in the process. Existing shareholders may even favor such managerial opportunism, which enables them to unload their ownership interest on outsiders, at a price inflated by misleading disclosures. Voluntary accurate disclosures can also be a tool of future opportunism. By establishing a perception of credibility in the first instance, a con-man can attract more money to be stolen at a later date.

It is even possible that a reliable voluntary disclosure of certain information would not be as valuable as a mandatory disclosure of exactly that same information, especially if the mandatory disclosure were backed with greater sanctions for inaccuracy. A mandatory disclosure regime can reduce transaction costs for investors. A company's past history of accurate, voluntary disclosures is no guarantee of its future performance. Reliance on voluntary disclosure raises all the same shortcomings, risks, and transaction costs of any relational, reputational system, described above in the context of foundational contract law. Although Easterbrook and Fischel are somewhat dubious of mandatory disclosure provisions, they concede that "[i]f federal disclosure laws reduce the costs of investors becoming informed, they will increase investors' net returns, and capital markets will be able to allocate funds to higher valuing users."[64] Thus, the reduction of transaction costs can justify a mandatory disclosure regime.

Another valuable feature of the mandatory disclosure provisions of the securities laws lies in their facilitation of *post facto* fraud enforcement actions. Issuers may engage in a wide range of opportunistic dishonesty, ranging from blatant lying to more subtle shading of the truth or convenient omission of important but negative information. The basic fraud laws can help protect against the most blatant lying. The generalized legal principle that silence will not be fraud, however, makes enforcement against subtler opportunism much less effective. The mandatory disclosure requirements help counteract this form of opportunistic behavior, by limiting the option of silence or incomplete voluntary disclosures. Mandatory securities law disclosures demand that companies provide specific information periodically and back that requirement with legal enforcement, should the information be omitted or dishonest.

Bernard Black has stressed that for companies to sell shares to third party investors, they must be able to "convey *credible* information to those parties."[65] Even assuming that companies would provide exactly the same information to investors in the absence of any securities laws, the laws could still provide a credibility benefit. Because of the securities laws, issuers face a greater risk of both criminal and civil sanctions if the disclosed information is false and misleading, which means that investors can place greater trust in the veracity of the disclosures. The risk of legal enforcement thus benefits the honest parties who seek to inform the market truthfully as well as investors who rely on disclosed information.

The foundational common law fraud rules provided some protection against misleading disclosures for investors, even in the absence of federal securities fraud actions, but the common law rules had some serious shortcomings. Section 10(b) of the Exchange Act, the basic authority for securities fraud litigation, has been adapted by the courts to the specific circumstances of securities fraud, rather than the more general circumstances of "garden variety" fraud. In some circumstances, the requirements of section 10(b) are more pro-defendant than that of ordinary fraud. Only a seller or purchaser may sue under section 10(b), and a party that fails to buy or sell securities has no possible claim. In other circumstances, such as reliance, the federal securities fraud action is less restrictive of plaintiffs. By adapting fraud to the circumstances of broadly traded publicly-held securities, in tandem with a mandatory disclosure regime and SEC enforcement, securities fraud laws can be much more effective than common law fraud liability. By reducing informational asymmetries and providing protection for potential investors, such securities laws might reduce the cost of capital to firms.

One key advantage of the securities fraud cause of action is its incorporation of some of the principles of financial efficient market theories. At common law, investors had to prove reasonable reliance on the fraudulent misrepresentation, which meant that they must have read or heard its contents. This reading or hearing is exactly the sort of transaction cost to be avoided by efficient markets. For every single investor in the market to read every single prospectus and quarterly report of every candidate for investment would require very substantial costs. The theory of efficient markets suggests that market prices reflect this information, thanks to sophisticated large institutional investors and intermediaries, even when most investors are unfamiliar with the information. Hence, under the federal securities law, a party may sue for fraud based on his or her reliance, not on the exact misrepresentation, but on the efficient market's use of that information.

The relaxed reliance requirement has another very great benefit for federal securities law, enabling more class action fraud litigation. There are considerable transaction costs involved in enforcing rights through litigation, for plaintiffs as well as defendants. While many lament the overlegalization of our society, research in areas such as malpractice shows that the vast majority of *deserving* plaintiffs do not even sue to recover what they deserve. The costs of litigating can be especially great for fraud claims, because plaintiffs need not only demonstrate that a defendant made a material factual misrepresentation, they must also demonstrate that the defendant knew of the falsity at the time (*scienter* or at least recklessness). If each individual shareholder had to sue independently to recover his or her damages, most fraud cases would not be brought, because the costs and risk of litigation would exceed the recovery, even when fraud occurred. This would mean less deterrence of fraud, which in turn means that investors face more risk and are less likely to place their funds into securities with such risk. The class action procedure, by cumulating the claims of all defrauded shareholders, enables greater and more efficient enforcement. The securities' laws relaxed reliance requirement is crucial to enabling class actions.

Another incidental economic benefit of section 10(b) is the nationalization of securities fraud law. Every state has some cause of action for fraud, and their requirements are roughly similar, but each state's law has its nuances. Securities are traded in a national market and corporate representations are spread nationally. In the context of fraud, each alleged misrepresentation would have to be evaluated separately, perhaps under the law of each of the 50 states. Some of the state laws could even conflict, where one state might require disclosure of certain information, while another might prohibit its disclosure as unreliable. Being subject to all these state rules is highly inefficient for companies and adds transaction costs associated with compliance. The nationalization of fraud rules for a national market adds consistency and efficiency to the law.

One further key economic benefit from securities laws is the creation of a *uniform* mandatory disclosure and enforcement system for investors. While the free market celebrates diversity and choice, there are circumstances when coordination on a uniform mandated system has great benefits. Consider driving behavior. Highways are much more efficient (and safer) because the United States has a law dictating "driving on the right." A free market system, in which drivers individually negotiated "side of road" during each of their highway encounters would be far less efficient than the uniform government rule. Indeed, the government rule would probably be net beneficial even if it picked the "wrong" side of the road for efficient driving, simply by creating predictable uniformity in driving. Some obvious examples of this principle in economic relationships include the use of a common currency and standardized weights and measures.

Economically, the relevant issue involves what are sometimes called network effects. Network effects describe the efficiency benefits associated with everyone using the *same* system. The benefits arising from common use of the same system are sometimes called network externalities. When all participants in a market conform to the same system, transaction costs can be lessened. For this reason, product and service standardization is used to reduce uncertainties, and efficiency may call for the stipulation of a "minimum acceptable standard," leaving it "to the market to exceed those standards" where efficient.[66] The value of this coordination network externality can be seen in the development of private institutions, such as the New York Stock Exchange, to create common rules for securities transactions. Significantly, the NYSE, a private institutional intermediary, has many *mandatory* rules for its members, although most of these rules have been required or at least strongly encouraged by the SEC. This provides some market test for the virtue of mandatory rules.

Michael Klausner has argued that corporate law can be justified in part by network externalities.[67] He observes that the traditional contractarian paradigm of parties selecting the best rules for their transaction loses the external benefits of consistent contract terms and interpretation. He

stresses the benefit of not only the common language of the law and contracts, but also that of judicial rulings that interpret and clarify that language. Klausner is generally skeptical of mandatory legal rules, as opposed
to default rules, in corporate law, though he recognizes that they may sometimes be preferable.[68] His analysis of mandatory rules, though, is focused
on the identification of the best rule and not on transaction costs. Allowing
any deviation from the legal rules adds transaction costs for investors, if
only those costs associated with identifying the existence and meaning of
such a deviation. Rao thus notes that "[m]arginal additions to standardization usually lead to decreasing utilities or returns, suggesting the existence of an optimal level of standardization, conducive enough to lead to
the formation of expectations."[69]

The same network externalities that support a common corporate law
apply to securities law. Corporate law provides a coordination benefit that
protects investors against post-purchase opportunism, through reliable
legal rules. Securities law provides the same benefit, primarily for those who
have not yet invested and need protection against fraudulent inducement of
their investment. Federal securities law gives assurances that investors will
have certain disclosures, that certain key information will not be omitted
from those disclosures, and that they will have legally enforceable rights
against parties who make materially misleading disclosures. Private networks can provide some of these benefits but are not an adequate replacement for government. Because of the widespread positive external benefits
of the coordinated system, no private network can fully capture the utility
it creates, which means that private networks will underinvest in creation of
these benefits.[70] Free-rider prospects for those outside the network compound this problem, as do the problems of intermediary opportunism and
market power discussed above. Experience in Russia demonstrates that
private intermediaries cannot effectively capture the coordination benefits
provided by the law.[71]

Network effects have at times been lamented for their perpetuation of
inefficiency. It is true that the efficiencies of existing networks mean that a
less efficient incumbent technology might prevail in the market over a more
efficient new technology, because the less efficient incumbent had established network effects that deterred switching to the newer and better technology. In the free market, this need not be a serious problem, if the better
technology is significantly better, those benefits will outweigh the costs of
transitioning to it. There is ample historical evidence demonstrating that
network members will transition to form a new network around a demonstrably better product.[72]

It might seem like governmentally-imposed networks pose a greater risk
of this type of inefficiency than do private networks, because the law may

preclude the private transition to a better system of disclosures. However, this concern ignores the democratic government's own concern for an efficient system, to produce societal welfare. Moreover, the private parties subject to the government regulation are hardly without influence in the government. Issuers have successfully lobbied Congress to limit the scope of securities fraud actions, most recently in connection with the PSLRA and SLUSA. Likewise, issuers and intermediaries have successfully lobbied Congress to defeat efforts to impose stricter accounting rules, such as the expensing of stock options. Given the presence of this private influence in government, it seems likely that mandatory disclosure and other legal requirements, when imperfect, will be overly lax rather than overly strict. This imperfection of laxity, though, does not call for more private ordering but instead indicates that government action should be strengthened.

An interesting natural experiment on this effect arose when a regulatory change required firms on the Over the Counter Bulletin Board (OTCBB) to comply with SEC reporting requirements. These firms were relatively small, and many left the OTCBB rather than comply with additional disclosure mandates. However, according to a Wharton study, the compliant firms experienced increased market liquidity and, more importantly, the OTCBB firms who had already complied with these disclosure requirements experienced positive returns and increased liquidity, once all firms were forced to disclose.[73] This demonstrated the positive externalities associated with a mandatory disclosure regime and its contribution to market reputation.

Uniform legal requirements, such as those of mandatory disclosure, can serve to enhance affective trust. Such legalization can transform trust into a "commodity" that serves as an "entity that is familiar and subject to pressure to conform to established standards" and serves as a "dependable anchor for easier and more trusting relationships as trust becomes routinely and predictably available, formalized, and standardized."[74] Once the nature of the disclosures and the government enforcement system become regularized, investors need not expend the time, effort, and resources to fully understand the scope of the disclosures and their remedies for opportunism, thus substantially reducing the transaction costs of individualized investments. The fear of "betrayal" and concern for being played for a "sucker" will especially undermine trust.[75] To the extent that the law discourages such betrayals, it can promote greater affective trust. The requirements of securities law can also serve to enhance both cognitive and affective trust and the consequential economic benefits.

While a significant difference between corporate and securities law is the protection that the latter affords to outside investors, this distinction is not precise. Securities law contains regulation of proxy battles that goes to the internal questions of corporate governance and the rights of current share-holders. The "best price" rules of the Williams Act governing tender offers prevent acquirers from favoring corporate insiders at the expense of other existing minority shareholders. Similarly, the Sarbanes-Oxley legislation of 2002 involves matters of internal corporate governance in addition to regulation of transactions with prospective purchasers. These rules would be evaluated according to and justified by the analysis of agency problems discussed above in the context of state corporations laws, though the network effects analysis in this section is also relevant to their value. For example, an investor benefits from the ability to rely on a uniform set of mandatory restrictive legal proxy disclosure rules, rather than having to rely on continuously investigating and monitoring his or her contractual rights to information disclosure.

EMPIRICAL STUDIES OF SECURITIES LAW

Ultimately, the questions of the value of foundational, corporate, and securities laws requires empirical testing of the benefits and costs of the laws. Such laws have theoretical advantages and disadvantages, and practice enables us to ascertain which category of effects prevail. Chapter 5 of this book will review the growing empirical literature on the cross-country comparisons of different legal regimes and their effect on economic growth and capital markets and present our own empirical analyses of this effect. Other types of studies have been conducted on the consequences of securities law, though, ranging from historical analyses on the origin of this law to the use of this law by foreign firms. This chapter concludes by briefly reviewing these categories of empirical findings.

There have been some historical studies of the economic effects of some aspects of securities law that focused on the effect of the first introduction of the law. One famous early study questioned the value of the securities law, after finding that the passage of the Securities Act had no apparent effect on the average return earned by investors in new stock issues.[76] While this study is often cited as evidence that the securities laws did not provide any benefit, it might also be noted that it also calls into question the claims of critics that these laws were harmful. However, it is not clear that the study's measure, the average return on new issues, is the proper test for the effect of securities laws, as the effect of greater information should be a reduction in opportunistic behavior, which would appear as a difference in the dispersion of returns from new issues. When this issue was more recently studied, the research found that the new issues after the adoption of the Securities Act did not significantly affect the average return of New

York Stock Exchange issues, but found a dramatic effect for issues not traded on the NYSE which were often overpriced prior to the Securities Act's effect.[77] Moreover, the dispersion of returns and associated risk was lower after the Securities Act for all groups of shares studied, included those traded on the NYSE. The results indicated that the "information effects of securities regulation should be reflected in the risk borne by investors, and not the average risk-adjusted returns."[78]

The mandatory disclosure rules also have seen some historical study. George Benston studied the reaction of the market to the passage of the 1934 Exchange Act, by testing the subsequent results of firms which had previously made required disclosures of sales against those which had not.[79] He found no material effect from the legislation. The study has seen significant criticism,[80] though, and its implications are uncertain.[81] Even Benston's results indicated that the 1934 Act improved pricing accuracy in the market. Several studies found that the mandatory disclosure provisions "of the 1933 and 1934 Acts reduced underwriter costs and that the disclosure programs increased investor confidence and led directly to a large increase in investor participation in the stock markets."[82] A more recent study, however, found that the laws' passage did not markedly increase public disclosures.[83] We will examine this historical evidence further in Chapter 4. Any such historical analysis is somewhat constrained by limits on available data, but the record can provide some information.

These studies from the era surrounding the adoption of the securities laws may be expected to underestimate the value of those laws in today's world. As noted above, a new law takes some time to establish its market credibility and yield its positive effects. Moreover, the SEC and its rules were still relatively embryonic at the time period studied in this research (prior to 1953 or even earlier). Thus, a lack of effect immediately after passage of the laws does not mean much about the current operation of those laws. It seems reasonable to expect that the Commission's rules and enforcement activities have improved over time, as its staff has gained more expertise and experience with implementing the laws. Any positive benefits of securities law would also grow as private parties became more familiar with the regime and associated network effects affiliated with the law. The true benefits from the law increase as it establishes its reliability and credibility and compliance becomes routinized and therefore cheaper. In the process, heuristics of trust develop that increase market efficiency.

The historical empirical measurements of securities law may inevitably underestimate its benefits, because they test only the federal securities laws. Before the nation had a federalized Securities Act or Securities Exchange Act, the states had written their own securities legislation, called "blue sky" laws. These state laws had some significant limitations, which provoked the demand for uniform federal legislation. However, the state laws surely offered some portion of the potential economic benefits from securities laws, so that studies of the federal laws would only capture a portion of the benefit from such laws, rather than representing a comprehensive measure.

Some international research also sheds light on the economic virtue of securities laws. Corporate takeovers can help promote the efficient alloca-tion of capital, by displacing ineffective management. Acquirers typically pay a material premium over the market price of a stock, which is under-valued. The presence of such acquisitions evidences some shortcomings in internal corporate governance, suggesting that public shareholders are either unaware of managerial shortcomings or unable to do anything about them in corporate elections. The ability of outside acquirers to take over a company, through devices such as tender offers, can thus enhance efficiency beyond that achievable by existing shareholders.[84] Incidentally, the threat of a takeover may also influence managers to perform better and save their jobs. The overall effectiveness of acquisitions in promoting this efficiency, though, depends on a variety of factors, including transaction costs, agency costs, information problems, etc. Not all takeovers are efficient—the acquirer's managerial decision is also influenced by agency opportunism risk, but the presence of acquisitions can help discipline the market and enhance efficiency.

One test for the economic value of corporate and securities law is to observe its effect on the market for corporate control through acquisitions. A study at the European Corporate Governance Institute found that the volume of merger and acquisition activity from 1999 to 2002 was much greater in countries that had stronger shareholder protection and higher accounting standards.[85] In addition, hostile takeovers are more frequent in countries with greatest investor protection, the premium paid to share-holders is greater in these countries, and cross-border mergers are more likely if the target company is governed by stronger investment protection laws. While these investor protections themselves add costs to acquisition activity (such as mandatory disclosure requirements and restrictions on how the takeover is structured), they apparently offer much greater coun-tervailing economic benefit and consequently enhance the market for cor-porate control.

Evidence for the economic benefits of the securities law can also be seen from a natural experiment involving foreign issuers of securities. Foreign companies cross-list their securities, in the form of certain categories of American Depository Receipts (ADRs), on US markets, thereby sub-jecting themselves to some of the restrictions of this country's securities laws. Doing so has the economic benefit of providing more direct access to US capital, but given the globalization of financial capital markets, cross-listing is not vital to accessing US capital. Some countries, to encourage cross-listing on their markets, have advertised corporate-friendly legal rules, though the United States has maintained its strict securities law requirements. These stricter rules may well have enhanced cross-listing in the United States, implicitly demonstrating the economic advantages of its securities regulation.

John Coffee and others have suggested that such cross-listing in the United States is a form of "bonding" by foreign companies, in which they accept the relatively rigorous requirements of US securities law in order to demonstrate the quality of their company and credibility of their disclosures.[86] Cross-listing may take different forms but typically requires foreign firms to materially increase their disclosures. US securities laws can lend credibility to the cross-listing companies that enhances their investment appeal. Companies from countries with lesser legal requirements may reduce the agency risk costs of investment by binding themselves to tighter standards.[87] The existence of cross-listing provides another natural experiment regarding the value of US legal governance of corporate securities.

The phenomenon of cross-listing has been extensively investigated by financial economists. Much of the research shows a distinct benefit to cross-listing. An investigation of hundreds of cross-listings found that the process significantly reduced a company's cost of capital, and that the benefit was greater as the increased government regulation from cross-listing was greater (that is, as the home governance was weaker and when the cross-listing was with an American exchange that exercised greater supervisory power).[88] A study of Canadian firms found that cross-listed firms traded at a higher price than did their purely domestic counterparts.[89] Other studies have shown that cross-listings increase firms' market values.[90] The benefit is greatest for minority shareholders, as might be expected, because of their vulnerability to opportunism.[91] More specific accounting research demonstrates that the value from the US securities laws comes from the disclosure requirements, which enable more accurate projections of the company's prospects.[92]

Some additional research has found that firms from weak investor protection nations were less likely to cross-list in the United States, but that companies from those nations who did cross-list issued more equity.[93] While this result has been used to question the bonding hypothesis, it is consistent with the possibility that agency problems prevent even efficient bonding through cross-listing. The cross-listing test thus has some theoretical imperfections, because the individuals who choose to cross-list, a company's officers, are the very individuals whose opportunism is regulated by US securities laws. Hence, the firms that might most benefit from bonding may be the least likely to undertake the process. Perhaps for this reason, the empirical evidence on the bonding rationale for cross-listing is not entirely consistent, but the evidence gives substantial support for the claim that the costs of compliance with US securities laws are more than overcome by the benefits of such compliance.

The significance of the cross-listing research should not be exaggerated, many companies do not voluntarily cross-list (for reasons that may involve efficiency or managerial agency problems or some other factor). The presence of cross-listing simply provides evidence of the potentially empowering value of restrictive national laws, as foreign companies voluntarily choose to bind themselves with restrictions in order to gain the benefits of this action. Indeed, the research on the value of regulation for cross-listing could well understate the true effects of strict regulation, because the cross-listing decisions are made by managers who may have some self-interest to the contrary. The positive results for cross-listed companies further testify to the value of the SEC requirements. Other research has found that firms providing more disclosures have a lower cost of capital,[94] but again this research is limited to voluntary disclosures. Evidence of such benefits of voluntary disclosure could overstate the value of mandatory rules (which might require inefficient excessive disclosure) or understate their value (because agency problems make voluntary disclosure insufficient and inefficient).

Some international evidence supports the economic value of compulsory provisions of securities laws. When the developing market economies of the Czech Republic, Hungary, and Poland created rules for their economies, the latter two countries adopted strong investor protection securities laws with an independent regulator, while the Czech Republic did not do so.[95] Some argued that the Czech approach was superior and that the securities regulations would "suffocate" the developing equity markets of Hungary and Poland.[96] In reality, the Hungarian and Polish markets outperformed the Czech market, even though the latter nation's privatization strategy should have enhanced the development of stock markets.

These studies are limited in scope but clearly support the economic value of securities regulation. It seems that US legal governance enhances the efficient market for corporate control via acquisitions. US legal governance appears to provide considerable value to firms, as evidenced from the economic value of cross-listing and bonding with federal securities laws. The small test of emerging East European nations generally supports greater securities legislation. The available evidence suggests that US laws are economically beneficial, even when they appear to restrain private choice. Chapter 5 will contain much broader cross-country studies of the association of various legal restrictions and market development, and this research will demonstrate the economic value of securities regulation.

COSTS OF CORPORATE AND SECURITIES LAW

The benefits of the law discussed above must be weighed against the costs of the law. Critics of securities law have lamented the purportedly unnecessary costs of SEC compliance, but they have not examined those costs closely. While there are no precise cost estimates for particular corporate or securities laws, the law firm of Foley & Lardner has surveyed companies on the cost of being "public" companies, which provides a rough proxy of the costs associated with compliance with corporate and securities law.[97] Companies would have significant going public costs, even absent the law, because of their need to attract external shareholders, but many of the costs of going public are legally compelled. The Foley & Lardner survey found that average 2003 costs for companies with annual revenue under US$1 billion were US$2.862 million, and average 2003 costs for companies with annual revenue over US$1 billion were US$7.408 million.[98] The largest single component of these costs for the larger companies was lost productivity, though accounting costs and the costs of directors' and liability insurance were also substantial.

One can estimate the total societal costs of going public, as a rough proxy for costs of compliance with corporate and securities law. The Mergent Online database shows that in 2003, there were 1159 US public companies with revenues over US$1 billion, and 5484 US public companies with revenues of less than US$1 billion. Multiplying these times the survey estimates yields a total national going public cost for all US companies of about US$24.2 billion. This number estimates all going public expenses and substantially overestimates the costs of the laws themselves. Companies would have some material accounting and voluntary disclosure costs even without any law, in their attempt to persuade outside investors to invest. The amount of the overstatement would depend on the extent of voluntary disclosure that companies would make, and many critics of the law assume that this would be significant. Hence, this US$24.2 billion estimate is an upper bound that may considerably overstate the effective costs of legal compliance. While these costs of going public, whether legal or voluntary, seem substantial, they must be viewed in context, as illustrated by the following analysis of companies listed on the New York Stock Exchange.

In 2002, there were 2783 companies listed on the New York Stock Exchange, of which 941 had over US$1 billion in revenues, according to the Exchange's factbook and Mergent Online. Taking the cost estimates from the Foley & Lardner study and applying them to these company numbers yields a cumulative going public cost for NYSE companies of slightly more than US$12.2 billion. As noted above, this is an upper bound for the costs of corporate and securities law, overstating the true costs by some unknown but possibly substantial amount. The true cost of the corporate and securities laws for NYSE-listed companies is something below US$12.2 billion.

To put this in context, the total market value of NYSE-listed companies at the time was nearly US$10 trillion, according to the Exchange's factbook. The total costs of going public for these companies are thus less than 0.00012 of the companies' market capitalization. Hence, only a miniscule marginal benefit from the law of 0.00012 would be required to economically justify their costs. Given the context of equity markets, the absolute cost of going public is plainly quite small, and the potential net benefit of corporate and securities law is easily seen. The cost of the laws could be justified by any market benefit, even a proportionally tiny one. If the laws work in the manner hypothesized above, they should pay for themselves many times over.

CONCLUSION

Much conventional economic analysis of law rejects mandatory rules, because they limit private choice. This analysis can approach the Panglossian, claiming that a laissez faire result is the best possible result and not to be questioned, simply because it is the product of a free market. While there is obvious truth in recognizing the value of private choice, such choice does not necessarily yield perfect results, and a government regulatory system can still offer additional economic benefits even when it restricts some aspects of that private choice. Government action can enhance trust, can reduce transaction costs, and can contribute to valuable network externalities that promote the development of financial markets.

There is a strong theoretical case that legal rules, including restrictive rules, contribute to economic efficiency and developed capital markets. While some economists argue that our rules are too restrictive and interfere with the development of free markets, their case is an abstract one that does not seem consistent with the experiential evidence. To the contrary, the best case against our laws may be that they are insufficient and permit too much opportunism to continue unchecked. Certainly the corporate scandals of recent years do not imply that our legal requirements are unduly rigorous. This is an imperfect human world, though, and no procedure, legal or private, will succeed in exterminating objectionable behavior. Decisions are made on the margin, and legal rules, both empowering and restrictive, can facilitate markets and economic development at this level, notwithstanding their imperfections.

The economic case for basic, corporate, and securities laws laid out in this chapter is theoretical and does not reach the level of proof. Given the very small costs of the laws, it seems a plausible case, but it is not yet proved. If the assumptions about trust and relative transaction costs and the costs of government intervention that underlie this chapter were modified, one could reach different conclusions about the economic value of these laws, as many have. The issue of the relative accuracy of the various assumptions and the economic effect of the law is ultimately a consequentialist one, which requires real world empirical testing of the effect, of which this chapter includes only little. The empirical research cited in this chapter supports the role of the laws we discuss. Additional empirical support for this chapter is found in the history that will be supplied in Chapter 4 and the quantitative studies addressed in Chapter 5. At present, we maintain only that there is a valid economic theoretical reason to believe that the laws we examine do indeed enhance efficiency and economic development. The critics' economic case, which itself is almost entirely theoretical, is not a sufficient or compelling answer to the claim that the laws have value.

Before turning to our own empirical investigation of the theories, however, we consider the behavioral analysis of economic decisionmaking. While classical economic analysis has considerable validity, it rests upon certain rational choice assumptions about individual decisionmaking that are not entirely accurate. Considerable psychological research demonstrates that the assumptions of self-interested rational choice economic analysis do not inevitably govern human actions. These findings have implications for the choice between relational private and rule-based legal governance. The behavioral analysis builds upon and complements the classical economic analysis of this chapter to set forth the theoretical basis for the benefits of law, including the mandatory restraining legal rules of corporate and securities law.

NOTES

1. P.K. Rao, THE ECONOMICS OF TRANSACTION COSTS 9 (2003).
2. Robert D. Putnam, BOWLING ALONE: THE COLLAPSE AND REVIVAL OF AMERICAN COMMUNITY 145–46 (2000).
3. George Dent, *Lawyers and Trust in Business Alliances*, 58 BUS. LAWYER 45, 45 (2002).
4. Michael Taylor, THE POSSIBILITY OF COOPERATION (1987).
5. Sim B. Sitkin & Nancy L. Roth, *Explaining the Limited Effectiveness of Legalistic "Remedies" for Trust/Distrust*, 4 ORG. SCI. 367 (1993).
6. Sumantra Ghoshal & Peter Moran, *Bad for Practice: A Critique of the Transaction Cost Theory*, 21 ACAD. MANAGEMENT REV. 13, 24 (1996).
7. *See* Stewart Macaulay, *Non-Contractual Relations in Business: A Preliminary Study*, 28 AM. SOCIOL. REV. 55 (1963).
8. David Charny, *Nonlegal Sanctions in Commercial Relationships*, 104 HARV. L. REV. 373 (1990).
9. World Bank, BUILDING INSTITUTIONS FOR MARKETS 171 (2002).

10. Lisa Bernstein, *Opting Out of the Legal System: Extralegal Contractual Relations in the Diamond Industry*, 21 J. LEGAL STUD. 1 (1992).
11. Matt Ridley, THE ORIGINS OF VIRTUE 202 (1996).
12. *See* Gillian K. Hadfield, *Contract Law is Not Enough: The Many Legal Institutions that Support Contractual Commitments*, at 6, forthcoming in HANDBOOK OF NEW INSTITUTIONAL ECONOMICS (Claude Menard & Mary Shirley eds. 2004).
13. Avinash K. Dixit, LAWLESSNESS AND ECONOMICS 16 (2004).
14. George A. Akerlof, *The Market for "Lemons": Quality Uncertainty and the Market Mechanism*, 84 Q.J. ECON. 488 (1970).
15. *Id.* at 495.
16. Roy J. Lewicki, et al., *Trust and Distrust: New Relationships and Realities*, 23 ACAD. MANAGEMENT REV. 438 (1998).
17. Kathryn Hendley, Peter Murrell, & Randi Ryterman, *Law Works in Russia: The Role of Law in Interenterprise Transactions*, in ASSESSING THE VALUE OF LAW IN TRANSITION ECONOMIES (Peter Murrell ed. 2001).
18. *Id.* at 85.
19. John McMillan & Christopher Woodruff, *Courts and Relational Contracts*, 18 J. L. ECON. & ORG. 221 (2002).
20. *See* John Shuhe Li, *Relation-Based versus Rule-Based Governance: An Explanation of the East Asian Miracle and Asian Crisis*, 11 REV. INT'L ECON. 651 (2003).
21. *Id.* at 660.
22. *Id.* at 661.
23. Avinash K. Dixit, LAWLESSNESS AND ECONOMICS 12 (2004).
24. P. Milgrom & J. Roberts, *Economic Theories of the Firm: Past, Present, and Future*, 11 CAN. J. ECON. 444, 449 (1988).
25. John P. Powelson, THE MORAL ECONOMY 111 (1998).
26. Sitkin & Roth, *supra* note 5, at 371.
27. Putnam, *supra* note 2, at 350–63.
28. Alfred Chandler, SCALE AND SCOPE: THE DYNAMICS OF INDUSTRIAL CAPITALISM 286–87 (1990).
29. Frank H. Easter brook & Daniel R. Fischel, THE ECONOMIC STRUCTURE OF CORPORATE LAW 130–31(1991).
30. Roger Lowenstein, ORIGINS OF THE CRASH 153 (2004).
31. *Id.* at 190.
32. *See* Frank Partnoy, INECTIOUS GREED (2003).
33. *Id.* at 352.
34. Jonathan R. Macey, *A Pox on Both Your Houses: Enron, Sarbanes-Oxley and the Debate Concerning the Relative Efficacy of Mandatory Versus Enabling Rules*, 81 WASH. U. L. Q. 329, 342 (2003).
35. *See* Arthur A. Schulte, Jr., *Compatibility of Management Consulting and Auditing*, 40 ACCT. REV. 587 (1965).
36. *See* Robert A. Prentice, *The Case of the Irrational Auditor: A Behavioral Insight into Securities Fraud Litigation*, 95 N.W. U. L. REV. 133, 194 (2000).
37. *See* Stanley Bairman, *Discussion of Auditing: Incentives and Truthful Reporting*, 17 J. ACCT. RES. 25 (1979).
38. *Of Scolds and Conflicts*, WALL ST. J., June 22, 2004, at A18.
39. Dixit, *supra* note 13, at 84–85.
40. Donald Wittman, THE MYTH OF DEMOCRATIC FAILURE: WHY POLITICAL INSTITUTIONS ARE EFFICIENT (1995).
41. Rao, *supra* note 1, at 92.
42. Oriana Bandiera, *Land Reform, the Market for Protection and the Origins of the Sicilian Mafia: Theory and Evidence*, 19 J. LAW ECON. & ORG. 218 (2003).
43. *See* Frank B. Cross, *Law and Economic Growth*, 80 TEX.L.REV. 1751–52 (2002).
44. *See* L.J. Zucker, *The Production of Trust: Institutional Sources of Economic Structure*, 8 RESEARCH IN ORG. BEHAVIOR 55 (1986).
45. *See* Shuhe Li:, *supra* note 20.

46. Allesandro Arrighetti, et al., *Contract Law, Social Norms and Inter-Firm Cooperation*, 21 CAMBRIDGE J. ECON. 171, 175 (1997).
47. Peter Vincent-Jones, *Hybrid Organization, Contractual Governance, and Compulsory Tendering in the Provision of Local Authority Services*, in CONTRACTS, COOPERATION, AND COMPETITION 143, 158 (S. Deakin & J. Michie eds. 1997).
48. Rosalinde Klein Woolthuis, et al., *Trust and Formal Control in Interorganizational Relationships*, Erasmus Research Institute of Management Report 13-ORG (2002).
49. *Id.* at 12–13.
50. Richard A. Posner, ECONOMIC ANALYSIS OF LAW 90–91 (4th ed. 1992).
51. *Id.* at 411.
52. Easterbrook & Fischel, *supra* note 29, at 4.
53. Carlos E. Campos, Roberto E. Newell & Gregory Wilson, *Corporate Governance Develops in Emerging Markets*, MCKINSEY ON FINANCE 19, (Winter 2002).
54. Easterbrook & Fischel *supra* note 29, at 41–42.
55. Mark J. Roe, *Corporate Law's Limits*, 31 J. LEGAL STUD. 233 (2002).
56. *See* Cross, *supra* note 43, at 1737, 1747.
57. Easterbrook & Fischel, *supra* note 29, at 21.
58. *Id.* at 34.
59. Henry Hansmann, *Corporation and Contract*, 8 AM. L. ECON. REV. 1 (2006).
60. *See* Ralph K. Winter, Jr., *State Law, Shareholder Protection, and the Theory of the Corporation*, 6 J. LEGAL STUD. 251 (1977).
61. Posnet, ECONOMIC ANALYSIS OF LAW, *supra* note 50, at 444–45.
62. Larry E. Ribstein, *Law v. Trust*, 81 B.U. L. REV. 553, 573 (2001).
63. Art Durnev & E. Han Kim, *To Steal or Not To Steal: Firm Attributes, Legal Environment and Valuation*, 60 J. FIN. 1461 (2005).
64. Easterbrook & Fischel, *supra* note 29, at 299.
65. Bernard S. Black, *The Legal and Institutional Preconditions for Strong Securities Markets*, 48 UCLA L. REV. 781, 786 (2001).
66. Rao, *supra* note 1, at 94–95.
67. Michael Klausner, *Corporations, Corporate Law, and Networks of Contracts*, 81 VA. L. REV. 757 (1995).
68. *Id.* at 834.
69. Rao, *supra* note 1, at 94.
70. *See* Robert B. Ahdieh, *Making Markets: Network Effects and the Role of Law in Creation of Strong Securities Markets*, 76 SO. CAL. L. REV. 277 (2003).
71. *Id.*
72. S.J. Liebowitz & Stephen E. Margolis, *Network Externality: An Uncommon Tragedy*, 8 J. ECON. PERSP. 133 (1994).
73. Brian J. Bushee & Christian Leuz, *Economic Consequences of SEC Disclosure Regulations*, Wharton Financial Institutions Center Working Paper (February 2003).
74. Sim B. Sitkin, *On the Positive Effect of Legalization on Trust*, 5 RESEARCH ON NEGOTIATION IN ORG. 185, 190 (1995).
75. Margaret A. Blair & Lynn M. Stout, *Trust, Trustworthiness and the Behavioral Foundations of Corporate Law*, 149 U. PA. L. REV. 1735, 1767 (2001).
76. George Stigler, *Public Regulation of the Securities Markets*, 37 J. BUS. 117 (1964).
77. Carol J. Simon, *The Effect of the 1933 Securities Act on Investor Information and the Performance of New Issues*, 79 AM. ECON. REV. 295 (1989).
78. *Id.* at 309.
79. George J. Benston, *Required Disclosure and the Stock Market: An Evaluation of the Securities Exchange Act of 1934*, 63 AM. ECON. REV. 132 (1973).
80. *See* Irwin Friend & Randolph Westerfield, *Required Disclosure and the Stock Market: Comment*, AM ECON. REV. 467 (1975); Joel Seligman, *The Historical Need for a Mandatory Corporate Disclosure System*, 9 J. CORP. L. 1 (1983).
81. Easterbrook & Fischel, *supra* note 29, at 314.
82. Robert Prentice, *Whither Securities Regulation? Some Behavioral Observations Regarding Proposals for its Future*, 51 DUKE L.J. 1397, 1419–20 (2002).

83. *See* Paul G. Mahoney & Jianping Mei, *Mandatory vs. Contractual Disclosure in Securities Markets: Evidence from the 1930s*, University of Virginia Law School John M. Olin Program in Law and Economics Working Paper #25 (2006).

84. Easterbrook & Fischel, *supra* note 29, at 171–72.

85. Stefano Rossi & Paolo Volpin, *Cross-Country Determinants of Mergers and Acquisitions*, ECGI Finance Working Paper No. 25/2003 (September 2003).

86. *See* John C. Coffee, *Racing Towards the Top? The Impact of Cross-Listings and Stock Market Competition on International Corporate Governance*, 102 COLUM. L. REV. (2002).

87. *See* R.M. Stulz, *Globalization of Equity Markets and the Cost of Capital*, J. APPLIED CORPORATE FIN. 8 (1999).

88. *See* Luzi Hail & Christian Leuz, *Cost of Capital and Cash Flow Effects of U.S. Cross-Listings*, ECGI Finance Working Paper (May 2004).

89. *See* Michael R. King & Dan Segal, *Corporate Governance, International Cross Listing and Home Bias*, CAN. INVESTMENT REV. 8 (Winter 2003).

90. *See* Craig G. Doidge, Andrew Karolyi & Rene M. Stulz, *Why are Foreign Firms Listed in the U.S. Worth More?*, 71 J. FIN. ECON. 205 (2004).

91. *See* Craig G. Doidge, *U.S. Cross-Listings and the Private Benefits of Control: Evidence from Dual-Class Firms*, 72 J. FIN. ECON 519 (2004).

92. Mark Lang, Karl Lins & Darius Miller, *ADRs, Analysts, and Accuracy: Does Cross Listing in the United States Improve a Firm's Information Environment and Increase Market Value*, 41 J. ACC. RSCH. 317 (2003).

93. W.A. Reese & M. Weisbach, *Protection of Minority Shareholder Interests, Cross-Listings in the United States, and Subsequent Equity Offerings*, 66 J. FIN ECON. 65 (2003).

94. Christine Botosan, *Disclosure Level and the Cost of Equity Capital*, 72 THE ACCOUNTING REV. 323 (1997).

95. *See* Katarina Pistor, *Law as a Determinant for Equity Market Development: The Experience of Transition Economies* in ASSESSING THE VALUE OF LAW IN TRANSITION ECONOMIES, *supra* note 17, at 267.

96. *Id.* at 278.

97. Thomas E. Hartman, Foley & Lardner LLP, *The Cost of Being Public in the Era of Sarbanes-Oxley* (presented at the 2004 meeting of the National Directors Institute).

98. *Id.* at 14.

3. Behavioral analysis of law and corporate finance

Chapter 2 demonstrated how traditional economic analysis could justify various forms of law and regulation, including securities regulation, as advancing economic efficiency and capital market development. Some economists, however, have used similar versions of economic reasoning to argue for minimization or outright elimination of securities regulation, or even foundational and corporate law. These views may be based upon unrealistic assumptions regarding how people make decisions. Traditional economic analysis has great power but rests upon behavioral assumptions of rational choice that are at best debatable. Psychological research into human behavior has shown that the simple behavioral assumptions of traditional economic analysis often do not apply. The purpose of this chapter is to explore how these behavioral insights bolster the conclusions derived in Chapter 2. The chapter applies the general principles of behavioral psychology to highlight from a different perspective the value that well-designed, well-administered law can have in advancing the benefits of a market economy. The behavioral insights integrate well with the key concepts of trust and transaction costs and their influence on efficient economic outcomes.

INTRODUCTION TO BEHAVIORAL DECISION THEORY

In antitrust law and some other areas, economic insights have added substantial enlightenment to policy analysis and had some impact on the law. However, the rigorous logic of traditional economic analysis has often been based on inaccurate premises, such as the rational man hypothesis. If one grants the assumption that people are always rational maximizers of their expected self-interest, then one may conclude that contracting parties will always bargain to the most efficient outcome. As discussed in Chapter 2, some maintain that investors should need no law or at most a bare bones contract law with an efficient civil judicial system to protect their investments from the perfidy of securities dealers, corporate officers and directors, and other market participants. Corporation law and securities law become largely redundant and even counterproductive in this calculus. While Chapter 2 makes a traditional economic case for corporate and securities law, that case is enhanced and supplemented by an appreciation of the research on human behavior.

Called varyingly behavioral law and economics, legal decision theory, and related terms, what we shall call *behavioral decision theory* derives largely from the work of Nobel Prize winning psychologist Daniel Kahneman and his late colleague Amos Tversky. Through years of experiments that have been replicated and extended by psychologists around the world, Kahneman and Tversky demonstrated that individuals do not make decisions in the fully-informed, rational manner assumed by traditional economic analysis. Instead most individuals' reasoning is infected by biases and the tendency to use simplifying heuristics that often cause judgments to divert from the theoretically rational in systematic ways.

Behavioral decision theory can improve economic analysis by providing more realistic psychological foundations for its analysis. Behavioral decision theory and related research stemming from fields such as behavioral finance, behavioral economics, and cognitive psychology add depth to our understanding of the role that law can play in creating a just and efficient society. Traditional economic theory posits that man is a rational maximizer of his expected utilities. Freed of governmental interference, such a rational man could, some argue, freely bargain with sellers of securities for an optimal level of disclosure and an optimal level of antifraud protection to fit his risk profile.

In the last 30 years, a "mountain of experiments,"[1] largely performed in the Kahneman and Tversky "heuristics and biases" tradition, demonstrates that people tend to deviate *systematically* from rational norms when they make decisions. As the study of human judgment has expanded beyond the psychology discipline and given rise to behavioral finance and behavioral economics, several related schools of thought have come to the fore. Some psychologists and others, for example, have stressed how deviations from the rational man model can constitute "fast and frugal" heuristics that can be quite useful in certain decisionmaking settings.[2] Others have sought to steal the new field of decisionmaking away from psychologists and bring it back into economics by studying the "economics of irrationality."[3] This section presents an overview of some of the more important deviations from ideal rationality

Bounded Rationality and Rational Ignorance

While traditional economic theory assumes that decisionmakers have complete and perfectly accurate information, that is seldom the case. Collecting full information is sufficiently expensive in terms of time, money, and effort that most decisionmakers sensibly stop materially short of doing so. Because of the lack of full information and additional limitations on rationality it is fair to say, as Nobel Prize winner Herbert Simon did long ago, that people are *"intendedly* rational, but only *limitedly* so."[4] This insight is consistent with that of traditional transaction cost economics but goes beyond that analysis by recognizing that individuals may lack the ability to optimize the precise amount and nature of transaction costs that they should bear for perfectly rational efficiency.

Confirmation Bias

Even if decisionmakers had relatively easy access to full information, perceptual limitations would hinder their decisionmaking. The confirmation bias indicates that if people begin a decisionmaking process believing that, for example, ABC Company's products are technically superior to those of its competitors, they will tend to gather information that supports that belief and ignore information that undermines it. Even trained scientists judge research reports that agree with their views to be of higher quality than comparable research reports that disagree with their views.[5] This bias and those that follow cause individuals to misestimate the transaction costs they should undertake in contracting. They will tend to perform too little informational investigation if they have an *a priori* trust in the other party.

Self-Serving Bias

The confirmation bias is strongly related to the broader self-serving bias that indicates that when people gather, process, and even remember information, they tend to do so in ways that support their preexisting point of view or their perceived self-interest. Information that contradicts their previous viewpoint or that undermines their perceived self-interest in some other way, is less likely to be sought out, read carefully, considered thoroughly, or recalled later. Even sincere efforts to judge the fairness of a situation are inevitably colored by the self-interest of the person making the judgment. For example, people tend to overvalue their own contributions to a joint project. If a company is doing well, its CEO likely believes that he or she is uniquely talented and responsible for its success.

Cognitive Dissonance

Reinforcing the confirmation bias and other problems with objectively processing information is Festinger's concept of cognitive dissonance,[6] the notion that people prefer cognitive consistency and when they have made a decision their minds will tend to suppress information inconsistent with the decision they have made. Thus, an auditor who has publicly taken the position that her client's financial statements are accurate or an attorney who has publicly stated that his client is innocent will have great difficulty objectively processing new information that is inconsistent with those positions. This concept reinforces *belief persistence*, the tendency of people to hold to beliefs long after the basis for those beliefs has been thoroughly discredited.

Emotions

Emotions can and do affect people's reasoning. Even if a person had access to full information, sometimes emotions such as anger or sadness prevent or severely impede rational thought. The connection between emotions and reasoning is complex, and it is well known that damage to key emotional centers of the brain can make it difficult for people to make good decisions or, indeed, to make decisions at all.[7] One emotion that people do not enjoy is regret; therefore, they will take extensive steps to avoid feeling regret, a phenomenon termed *regret aversion*. Because humans tend to regret adverse consequences that stem from their actions more than adverse consequences stemming from their inaction (the *omission bias*), anticipated regret aversion can channel human decisionmaking in important ways. Regret aversion suggests that, absent any legal protection, many individuals will choose not to invest in the market for fear of suffering great losses, even if the risk of such losses is small. Relatedly, people possess an innate sense of *fairness* and will act in a way that damages their own self-interest in order to punish others whom the decisionmaker believes have acted unfairly. While emotions are not necessarily irrational, they are generally ignored by traditional economic analysis.

Undue Optimism and Overconfidence

It seems to be evolutionarily adaptive to be unduly optimistic, to believe that the bad things that occur in life will mostly happen to other people and not to us. There is some evidence that only the chronically depressed are well-calibrated in this regard. Newlyweds optimistically believe that there is a zero chance that they will get divorced, though 40–50 percent of marriages end in divorce. People also tend to think that they are more moral, more competent, better drivers, smarter investors,[8] and otherwise generally superior to their fellows. Because of undue optimism and overconfidence, people can make decisions that are ill-considered and occasionally unduly risky. Undue optimism might, for example, cause a party to be blindly trusting of another even when such trust was unwarranted.

Illusion of Control

Related to undue optimism and overconfidence is the illusion of control, the irrational belief people often hold that they can influence things that are truly out of their control. Because of this illusion, people tend to roll a pair of dice hard when they want a high number and softly when they want a low number, and they value more highly a lottery ticket that they chose from a bin as compared to a similar lottery ticket in that same bin that someone else chose for them.

Availability Heuristic

Because of the availability heuristic, people often think that events that seldom occur actually happen more frequently simply because they have been in the news recently or are otherwise particularly available to recall. Because murders make the headlines and strokes usually do not, people tend to think that more people die of murder than strokes when the actually ration is 11 to 1 in the other direction. This heuristic, like many others, will cause individuals to miscalculate the efficient transaction costs necessary for a particular decision.

Representativeness Heuristic

Because of the representativeness heuristic, decisionmakers tend to judge probabilities by flouting numerous rules of statistics and focusing instead upon the degree of similarity that an item seems to bear to a category or parent population. For example, in deciding whether a person is an accountant or a professional basketball player, people will tend to focus on how much the person fits the stereotype of the two professions (tall? mild-mannered?), ignoring the fact that there are many times more professional accountants than professional basketball players. The fact that the representativeness heuristic tends to cause people to ignore base rates creates many errors in statistical reasoning.

False Consensus Effect

People are often surprised that others do not share their views on issues ranging from capital punishment to the designated hitter. They expect others to share their views—if they believe ABC Co. is a good investment, they act as though others will believe that also.[9] They expect others to share their qualities: honest people expect other people to be honest; crooks have much lower expectations for their fellow man. Because of the false consensus effect, honest people are often insufficiently wary. A related phenomenon is the *personal positivity bias*—which is what causes people to think that although most politicians are crooks, their Senator is honest and although many stockbrokers are untrustworthy, the one they have chosen is a prince among men.

Insensitivity to the Source of Information

People have difficulty not taking into account information that they are exposed to, even if they are given evidence that the source of the information is biased or perhaps of dubious reliability. People adjust their perception of the information in light of the problems with the source, but typically do not do so sufficiently. For example, from May 2000 to February 2001, the NASDAQ stock index fell by more than one-third, yet Wall Street stock analysts sell recommendations held steady at 0 percent.[10] This was a clear signal to the market that many analysts were more concerned with opportunistic behavior, protecting the interests of the investment bankers in their firms, than they were with producing accurate reports. Nonetheless, the market did not adequately adjust for the unreliability of the stock analysts.[11] The SEC decried earnings management, yet issuers continued to practice it and generally fooled even professional investors.[12] This explains how even unreliable intermediaries may thrive, failing to correct for opportunistic behavior.

The Conformity Bias

People tend to look to others for cues as to how to act. When more forks than they are used to seeing are arranged around their plate at a fancy dinner, they tend to look to others to see which one to pick up first. In business as well, decisionmakers will be heavily influenced by the decisions and actions of those around them. Solomon Asch proved that subjects will often say that one line that is obviously shorter than another is indeed longer if several confederates of the experimenter have said that it is longer. In cooperation games, people tend to cooperate if they think that is what other participants will do; they tend not to cooperate if competition seems to be the expected conduct. People are so influenced by the actions and views of others that in some contexts *groupthink* occurs, where group loyalty in a homogeneous group and pressures to conform in a homogeneous group lead to "a deterioration of mental efficiency, reality testing, and moral judgment."[13] Reinforcing groupthink is the phenomenon known as *risky shift* wherein decisionmakers will tend to make more extreme (sometimes riskier) decisions when acting in small groups than when acting alone. Yet another related notion is *herding*, where decisionmakers such as hedge fund operators ignore their own judgment and even the underlying facts, focusing primarily upon other people's actions.

Low Probability Events

In calculating probabilities, not only do people tend to give undue weight to vivid events (as noted above), but they also tend to completely ignore some potentially significant but low probability events. For that reason, people tended not to wear seatbelts before the law required them to buckle up and tended not to buy flood insurance unless there had been a recent flood. When people do heed low probability events, they are likely to weight them improperly and may exaggerate their significance.

Anchoring and Adjustment

Although there is no particular reason for the last two digits of a person's social security number to influence their decisions, it will almost always do so if they are asked to think of those numbers and then make a judgment as to an uncertain numeric answer, such as the number of African countries in the United Nations or the number of miles from Denver to Memphis. If one of two negotiators first mentions a number, it often anchors the discussion and influences the ultimate outcome. Such anchoring may prevent parties from properly adjusting to information about matters such as managerial opportunism.

Framing

Under certain circumstances, people's answers to questions and solutions to problems tend to change depending on how the question or problem is framed, even if the substance of the query remains constant. For example, people would rather buy potato chips that are advertised as 90 percent fat-free than identical chips advertised as 10 percent fat.[14] Marketers of potato chips and securities often take advantage of this weakness that most buyers exhibit in making decisions—Fidelity Investments recently advertised that 6 of its 24 funds were "highly rated" when it would have been as true to say that 75 percent of its funds were not.[15] The framing bias is one that facilitates fraud by those who are clever enough to take advantage of the bias in others.

Loss Aversion

A major implication of framing is that people's decisions can be greatly impacted by whether a problem is presented in a "gain frame" or a "loss frame." The reason is that people suffer from the impact of losses about twice as intensely as they enjoy gains. They will often, therefore, make seemingly irrational decisions in an effort to avoid sustaining losses. As with regret aversion, this heuristic will cause individuals to underinvest in markets, harming the economy, as the relative risk of loss grows.

Endowment Effect

Loss aversion is exacerbated by the endowment effect. Although a pen would appear to be a pen and a candy bar a candy bar, hundreds of studies show that if the pen or candy bar are ours, if we consider them part of our endowment, we will often demand many times as much money to part with them as we would have paid to acquire them in the first place. Because people do not feel that they were endowed with money they do not have on account, hidden taxes flourish in our economy. Consistent with this research, mutual funds continuously charge customers with hidden fees. Investors avoid high front-end load fees that are quite visible, but tend to ignore seemingly smaller ongoing operating expenses and other fees that are hidden by the volatility of equity returns.[16]

Prospect Theory

Loss aversion, the endowment effect, *reference dependent utility* (the fact that we are often more concerned with our position relative to other reference points—such as the status quo or the wealth of our neighbors—than with our absolute position), and framing are four pieces that help make up prospect theory, Kahneman and Tversky's proposed improvement upon rational man economics' subjective utility theory. Although not perfectly satisfying, prospect theory suggests, in part, that the notion of utility should be replaced with "value," which is defined in terms of gains and losses from a reference point with the value function being greater for gains than for losses. Preferences will depend on whether a problem is presented in a loss frame or a gain frame.[17]

Mental Accounting

Although to *homo economicus*, a dollar is a dollar, *homo sapiens* often treats dollars differently by placing them in separate mental accounts. Thus, for

example, people may be willing to spend money won in a raffle in a frivolous way when they would not willingly spend money from their regular
paycheck in that way. Stocks may be treated differently as well. One study
found that when employees' options in pension funds are limited to stocks
and bonds of other companies, they average investing 51 percent of their
money in the stock funds and 49 percent in the bond funds. If a third choice
is added in the form of their own company's stock, they tend to invest 42
percent in their company's stock, and then 29 percent in the other stock
funds and 29 percent in the other bond funds. They account differently for
their own company's shares, leading to a much different balance between
stocks and bonds.[18] As noted above, a feature such as this will cause the
misallocation of the efficient optimization of transaction costs.

Status Quo Bias

All things being equal, people prefer the status quo, the familiar. They tend
to stick with the old favorite, even if they might choose an alternative were
they choosing for the first time. Related to this is the *habit* heuristic. As a
handy mental shortcut, many people choose to drive a certain route to work
or to order a certain dish at a restaurant because they "always" do it and
need not expend mental energy reweighing the advantages and disadvantages of alternate choices.

Sunk Cost Effects

Assume that a couple has purchased tickets to a play whose traveling cast
is visiting their city from New York. On the day of the performance they
both feel sick and are told by reliable sources that the show really stinks. If
they had been given the tickets, the couple might well choose to stay home.
But if they paid for the tickets, they will hesitate to "waste" their money and
so they are much more likely to go to the play and suffer loss of time that
will compound their loss of money. Rational people would not do this,
economists counsel, but most real people honor sunk costs.[19] Indeed, once
costs are sunk, individuals and groups often decide to pour more and
more resources into a deteriorating situation in an irrational *escalation of
commitment.*

Time Delay Traps

When an action has short-term and long-term consequences, people tend
to underappreciate the impact of the latter. They tend to value immediate
over delayed gratification and often have great difficulty making rational

intertemporal choices.[20] According to Professor Kraakman, "The *Wall Street Journal* reports almost daily on at least one controlling executive from a substantial firm who (now to his regret) chose to gamble personal liability against the returns on bribery, price-fixing, or third-party fraud."[21] The time delay trap certainly plays a role in many of these criminal acts where *homo sapiens* fails to act as *homo economicus*.

Bounded Willpower

Theoretically, a rational man who has made a decision as to what is in his best interests can then execute that decision. Unfortunately, the very existence of smoking clinics and fat farms indicates that because of bounded willpower, humans often are unable to act consistently with their own best interests, even if those happen to be perceived accurately. Because of time delay traps and bounded willpower, even a dominant efficient strategy (such as the universally honest behavior of Figure 2.2 above) will not always prevail.

Other flaws in human judgment and decisionmaking could be added to this already lengthy catalogue, but the obvious point is that people do not act as traditional economic theory assumes. While all people are not affected by all of these heuristics and biases in all circumstances, they do tend to systematically depart from optimal decisionmaking in a variety of settings. This extensive list reveals the limits of rational choice assumptions.

The implications of behavioralism should not be exaggerated. While the long list of behavioral exceptions to rational choice might leave one thinking that we live in a wildly irrational world, markets do operate in at least a roughly rational manner. Successful companies generally draw more investment, and obviously failing companies are shunned. Many economic predictions are confirmed in practice. Neither should the implications of behavioralism be ignored, though. Imperfectly rational efficient behavior leaves room for improvement. To the extent that the law can help counteract some of the systematic behavioral biases, it may produce a more extensive and more efficient system of capital markets.

ILLUSTRATIVE IMPACT OF BEHAVIORAL DECISION THEORY

Although many of these heuristics and biases have been discovered in the laboratory, most have been uncovered as psychologists attempted to determine explanations for real-life conduct that appeared to be inconsistent with the economist's rational man model. Most have been replicated in studies of real-world decisionmakers.[22] As an indication of the significance of behavioral decision theory, consider its impact on just one aspect of economic analysis—the efficient market hypothesis.

Some believe that the stock market is strong-form efficient, that securities prices respond to all relevant information, public or private. More popular is semi-strong form efficiency—that current prices reflect everything that can be learned by studying public information.[23] In 1978, Professor Jensen announced that "there is no other proposition in economics which has more solid empirical evidence supporting it than the Efficient Markets Hypothesis."[24]

Although securities markets are certainly efficient and for many purposes of analysis it makes sense to assume their more complete efficiency, in real life many departures from theoretical models are observed. The work of Kahneman and Tversky, of Richard Thaler (founder of the field of behavioral finance),[25] and of Colin Camerer and many others (developers of the subdiscipline of behavioral economics)[26] has demonstrated that Jensen's statement was premature. That economists today admit that behavioral studies demonstrate that investors are often far from rational, that the judgment biases of even sophisticated institutional investors "are not isolated quirks but consistent deep-rooted and *systematic* behavioral patterns"[27] counsels against overstating the efficiency of the market, especially the unregulated market.

Consider, for example, the equity premium puzzle. Since 1926, the annual real return on equity securities has been approximately seven times as large as the real return on treasury bills. Risk coefficients cannot explain the difference. Within the standard expected utility-maximizing paradigm, this persistent premium presents a conundrum. Why is anyone willing to hold treasury bills and other bonds? The best explanation developed to date is that proposed by Thaler and Benartzi that rests upon two behavioral concepts: (a) loss aversion, and (b) mental accounting. As noted earlier, mental accounting means that, contrary to economic reasoning, people do not treat all money as fungible. Combined, these two factors create what Thaler and Benartzi called myopic loss-aversion. Over the long run equities will do better than bonds, but in the short run they have much greater variability. Because people, including sophisticated investors such as pension funds and university endowments, hate to sustain losses, even in the short run, they will demand a large premium to accept the return variability of equity securities.[28]

Or consider that there is considerably more frequent trading on securities markets than rational models predict. One of the leading explanations for why so much trading occurs is the overconfidence of traders. Whereas rational investors would not make trades if projected returns are insufficient to cover information and transaction costs, overly confident investors would have unrealistic beliefs regarding their projected trading profits. This hypothesis has been advanced by several scholars and confirmed in an empirical study involving investors with discount broker-age accounts.[29] And the more frequently investors trade, the worse they tend to do.[30]

Or consider the disposition effect. The evidence is quite strong that loss aversion and related phenomena cause investors to be reluctant to sell shares when to do so would sustain a loss. Rather than suffer the pain of the loss, investors tend to hold on to the shares too long a time (and often end up sustaining a much larger loss). In complementary fashion, investors tend to sell shares that have accumulated small gains quickly in order to lock in a gain and insure against a loss. In both regards, investors' activity contradicts models of efficient investing behavior.[31]

When empirical studies in finance demonstrated that investors tended to underreact to releases of good news or bad news but overreact to a series of releases of news, behavioralists indicated psychological grounds for these inefficient tendencies. Tversky and others had already demonstrated that in making projections, people tend to pay too much attention to the strength of evidence they consider and too little attention to its statistical weight.[32] Barberis, Shleifer, and Vishny developed a "model of investor sentiment" that showed how this psychological tendency could account for the market's under and overreactions.[33]

Why did the securities markets not react rationally during the dot.com boom, when information surfaced that Enron seemingly owed no taxes, and when WorldCom repeatedly met earnings projections by fractions of a penny per share? Why was Alan Greenspan's observation that the markets suffered from "irrational exuberance" so prescient? Ribstein sensibly sug-gests overoptimism as an explanation. In bubbles, investors tend to under-estimate the likelihood of loss and are optimistic that even if the train crashes, they will be one of the last ones to jump off before the collision.[34] The availability effect and the representativeness heuristic can also lead people to see trends that are not always there and to expect prices that have been rising to continue to rise even in the absence of sound economic reasons for them to do so.[35]

The most common response to these demonstrated errors is the claim that sophisticated investors dominate the market, and their judgment and expertise should always move the market to the efficient level. But in the dot.com bubble, virtually all those sophisticated investors rode Enron stock from its market high of 90 dollars right down to its bargain basement price of 90 cents. They made the same cognitive mistakes as lay investors and lost hundreds of millions, if not billions of dollars when the bubble burst.[36] The fact that institutional investors were as prone to the hysteria of the dot.com bubble as lay investors was not surprising to behavioralists. A wide array of studies have indicated that experts with sophistication and experience, including physicians, statisticians, judges, auditors, engineers, securities analysts, financial analysts, institutional investors, and others are often nearly as subject to (and, occasionally, more subject to) the problems caused by heuristic-driven and biased thinking as are lay people.[37] In the words of Hersh Shefrin, "Wall Street strategists are prone to committing a variety of behavioral errors and biases: gambler's fallacy, overconfidence, and anchoring."[38]

Research has found that investing professionals are boundedly rational; "operating under conditions that have both financial and ego consequences and where information acquisition costs are virtually zero, even professional security analysts deciding on which securities to select do not acquire most (or even much) of the information available."[39] Even institutional investors tend to base their investing decisions on hunches, emotions, and intuitions.[40] Professional investors, like others, are subject to the availability heuristic, meaning in part that they are more likely to buy the stocks of companies that are easy to recall, perhaps because they have been mentioned in the newspaper recently.[41] Professional investors are also subject to the representativeness heuristic, meaning that they are more likely to judge some probabilities based not on statistical likelihood but upon the similarity that an item seems to bear to a category or parent population. This heuristic is part of the reason that professional investors irrationally believe in the proverbial "hot hand," the erroneous notion that a money manager or security analyst who has been on a roll will stay on a roll.[42] It appears that investing professionals tend to ignore low probability events.[43]

This above discussion is far from exhaustive but should suffice to illustrate that institutional and other sophisticated investors' behavior does not overcome the effects of psychological heuristics. If people are not models of rationality and even institutional and other sophisticated investors can make systematic misjudgments that prevent the financial markets from being as efficient as economic theory presumes, there is room for law and regulation to play a role in improving market efficiency.

BASIC LAW AND BEHAVIORAL DECISION THEORY

Economic analysis has dominated interdisciplinary legal research in recent years, in part because it adds rigor to legal analysis. However, a limitation on economic analysis is that the law attempts to influence human behavior, but economists often proceed from an incomplete understanding of why humans act as they do. As already noted, the most frequent and significant misassumption of economic analysis is that human beings are optimally rational maximizers of their expected utilities. Behavioral decision theory, which starts from more realistic assumptions as to why people act as they do, can help explain the role of law in advancing the efficiency of markets.

Consider contract law. An overarching premise of economic analysis of contracts, including those used to embody rights in corporate structures and purchases and sales of securities, is found in an aspect of the Coase Theorem which provides that the initial assignment of legal rights does not determine which use will ultimately prevail because the parties will bargain to the most efficient state of affairs.[44] In other words, if left to their own devices and without transaction costs, free of government interference, promoters of and investors in enterprises will negotiate to the most efficient possible contract.

However, research from behavioral psychology indicates that the initial assignment of legal rights matters significantly in contractual bargaining. Evidence indicates that people are both loss averse and impacted by the endowment effect. Together, these concepts indicate that the initial distribution of rights will greatly impact negotiation between two parties.[45] For example, if a statute provides that employees will presumptively have certain types of benefits unless they agree to forfeit them, they are much more likely to be accorded those benefits by an employer than if the statute provides that employees presumptively will *not* have those benefits unless they bargain with the employer to achieve them.[46] Therefore, it is likely that under a corporate code that assumes shareholders will not have inspection rights or voting rights unless they take measures to have the Articles of Incorporation amended, then they are much less likely to have such rights than if the corporate code assumes that such rights exist. Economists recognize that transactions costs mean that the simple Coase Theorem cannot describe reality but behavioral psychologists go further and recognize that even in the absence of material transaction costs, such a renegotiation is not likely to occur.

Besides loss aversion and the endowment effect, the related concept of the status quo bias plays a role here. *Ceteris paribus*, people prefer the status quo.[47] Part of the reason is regret aversion—that they are more likely to regret bad consequences that stem from their actions than from their inactions. By sticking with the status quo they reduce the risk of feeling regret in the future.[48] Thus, when New Jersey reduced the price of automobile insurance along with coverage but gave insureds the option to opt into a more expensive policy with broader rights and Pennsylvania did the opposite—enacted an expanded-rights presumption that gave insureds the option to opt into a cheaper regime with fewer rights to sue, in each state most insureds chose what they perceived to be the status quo. A large majority of New Jersey residents chose cheaper insurance and less coverage while a large majority of Pennsylvanians chose more expensive insurance and more coverage.[49] As Korobkin has demonstrated experimentally, parties tend to treat form contracts as the status quo and to accept them with little question or negotiation.[50] Consumers may well accept a warranty disclaimer or arbitration clause that is part of a form contract because it seems to be the status quo, where they would object loudly to the suggestion that such a provision be penciled into a form contract that did not contain them.[51]

Some argue that although the status quo bias might explain why Coasian bargaining does not occur in real life when economists theorize that it should, it does not explain why abusive terms persist. The notion is that competition should force merchants to place pro-consumer provisions in their contracts. Unfortunately, the reverse is often true. Because consumers and investors tend not to pay attention to nonprice terms and often believe that unfair collateral terms such as waivers of rights or arbitration provisions will never apply to them (because of the tendency people have to be unduly optimistic and to ignore low probability events), competition actually forces merchants to include such terms so they will not miss out on the profits their competitors are achieving by scalping customers. The simple fact is that contract renegotiation is quite rare, indicating that contracting parties do not, when faced with a contract that is not optimal, reopen bargaining to work toward a better solution, indicates that the Coase theorem is unduly optimistic. If parties cannot be counted to bargain to the most efficient result, then there may well be a role for law and regulation.

As indicated in the previous chapter, trust is an important part of a business environment, and law can foster trust. People do not wish to do business in a crooked marketplace. This is true in part because of rational fears of being exploited by dishonest companies and individuals. In addition, it is true because people inherently value fairness. "Humans are guided by an innate sense of fairness that drives their actions, attitudes and behaviors."[52] Although it is not always rational for people to act fairly toward others in a one-shot ultimatum game context, they often do. They do because fairness matters, as research in behavioral decision theory indicates. In the experimental ultimatum game, A may be given US$100 with the power to offer any division between himself and B. But if B rejects the division, neither party receives anything. Rationally, economists say, A should offer US$1 to B and propose to keep US$99 for himself. B should accept this because US$1 is better than nothing. However, typically offerors propose much fairer divisions of the US$100 (often 50/50) and offerees who are offered a very small share often reject it. They would rather receive nothing in order to punish the offeror for acting inequitably than to receive an amount they perceive as unfair. Many offerees are willing to suffer an economic loss in order to promote perceived fairness.[53]

Contract rules that promote fairness can not only benefit society by recognizing that efficiency is not the only value that policy should be concerned with; they can also promote efficiency by creating the type of economic atmosphere in which people wish to do business. To promote fairness, contract law allows incapacitated people to disaffirm their contracts.[54] Not only does this policy deter and punish inequitable conduct and prevent the government's enforcement mechanism from being used for an inappropriate purpose,[55] it also advances efficiency because incapacitated people are unlikely to allocate their resources in an optimal manner. To promote fairness, contract law prohibits fraud. As Farnsworth points out, intentional misrepresentation is the type of act that invites courts to make moral judgments.[56] Fortunately, this rule also promotes efficiency, for fraud undermines the efficient allocation of resources.

The importance of law in this regard is difficult to overstate, for an unregulated system of private contracting can lead to rampant opportunism. For several reasons, many having to do with the tenets of behavioral decision theory, a lawless market is suboptimal. First, people are usually unable to tell when they are being lied to. Many studies show that few people can guess at a better than chance level as to when people are lying to them.[57] Worse yet, because of overconfidence, people think they are adept at lie detecting, leaving them particularly vulnerable. The consensus effect exacerbates an already bad situation by increasing an honest person's vulnerability when they are dealing with someone they perceive to be "like them" (hence the popularity of affinity frauds). And even if people learn that the person they are contracting with is untrustworthy, insensitivity to source means that they may well fail to take adequate steps to protect themselves. Those who do not fall prey to fraud may be overly cautious and frightened of any investment, for fear of being defrauded, even when the other party is honest. Contract rules that refuse to enforce unfair and inefficient contracts and that punish fraudsters advance fairness and efficiency concerns.

In both contract law and tort law, it is often argued that governmental regulation and law-imposed liability are unnecessary because reputational constraints will suffice to discipline contract breakers and tortfeasors. Contracting parties will not commit fraud because it will ruin their reputation in the marketplace. Sellers will not market defective products because word will spread and no one else will buy from them.

Because a rational person has concern for his or her long-term reputation, some economists have presumed that government regulation of fraud is unneeded in securities and other markets. Repeat players must act properly or else they will be punished. As just one example, Judge Easterbrook, a leading law and economics scholar as well as a federal judge, has opined that even in the face of a financial scandal with a busted audit, judges should presume that the auditors were not reckless because their long-term reputational interest makes it "irrational" for them to do anything other than make their clients toe the line.[58] Chapter 2 has demonstrated how reputational sanctions cannot produce an efficient level of honesty, and behavioralism only enhances the economic problem.

Unfortunately, the past few years have made it surpassingly clear that too many actors in our capital markets, perhaps because of time delay traps or other problems with intertemporal decisionmaking, are more than willing to sacrifice long-term reputational capital for short-term financial gain. Corporations such as Enron, WorldCom, Global Crossing, HealthSouth, and Tyco had wonderful reputations in the late 1990s. Enron was widely known as the world's most innovative company. WorldCom was a marvel of the hot new telecommunications sector. Yet all these companies, and many others, ruined their own reputations by financial skullduggery. Enron moved debt off its books and engaged in transactions designed to produce the temporary appearance of income, ultimately costing its investors US$70 billion. WorldCom inflated earnings by US$11 billion. Global Crossing collapsed under US$12.4 billion in debt that it had hidden. Quest restated US$2.5 billion in revenue in 2000 and 2001. Indeed, 10 percent of NYSE-listed companies had to restate their financials between 1997 and June 2002, and writeoffs of US$148 billion erased virtually all of the profits reported by NASDAQ companies between 1995 and 2000. While recognizing that empirical studies show that there are long-term benefits to building a reputation for providing reliable and timely disclosures, Professor Dechow and colleagues noted after a recent empirical study that "the sample of firms investigated in this study chose to risk (and ultimately lose) those benefits for the prospect of short-term gain."[59]

Of course, the actions of corporations are really the actions of individuals. What about their reputational capital? Enron officers sacrificed their long-term reputation in order to loot the firm of hundreds of millions of dollars in bonuses and stock options that they pretended to earn by entering the firm into deals that ultimately lost billions and by fraudulently inflating the stock price through all manner of devious accounting maneuvers. Enron's outside directors damaged their own long-term reputations by negligently and perhaps recklessly failing to detect the officers' shenanigans and by foolishly waiving the firm's conflict-of-interest policy. Enron's law firm also suffered serious reputational injury when its attorneys forgot that their ultimate loyalty was to the corporate entity and the shareholders rather than to the individual officers whom they aided and abetted in many of their more spurious transactions. Stock analysts chose short-term lucre over long-term reputation by publicly hyping (while privately condemning) stocks of companies like WorldCom as their share price tanked, in order to cultivate investment banking business for their employers.

In the face of such gatekeeping failures, one response is to take refuge in mutual funds. However, even sophisticated investors were victimized nearly as much as lay investors by the frauds of these various actors. In addition, mutual funds have victimized unsophisticated investors in a wide variety of ways. Former SEC head Arthur Levitt has termed some of these abuses "the most egregious violation of the public trust of any of the events of recent years."[60] There is substantial evidence that market timing abuses were systemic, and that industry professionals knew about the abuses and did nothing. Jack Bogle, founder of Vanguard Group, notes that "increasingly everything in the fund industry is favoring the manager at the expense of the shareholder."[61]

Nor can the reputational concern of auditors adequately protect investors. While Judge Easterbrook assumes that auditors would not risk their long-term reputations by acting recklessly, behavioral research provides a plethora of potential explanations for why reckless and fraudulent auditing is hardly an infrequent occurrence. In addition to the rational reasons discussed in Chapter 2, several explanations for auditor failings arise from 30 years' worth of behavioral research in accounting.[62] Among those are the following:

- *Confirmation bias*: Numerous studies indicate that auditors are prone to the confirmation bias and tend to perceive evidence and emphasize results that confirm their initial hypothesis, which is often established by the client's documents or their work from the previous year's audit.
- *Cognitive dissonance*: Once an auditor has taken a public position by certifying the accuracy of a client's financial statements, it becomes very difficult to process information that undermines the conclusion that the client is in sound financial shape and that its financial statements accurately reflect its financial condition.
- *Memory limitations*: As noted earlier, people are more likely to remember facts that support their beliefs than facts that undermine them. Memory of documents is extremely important to the audit process, and problems can arise from this tendency to remember selectively, especially because studies show that auditors are overconfident regarding the accuracy of their memories.
- *Undue optimism and overconfidence*: 83 percent of auditors, in one study, believed that they possessed above average skills. Such

overconfidence about their abilities and undue optimism about how things will turn out for themselves and their clients can cause auditors to cut corners and thereby create problems.

- *Insensitivity to source*: Studies indicate that auditors are better than most people at discounting information that comes from questionable sources, however even they tend to overweight client-provided explanations in situations where the client obviously has a strong interest at stake.
- *False consensus effect*: Because of the false consensus effect, honest auditors, like other people, have difficulty believing that the people they deal with are dishonest. This tendency can cause major problems for an honest auditor with a crooked client.
- *Anchoring and adjustment*: Innumerable studies show that people's judgments become easily anchored by irrelevant numbers. This tendency can cause obvious problems for auditors who are often anchored by the numbers provided by the client that they then must audit.
- *Self-serving bias*: As noted earlier, auditors and everyone else tend to gather, process, and recall information in ways that advance their own interests, even when they try to be fair. This bias is extremely robust and studies show that auditors suffer from it. For example, studies show that if there is any question as to the appropriate outcome auditors tend strongly to favor the client in order to keep the client happy and the stream of revenue coming in. Even if there is a strong conflict between the client and the auditor as to an appropriate treatment for a transaction, the auditor tends to defer to the client *unless* the client is in financial trouble and thereby presents a significant litigation risk for the client.
- *Tangible vs. abstract*: Not only does the time delay trap prevent people from assessing future consequences rationally, auditors also suffer from the fact that if they stand up to their client they may cause current, tangible harm to people whom they know and like, including their clients' employees and their colleagues. The potential victims of reckless auditing, on the other hand, are nameless and faceless and may, after all, never materialize.

Put all these factors together and it is not terribly surprising that auditors act recklessly from time to time. As Professor Loewenstein has noted, "if one wanted to create a business setting that would virtually *guarantee* unethical behavior, it would be difficult to improve on the existing case of independent auditing."[63] It is Pollyanna-ish to believe that the reputational constraint is sufficient in light of these behavioral tendencies.

Similar analyses could be done of each of the other gatekeepers who dropped their respective balls during the Enron scandal. It should be clear that it is easy to rest too much reliance on securities actors' rational incentive to preserve their long-term reputations as a substitute for government regulation. "[T]here are limits to reputation."[64] Reputation added to legal constraints were insufficient to prevent major frauds in the 1990s. Take away the legal constraints, and things would have been much worse.

CORPORATE LAW AND BEHAVIORAL DECISION THEORY

Behavioral analysis can inform many aspects of corporate law. In this section, we touch upon a few. As noted in Chapter 2, the principal concern of corporate law is solving the agency problem so that officers and directors will operate the corporation in the best interests of the shareholders. Corporate law helps by imposing fiduciary obligations on the managers of the corporation and punishing them for breach. Presumably this would be unnecessary if the shareholders and promoters could simply bargain to an optimally efficient result, but this is unrealistic for logistical reasons in public corporations and unrealistic for behavioral reasons in smaller corporations.

Consider the investor who is asked to invest in a neighbor's small but growing corporation. The neighbor is a promoter and CEO. For reasons of bounded rationality and rational ignorance, the investor's investigation of the company's condition will likely not be optimal. Judge Posner has explained why information costs render ignorance rational:

> Contracts are costly to make and . . . costs may well exceed the benefits . . . when the contingencies that would be regulated by contract—death or personal injury from using a product—are extremely remote. [When a consumer purchases an expensive item like a car] the greatest [contracting] cost [is] not the direct cost of drafting; it [is] the cost of information. The inclusion of . . . a clause [specifying rights and duties in the event of a remote contingency such as death or personal injury] would not serve its intended purpose unless the consumer knew something about the costs of alternative safety measures that the producer might take and about the safety of competing products and brands. But the cost of generating that information, and particularly the cost to the consumer of absorbing it, may well be disproportionate to the benefit of a negotiated (as distinct from imposed-by-law) level of safety.[65]

If fraud seems a remote contingency to the investor, then the cost of an optimal investigation of the investment will seem disproportionate to the perceived benefit. And if the investor likes the CEO he will probably, for reasons of the false consensus effect, trust him too much. The investor is

unlikely to detect if he is being lied to, and to be overconfident in his conclusion that the promoter has been truthful. Once he has decided to trust
the promoter, he is unlikely to discount sufficiently representations made if
any evidence appears as to the untrustworthiness of the CEO. Cognitive
dissonance and belief persistence will impede his processing of information
that undermines his initial conclusion that the promoter is honest and that
the company is a promising one. Overconfidence and undue optimism will
bolster this conclusion. All these factors put together paint a picture of a
vulnerable investor whose fate is uncomfortably in the hands of another. A
legal regime that imposes duties of loyalty upon the CEO and other managers and punishes violations provides protection for the investor that
would otherwise be lacking. In so doing, it encourages investment.

Professors Blair and Stout have pointed out that just as shareholders
cannot be omnipresent to monitor the stewardship of their investment,
neither can the law be everywhere (nor can it be perfectly enforced).[66]
Therefore, trust remains an important factor in the corporate governance
calculation. As those commentators note, however, trust derives largely
from social norms. The law dramatically impacts those norms. Professors
Donaldson and Dunfee point out that "[o]utside sources may influence the
development of norms. Law, particularly when it is perceived as legitimate
by members of a community, may have a major impact on what is considered to be correct behavior."[67] Thus, when the Civil Rights Act of 1964 outlawed racial discrimination, people's views of the acceptability of such
discrimination was significantly altered. Because of the conformity bias,
what is considered correct behavior exerts a major influence upon how
people act.

For present purposes, corporate law establishes that managers and directors are to act in the best interests not of themselves, but of shareholders.
In so doing, the law not only gives them external incentives in the form of
liability rules to act in this way, it also changes their internal preferences by
helping to establish trustworthy actions as the societal norm. Thousands of
cooperation games administered by psychologists over the years establish
that people are more willing to cooperate (irrationally, according to economic incentives) if they are instructed to do so, and/or if they believe that
others will cooperate (the conformity bias). The law instructs managers to
act in a fiduciary capacity and thereby increases the odds that they will do
so. This message is repeatedly sent to managers by judges who often
describe the manager's fiduciary duty in the strongest terms. The law also
helps to establish the social norm, reinforcing the likelihood that managers
will choose to act as fiduciaries.

While contractarians argue that the fiduciary duty is just another in the
"nexus of contracts" that comprise corporate law, Blair and Stout argue

convincingly that it is much more. To allow managers to opt easily out of the fiduciary duty via simple contract would "undermine trust among corporate participants by implying that trustworthy behavior is not important, not common, and not expected."[68] Fortunately, most corporate law does not allow such contracting out. As Blair and Stout note:

> The phenomenon of trust behavior suggests that fiduciary relationships are created by the law in situations in which it is efficient or otherwise desirable to promote other-regarding, trusting and trustworthy behavior. Moreover, the key to a successful fiduciary relationship lies in framing both economic and social conditions so as to encourage the fiduciary to make a psychological commitment to further her beneficiary's welfare rather than her own. For example, by making directors and officers who violate their duty of loyalty to the firm liable for damages, the law encourages trustworthy behavior in corporate fiduciaries by reducing the expected gains from malfeasance (thus reducing the fiduciary's cost of behaving trustworthily). At the same time, case law on the duty of loyalty unambiguously signals that the fiduciary relationship is a social situation that calls for other-regarding behavior, to the point where the fiduciary is discouraged from even thinking about her own interest through a prophylactic rule that bans unauthorized personal gains even in circumstances in which the fiduciary could arrange this without harm to her beneficiary. Similarly, the sermonizing tone typically adopted by courts in fiduciary cases reinforces the social message that other-regarding behavior is demanded.[69]

By setting up a system where shareholders believe they can trust managers given the social norms (formed in part by the law) and the legal liabilities (established by the law), investors do not have to expend substantial time, effort, and money to investigate whether their managers do or do not purport to act in the investors' best interests, avoiding an "information externality" created if contracting out of the fiduciary relationship is permitted.[70]

The agency problem is composed not just of intentional wrongdoing by managers. Behavioral considerations highlight numerous other pitfalls that make corporate law extremely helpful for disciplining managers, compensating investors, and encouraging investment. Consider the subject of executive compensation. Because of the self-serving bias and general overconfidence, officers tend to think that they are worth what they are being paid, especially because the high compensation that other officers were receiving indicated through the conformity bias that this was the appropriate standard and because reference-dependent utility made the matter important to the managers. Numerous abuses have ensued, in part because incentive compensation was largely untethered from actual firm performance. Stock option grants tend to be timed to precede favorable firm-specific news announcements, allowing company executives to profit arguably unfairly.[71] Stock options that were under water because of poor performance were often repriced. At the highest levels, CEO compensation alone absorbed most corporate profits at some companies that were doing comparatively well.[72]

Because of the same behavioral considerations, such as the conformity bias and undue optimism affecting the judgments of directors, current corporate law rules were insufficient to prevent tremendous abuses. However, in the absence of fiduciary duties, the situation would likely have been many times worse. One of the Sarbanes-Oxley Act's corporate governance provisions requires officers and directors of companies that have to restate their earnings (323 public companies in 2003) to forfeit their stock profits and bonuses gained on the basis of the bogus numbers. Before this provision, often companies would announce record profits, the officers would pocket record bonuses, the companies would later restate their financials, but the officers would retain the unearned bonuses. Sarbanes-Oxley's forfeiture provision changes that situation.

When contemplating why 300 companies a year are restating their financial statements, again consider the possibility that not all are blatant frauds. Because of the behavioral factors noted above, it is possible that the top brass of companies often times really believe (or talk themselves into believing) that their firms are doing well. Professor Langevoort used behavioral analysis to suggest that in organizations, optimistic, self-confident, "can-do" people tend to be promoted and that people prefer to send good news up the corporate ladder over bad news. When biased information is fed to unduly optimistic, overconfident managers who suffer from the illusion of control, they often end up misperceiving risks and harboring unrealistically optimistic views about their company's status and prospectus. The self-serving bias also helps these officers to see what they wish to see, especially if they have previously committed to a particular course of action. Sunk cost effects and cognitive dissonance can make it particularly difficult to change course.[73]

All of these are difficult biases to overcome, but Sarbanes-Oxley's section 404 provision for internal controls could help. It is a corporate governance provision aimed primarily at improving the odds that full and accurate information relating to the financial situation of the company will rise to the top of the corporate chain of command. Perfection will never be achieved, but a corporate governance provision such as this, coupled with the fiduciary duties imposed upon officers and directors, should improve the quality of corporate decisionmaking over what would occur in their absence.

The most difficult aspect in all of this is striking the proper balance. Managers must be constrained and monitored to ensure that they are working in the best interests of shareholders. At the same time, if monitoring is excessive, managers cannot work efficiently. Economists Easterbrook and

Fischel propose an efficiency rationale for the business judgment rule—the courts' refusal (with rare exception) to second-guess the decisions of a company's managers unless there exists a conflict of interest.[74] There is a behavioral reason as well—the hindsight bias. Courts realize that not only are they not business experts, but they should not impose liability upon managers for merely careless decisions based on second-guessing those managers with the benefit of 20–20 hindsight.[75]

SECURITIES LAW AND BEHAVIORAL DECISION THEORY

The securities industry is so rife with potential conflicts of interest that only the most strident of SEC opponents propose that the SEC deregulate investment advisers, stockbrokers, stock exchanges, and other industry actors. Honest actors in these industries oppose full deregulation. Because of the self-serving bias, even investment advisers, stockbrokers, or stock analysts who tried to be honest and objective would have great difficulty doing so. In most instances, their interests are ill-aligned with those of their customers and the results are often greatly damaging to investors' interests.

Consider, for example, stockbrokers.[76] Is the reputational constraint sufficient to ensure that brokers act in the best interests of their clients? While it is generally in investors' interests to buy high quality stocks and hold them for the long term, stockbrokers do not make much money that way. It is in the brokers' interests to persuade their clients to do some trades from time to time. And that is just the beginning of the conflicts of interest. The brokers make more money if the products they convince investors to buy are "house products" or riskier products, regardless of whether they are the best products or the best fit for the investor's risk profile. On Wall Street, where "bonuses are in the millions of dollars, there are strong rational reasons to push the limits of normative behavior."[77]

The reality of practice reveals one Morgan Stanley employee expressing enjoyment at "ripping [the client's] face off"[78] and Salomon Brothers employees becoming "minor heroes" in their offices by "blowing up" their customers by selling them low quality securities that Salomon wished to dump out of its own portfolio;[79] Dean Witter selling US$2 billion of high risk bond funds by targeting elderly clients and misrepresenting the funds as safe and secure investments;[80] large numbers of brokers convincing elderly people to purchase variable annuities inappropriate for their needs,[81] and Republic New York Securities Corporation assisting a financial adviser in bilking more than 100 institutional investors out of

US$700 million even though the president of its futures division stated on tape that "a doofus flipping a . . . coin every day" would have had more success than the adviser (who lost US$556 million while trading).[82]

Among the reasons for the inadequacy of the reputational constraint for remedying the misalignment of interest between broker and customer is that even when brokers pursue their own interests at their clients' expense, their reputations may not suffer much or at all. During the bubble of the 1990s, the stock market rose so dramatically that it was difficult for even dishonest and incompetent brokers to lose money for their clients. Because people make decisions in relation to a reference point,[83] investors tend to be much more upset if they lose money in an absolute sense than if they are simply not making as much money as other investors.

Additionally, because of cognitive dissonance and other factors, investors often will remember having made more money than they truly did. Studies show that investors frequently remember that their mutual fund performed better than it really did. Even if they do notice that their broker has done a poor job, regret theory predicts that they will often not complain. If they did, it would highlight in their own mind the mistake they made in hiring this broker and they would suffer regret that they would just as soon avoid. Even if investors do notice the poor decisions made by their brokers and do complain, the ability of any firm to trade on its reputation depends on appearance rather than fact. By shunting claims to arbitration and settling cases without admitting or denying wrongdoing, firms are able to minimize the publicity for many of their brokers' wrongs. Due to the availability heuristic, investors bombarded with advertisements about the reliability of a brokerage firm are likely to believe them despite the occasional public report of a problem, especially because most other firms that a customer might choose to do business with may have recently been involved in scandals as well.

A final point is that most stockbrokers leave the industry within three years of starting. How can they be concerned with their long-term reputational capital? Even if they plan on staying around, "[r]eputational sanctions also have limited effect on especially venal parties."[84] The bottom line is that empirical evidence indicates that the reputational constraint affects brokers, but weakly.[85] Legal regulation is needed as an important supplement. Similar analyses could be done regarding investment advisers, stock analysts, stock exchanges, and other professional securities actors.

Corporate Disclosure

"Mandatory disclosure is a—if not the—defining characteristic of US securities regulation."[86] The primary justification for mandatory disclosure is economic, not behavioral. Still, behavioral insights can be valuable. The optimistic, confident managers who interpret the world through a self-serving lens (like everyone else) will tend to believe that they are only hindered by the oversight of others. They will view disclosure as only a hindrance not a help.

In a recent "thought experiment" involving a hypothetical country without a securities law regime, Professor Bainbridge examined behavioral factors in order to determine whether full disclosure would evolve on its own. While he is a critic of the US mandatory disclosure system,[87] Bainbridge made some points that suggest that full disclosure would not come about on its own. Bainbridge first notes that the intense tendency people have toward conformity can cause even seemingly rational decisionmakers to engage in herd behavior, to imitate the actions of others rather than utilizing one's own information and judgment. He notes that herd behavior may be particularly common in markets with inadequate disclosure by firms.[88] Bainbridge suggests several reasons why voluntary disclosure might be suboptimal—not emphasizing one of the most obvious: that the company's managers want to minimize oversight. Given a herd mentality that reinforces a practice of minimal disclosure and no strong reason for voluntary disclosure to increase, Bainbridge observes that a mandatory disclosure rule could have three beneficial effects by (a) beginning a cascade of disclosure by shifting the disclosure norm, (b) making disclosure credible by adding an antifraud feature, and (c) providing a standard around which disclosure practices can cluster. As noted in Chapter 2, one of the most powerful benefits of a mandated disclosure system is the comparability of data that a legal requirement can best provide.

Bainbridge points out that if corporate managers are used to nondisclosure or limited disclosure, the habit heuristic, the status quo bias, the anchoring effect, the endowment effect, loss aversion, and regret aversion would all influence them to hew close to the established standard of minimal disclosure.[89] All of these factors cause people to make decisions where the current regime is a heavily influential reference point. While Bainbridge suggests that there is little evidence that the status quo bias is a serious problem in US capital markets, the existence of this bias has been repeatedly demonstrated and is extremely robust. When Samuelson and Zeckhauser gave subjects several different ways to allocate a portfolio of securities they had inherited from their uncle, alternatives became more attractive as soon as they were designated as the status quo and the more alternatives there were, the stronger was the effect.[90] There is every reason to believe that the status quo effect would impact the decisions of corporations regarding how much to disclose, just as it has been shown along with anchoring and adjustment to impact the decisions of auditors who tend to pattern this year's audit plan after last year's audit plan,[91] which can give dishonest clients a road map for cloaking their fraud.

Finally, Professor Bainbridge observes that social norms affect decision-makers.[92] If the norm among companies is not to disclose, is it not more difficult for full disclosure to evolve? Bainbridge suggests that legal reform probably could not precede cultural change in most societies, especially since managers of companies have substantial political influence. This is a fair point but in other nations legal change may well happen as it does in the United States—an episode of major corruption or a traumatic break in the markets can create the conditions needed for political change. That is how the 1933 and 1934 Acts and Sarbanes-Oxley Act were passed. We have seen how a change in the law can indeed alter norms, as in passage of the Civil Rights Acts. Indeed, full disclosure was not the norm in America before the 1933 and 1934 securities laws were passed, but quickly became the norm thereafter. Before 1933, prospectuses in America were little more than notices. Afterwards, issuers soon embraced the full disclosure norm, although perhaps not enthusiastically. The law created a requirement that was followed under the pain of liability, and gave rise to a norm, such that even domestic issuers in exempt offerings and foreign issuers operating under their own exemptions often provide prospectus-like disclosure today. They do so not because the law requires it, but because it has become the expectation, what investors are used to seeing. By setting the standard for registered domestic public offerings, Congress actually raised the disclosure bar in many other settings.

Bainbridge suggests that because the legal requirement of full disclosure has become the norm in America there is no longer justification for manda-tory disclosure in the United States. It is in fact likely that if mandatory dis-closure were repealed, social norms, the status quo bias, and other factors would ensure that voluntary disclosure would remain substantial. But, in the absence of the reinforcement of legal requirements, it would likely decay over time although it is unlikely that it would ever sink to pre-1933 levels. And obviously the first to start disclosing less would be the compa-nies that have bad news. Investors would realize this, of course, but typi-cally would not discount for it sufficiently. If the law has successfully created a valuable norm, that is not much of an argument for abolishing the law, at least given its relatively low cost.

For all the reasons just explored, it is difficult for corporate managers to choose to fully disclose in the absence of legal requirements. It is true that even if the law does not require disclosure, managers might choose to do it voluntarily if sufficient pressure were exerted by investors. However, behav-ioral analysis not only indicates why issuers will not voluntarily disclose information at an optimal level, it also explains why investors will not necessarily demand such disclosure before investing. The same behavioral factors discussed in the corporate governance section that might well induce a person to invest in a neighbor's corporation without providing for any protection from breach of fiduciary duty will also often lead to an investment decision made upon the basis of inadequate disclosure. Cognitive conservativism in the form of rational ignorance, undue optimism, and overconfidence, the illusion of control, and other factors can all lead investors to pay their money without being given full disclosure. Investors, like everyone else, view the status quo as the standard reference point. If minimal disclosure is the standard, investors tend to anchor on it and not to demand much more. Why, after all, should an investor who trusts a promoter to be honest and not cheat him require that promoter to go to the expense of producing audited financial statements and other expensive disclosure materials?

Fraud Protection

The other bulwark of federal securities laws, in addition to mandatory disclosure, is fraud protection. Both the 1933 and 1934 Acts forbid misrepresentation in the purchasing and selling of securities and section 10(b) of the 1934 Act, the statute's key antifraud provision, is quite likely the most influential securities law provision ever enacted. Congress's main goal in passing the 1933 and 1934 Acts was to restore confidence in the integrity of the securities markets so that investors would return to "play the game." The Congressional instinct was a sound one. Studies of trust, cooperation, and social dilemmas establish that people will cooperate and trust if they believe others will cooperate and trust. But trust is a fragile commodity. People wish to avoid "being a sucker."[93] They will not play if they believe the game is crooked.

If fully-informed, rational investors invested in efficient markets where securities sellers were adequately constrained by reputational concerns, there would arguably be little need for securities regulation. Unfortunately, those conditions do not obtain in real markets. Therefore, it is questionable whether the SEC should sit on the sidelines and allow investors to bargain for their desired level of fraud protection or be able to choose a legal regime that contains their desired level of fraud protection. Even those who are the strongest believers in private ordering usually agree that public enforcement mechanisms are needed to investigate fraud claims and punish wrongdoers. But they trust that investors will bargain for their desired level of disclosure and their desired level of fraud protection. In addition to ignoring the transaction costs associated with such individualized bargaining, behavioralism demonstrates the deficiencies of reliance on such bargaining.

The next chapter will indicate that history contradicts the assumptions of purely private ordering. But consider a contemporary scenario in which a promoter of ABC Co. makes glowing oral representations to an investor about ABC. Those oral representations convince the investor that he should buy the stock. The promoter then produces a form contract. One thing that is extremely unlikely to happen at this point is for the investor to refuse to buy the stock unless the promoter provides just the level of antifraud protection that the investor desires. The investor might desire a negligence or recklessness standard of liability. The promoter might prefer that he be liable only if he acted with *scienter*. The promoter might wish to require that all claims be arbitrated, while the investor might wish to have the right to go before a jury.

Despite the parties' different desires, the most likely thing that will happen is not a haggling over these terms. Instead, it is mostly likely that the investor will sign the contract, even if it contains a provision stating that "ABC Company and its agents make no representations other than those contained in writing in this document and the investor acknowledges that he is relying on no other statements and that this document represents the entire agreement between the parties."

Because Congress understood human nature and the fact that any con-man who could induce an investor to put money into a bogus deal also had a good chance to convince the investor to waive any antifraud rights he enjoyed, it placed in both the 1933 Securities Act and the 1934 Securities Exchange Act provisions that sought to prevent investors from waiving rights accorded them by the Acts. Most courts have refused to enforce such waivers as inconsistent with the antiwaiver provisions of the 1933 and 1934 Acts, but a substantial number of courts have enforced them, functionally allowing investors to waive any substantive protection from securities fraud.

But why would seemingly rational investors blithely sign away their rights? Why do they so often elect to sign contracts that give them no protection from fraud? Why are they unlikely to bargain for just the "right" level of antifraud protection? The short answer is: For the same reasons that product consumers bought products such as automobiles under contracts that contained virtually no warranties and no significant protection from defective products before courts and legislatures devised modern product liability law. The longer answer requires a little more behavioral analysis.[94] Contemplate these behavioral considerations, among many others that could be discussed:

- *Rational ignorance*: Whether renting a car or purchasing securities, few people read form contracts that are placed before them. Often they are told by the other party that the contracts just contain "boilerplate" and they should not bother to read them. Usually they are dealing with a seller's agent who does not have the authority to bargain over their terms anyway. As Judge Posner has noted, the information costs of reading a form contract typically make it not worth the time to do so.[95]

- *Overconfidence, undue optimism, and illusion of control*: People tend to believe that they are better than they really are at judging character, that the bad things like being victimized by fraudsters that happen to other people will not happen to them and that they can control situations that are not truly controllable, such as by selecting the seller of the securities they buy. For these reasons, as Ribstein has noted, "[i]nvestors, like others, may be overly optimistic in the sense of discounting risks, including the risk of fraud."[96] These factors often cause investors to sign contracts that irrationally waive protection from fraud because they believe that they will not be victims of fraud. Studies show that when asked about the contracts that they have signed people believe that they are more favorable to them than they actually are.

- *Probabilities and future events*: As noted earlier, most people are not particularly good at calculating probabilities, often substituting rule-of-thumb heuristics for more rigorous statistical analysis. They tend especially to ignore low probability risks, such as the chance that the seller of their securities is ripping them off, even when large amounts of money are at stake. Just like product purchasers, investors in securities seldom consider that they might have to bring a lawsuit later on to vindicate their rights.

- *False consensus effect and personal positivity bias*: As noted earlier, both false consensus effect, which causes honest people to believe that others are honest as well, and the personal positivity bias, which causes people to generally view others favorably, work together to lead people to be insufficiently wary of fraud. Because these tendencies are reinforced by the concept of cognitive dissonance, once investors decide that they wish to do business with a particular promoter or stockbroker, they will have great difficulty properly processing information that begins to indicate that that promoter or stockbroker is a crook.

- *Inability to detect deception*: People's belief that they can detect when they are being lied to, coupled with their typical utter inability to do so, often causes them to be insufficiently cautious regarding fraud. In business, lies are particularly hard to detect "because people regard lies as part of playing a complex game."[97] If people "just know" that they are not being lied to, they will be unduly willing to sign a contract waiving protection from fraud.

- *Insensitivity to source*: As noted earlier, even when people are told that those they are dealing with are unreliable or have an incentive to deceive them, they are not adept at taking that information into account in their decisionmaking. They may adjust in the right direction some of their conclusions, but typically not nearly far enough in the right direction.
- *Salience of oral communications*: It is a simple fact that people find oral communications to be much more salient than written communications. The oral representations that a sales representative makes tend to drown out substantially any written disclaimers of those representations.
- *Status quo bias*: As noted earlier, all things being equal, people prefer the status quo. When a seller of securities hands the buyer a form contract, that contract represents the status quo. It anchors the buyer's judgment. A dense form contract has an "authoritative legality"[98] about it that induces deference and makes it unlikely that the buyer will bargain over terms. Consistent with the effects of the status quo bias, Choi and Gulati have found that even the most sophisticated investors often adopt contract provisions not out of preference but because they are the "standard" provisions.[99]

For all these reasons and others, it is easy to see why investors did not before securities regulation existed and likely would not today adequately bargain for antifraud protection. For reasons noted immediately above, people are not facile at telling when they are being lied to and not adept at accurately adjusting their conclusions when they learn that the source of information upon which they are relying is not trustworthy. Therefore, their adjustment in price will typically be insufficient to account for the risk of fraud they face. There are no formulas that can be applied or computer programs that can be run to accurately adjust the price of the securities to compensate for the risk of fraud. How does one efficiently discount the difference between a recklessness standard and a negligence standard, between an arbitration clause and the right to a jury trial? Professor Sale has pointed out that the markets did not accurately discount for the possibility of gatekeeper failure in the 1990s,[100] and Professor Choi admits that unsophisticated investors would probably not be able to value different protective devices that issuers might adopt.[101]

Effective antifraud provisions are therefore necessary and efficient—private ordering cannot restrain fraud. Because of behavioral tendencies, people do not always rationally play the game as described above in Figure 2.1. Many invest notwithstanding the risk of fraud, and some of them suffer the consequences of fraud. For others who are more cautious, behavioral concerns such as regret theory and loss aversion mean that no investment will take place, as in Figure 2.1. The more fraud that transpires at the expense of the risk-taking population simply highlights to the cautious the dangers of placing their savings in equity securities.

THE ROLE OF GOVERNMENT

This chapter's discussion has thus far aimed primarily at demonstrating that behavioral considerations can clarify some of the strengths and weaknesses of economic analysis of private ordering. Law and economic analysis does not have a single prescription, but those forms that have been used to argue in favor of substantially less or no securities regulation are based on various premises that behavioral evidence greatly undermines. Investors are not as rational and securities professionals' concerns for reputation are not as potent as many have supposed. That said, behavioral considerations do not automatically validate securities regulation or easily guide us to conclusions about what form securities laws should take.

Lawmakers who pass statutes and bureaucrats who supplement them with rules and enforce them are also humans with all the foibles—overconfidence, undue optimism, honoring of sunk costs—of others. Just as an audit firm that has hired several new auditors and trained them for a large client that is an energy company will have difficulty flushing that investment in the face of evidence that the energy company is an extremely high risk client which is probably transgressing important accounting rules, so will a securities agency that has established a branch to regulate a particular activity have difficulty making the decision to eliminate that branch and reassign its employees in the face of evidence that the regulation is simply not accomplishing its goal.[102]

At a minimum, behavioral considerations should be used to analyze current disclosure rules to determine how they can be improved. The amount and form of disclosures can no doubt be improved by behavioral analysis. Behavioral considerations arguably counsel for greater expenditures by the government for investor education even while they provide a sobering assessment of the limits of the improvement that education can bring. The virtue of government action is not that it is free of behavioral shortcomings but that the imperfect government action may nonetheless combat private behavioral shortcomings and produce a more efficient market. Perhaps the main problem of government action is that it does not go far enough to combat the limitations of private ordering.

Political concerns can minimize the effectiveness of securities regulation. There is substantial evidence that the SEC was not active enough in the 1990s. Because of political pressure, it was underfunded, understaffed, and under the gun in many situations when it tried to improve corporate performance. As an example, in 2000, the SEC compromised in a battle with the Big Five auditing firms and allowed them to continue providing consulting services to audit clients. Just about the only concession the SEC extracted from the politically-charged battle was a requirement that the clients disclose in their proxy statements all the fees that they paid to their auditors. The amounts disclosed showed shocking levels of consulting fees and clearly should have drawn into question the independence of these auditors. But, of course, the discussion earlier in the chapter explained that when investors learn of the questionable nature of a source of information, they tend not to accurately discount the information itself. In light of what happened with Enron, WorldCom, Global Crossing, and all the others, it appears that the eventual ban on most consulting services enacted in the Sarbanes-Oxley Act should have been instituted earlier.

The SEC has the benefit of a decisional process that effectively gathers information from all points of view. The Commission also has significant formal and informal avenues of communication with the securities industry, ensuring that it has the input and often the support of market professionals it seeks to regulate. The Commission's staff generally keeps in close contact with those it regulates via informal meetings with securities professionals.

When new rules are considered, the SEC has a decisionmaking process that insures substantial infusion of the views of all parties. Unlike an individual decisionmaker prone to the confirmation bias, seeking out only information that supports preexisting views, the Commission publishes proposed rules, has a lengthy comment period, examines and responds to the comments. If a controversial rule is proposed, literally thousands of comments may be lodged by advocates and opponents, investors and securities professionals, academics of all viewpoints, and many others. The process often results in the Commission substantially adjusting, amending, or even scrapping its original proposals. The fact that the Commission itself must contain members from both major political parties also helps to foster the give and take that improves the decisionmaking process.

Additionally, the SEC uses two simple decisional heuristics that have served it well over the years: (1) disclosure is good; and (2) fraud is bad. These are the very heuristics that help combat the shortcomings of purely private ordering. Although it is certainly true that too much disclosure can be inefficient and that too many resources could be invested in trying to deter or punish fraud, as a matter of first principles the SEC is on pretty solid ground.

CONCLUSION

In our imperfect world behavioral decision theory makes it clear that investors do not typically demand full disclosure or protect themselves adequately from fraud, even within the constraints of limited information and transaction costs. And corporate officers and directors sometimes fail to fully disclose, breach their fiduciary duties, and even commit securities fraud. Sometimes these actions serve their own rational interests; other times they are simply manifestations of poor intertemporal decisionmaking or bounded will power.

In a world populated by imperfect decisionmakers, law can advance fairness goals and market efficiency. For example, corporate law encourages the trust that is so critical to investment by helping establish the social norms that signal proper conduct for managers. Legislation changes what people believe about approval patterns in their society and because people value approval (the conformity bias), their new beliefs lead to different behaviors.[103] When Congress twice in the 1980s passed legislation to punish insider trading, people's views of the acceptability of that practice changed. When the SEC bans misleading and manipulative conduct, "financial morality" evolves.[104] These unfair and inefficient acts become less acceptable and people become less likely to engage in them for both legal and moral reasons. In Professor Welle's words, "[b]y prohibiting fraud and mandating disclosure, the securities laws protect investors and promote honesty, trust, and ethical behavior in commercial transactions. The securities laws set standards that serve to socialize, to educate and to direct individuals toward more morally appropriate forms of behavior."[105] It is widely acknowledged that when Congress legislated against securities fraud by passing the 1933 and 1934 Securities Acts, the level of such fraud was reduced.[106]

No mechanism of social control is perfect and there will be times, as during the dot.com bubble, when substantial numbers of actors will forget the rules. It will seem that earnings management is at least "kind of ok" because so many competitors are doing it. Bullying auditors into accepting aggressive accounting measures won't seem so bad, because others' actions are sending the cues that this is acceptable. Round-tripping by telecom companies and manipulating deregulated markets by energy traders will temporarily become accepted within the industry. Then it takes action, such as passage of the Sarbanes-Oxley Act, to remind economic actors what the social and legal norms truly are.[107]

NOTES

1. Conlisk notes: "There is a mountain of experiments in which people: display intransitivity; misunderstand statistical independence; mistake random data for patterned data and vice versa; fail to appreciate law of large number effects; fail to recognize statistical dominance; make errors in updating probabilities on the basis of new information; understate the significance of given sample sizes; fail to understand covariation for even the simplest 2×2 contingency tables; make false inferences about causality; ignore relevant information; use irrelevant information (as in sunk cost fallacies); exaggerate the importance of vivid over pallid evidence; exaggerate the importance of fallible predictors; exaggerate the *ex ante* probability of a random event which has already occurred; display overconfidence in judgment relative to evidence; exaggerate confirming over disconfirming evidence relative to initial beliefs; give answers that are highly sensitive to logically irrelevant changes in questions; do redundant and ambiguous tests to confirm an hypothesis at the expense of decisive tests to disconfirm; make frequent errors in deductive reasoning tasks such as syllogisms; place higher value on an opportunity if an experimenter rigs it to be the "status quo" opportunity; fail to discount the future consistently; fail to adjust repeated choices to accommodate intertemporal connections; and more." John Conlisk, *Why Bounded Rationality?*, 34 J. ECON. LIT. 669, 670 (1996). *See also* Larry T. Garvin, *Adequate Assurance of Performance: Of Risk, Duress, and Cognition*, 69 U. COLO. L. REV. 71, 145 (1998) ("Cognitive psychology and experimental economics have found a smorgasbord of cognitive errors, which collectively falsify most of the axioms of rational choice theory.").
2. *See* BOUNDED RATIONALITY: THE ADAPTIVE TOOLBOX (Gerd Gigerenzer & Reinhard Selten eds. 1999).
3. *See* THE ECONOMICS OF IRRATIONAL BEHAVIOR (Francesco Parisi & Vernon Smith eds. forthcoming).
4. Herbert A. Simon, ADMINISTRATIVE BEHAVIOR xxiv (2d ed. 1957).
5. Max H. Bazerman, JUDGMENT IN MANAGERIAL DECISION MAKING 39–41 (3d ed. 1994).
6. Leon Festinger, A THEORY OF COGNITIVE DISSONANCE (1957).
7. *See* Antonio R. Damasio, DESCARTES' ERROR (1994).
8. *See* Werner F.M. De Bondt, *A Portrait of the Individual Investor*, 42 EUR. ECON. REV. 831 (1998).
9. Robert J. Shiller, IRRATIONAL EXUBERANCE 143 (2000).
10. Barbara Moses, *Research Analysts Under Fire*, ALI-ABA Broker Dealer Regulation Course study (January 10–11, 2002).
11. *See* Roni Michaely & Kent L. Womack, *Conflict of Interest and the Credibility of Underwriter Analyst Recommendations*, 12 REV. FIN. STUD. 653 (1999).
12. *See* Andrei Shleifer, INEFFICIENT MARKETS: AN INTRODUCTION TO BEHAVIORAL FINANCE 187 (2000).
13. Irving L. Janis, GROUPTHINK: PSYCHOLOGICAL STUDIES OF POLICY DECISIONS AND FIASCOES 9 (2d ed. 1982).
14. *See* Max Sutherland, ADVERTISING AND THE MIND OF THE CONSUMER 21 (1993).
15. *Showing Fidelity*, FINANCIAL TIMES, June 9, 2004, at 14.
16. *See* Brad M. Barger, et al., OUT OF SIGHT, OUT OF MIND: THE EFFECTS OF EXPENSES ON MUTUAL FUND FLOWS 1 (December 2003), *available at* http://ssrn.com/abstract=496315.
17. Daniel Kahneman & Amos Tversky, *Prospect Theory: An Analysis of Decision Under Uncertainty*, 47 ECONOMETRICA 263 (1979).
18. *See* Richard H. Thaler, *Mental Accounting Matters, in* ADVANCES IN BEHAVIORAL ECONOMICS 75, 99 (Colin F. Camerer, George Loewenstein & Matthew Rabin eds. 2004).

19. Hal R. Arkes & Catherine Blumer, *The Psychology of Sunk Cost*, 35 ORGANIZA-
    TIONAL BEHAV. & HUM. DECISION PROCESSES 124 (1985).
20. TIME AND DECISION: ECONOMIC AND PSYCHOLOGICAL PERSPECTIVES
    ON INTERTEMPORAL CHOICE (George Loewenstein, Daniel Read & Roy F.
    Baumeister eds. 2003).
21. Reinier H. Kraakman, *Corporate Liability Strategies and the Costs of Legal Controls*, 93
    YALE L. J. 857, 888 (1984).
22. *See* Robert A. Prentice, *Chicago Man, K-T Man, and the Future of Behavioral Law and
    Economics*, 56 VAND. L. REV. 1663, 1696–1702 (2003).
23. *See* Gary W. Emery, CORPORATE FINANCE: PRINCIPLES AND PRACTICE
    600–603 (1998).
24. Michael C. Jensen, *Some Anomalous Evidence Regarding Market Efficiency*, 6 J. FIN.
    ECON. 95 (1978).
25. *See* Richard H. Thaler, THE WINNER'S CURSE (1992); QUASI-RATIONAL
    ECONOMICS (1991); ADVANCES IN BEHAVIORAL FINANCE (R. Thaler ed.
    1993).
26. *See* ADVANCES IN BEHAVIORAL ECONOMICS (Colin F. Camerer, George
    Loewenstein, & Matthew Rabin eds. 2004).
27. Stephen C. Choi & A.C. Pritchard, *Behavioral Economics and the SEC*, 56 STAN. L.
    REV. 1, 5 (2003).
28. Sholom Benartzi & Richard H. Thaler, *Myopic Loss Aversion and the Equity Premium
    Puzzle*, 110 Q. J. ECON. 73 (1995).
29. Terrance Odean, *Do Investors Trade Too Much?*, 89 AM. ECON. REV. 1279 (1999).
30. *See* Richard Deaves, et al., AN EXPERIMENTAL TEST OF THE IMPACT OF
    OVERCONFIDENCE AND GENDER ON TRADING ACTIVITY 21 (2003), *avail-
    able at* http://ssrn.com/abstract=497284.
31. Terrance Odean, *Are Investors Reluctant to Realize Their Losses?*, 53 J. FIN. 1775 (1998).
32. Dale Griffin & Amos Tversky, *The Weighing of Evidence and the Determination of
    Confidence*, 24 COG. PSYCHOL. 411 (1992).
33. Nick Barberis, Andrei Shleifer & Robert Vishny, *A Model of Investor Sentiment*, 49 J.
    FIN. ECON. 307 (1998).
34. Larry E. Ribstein, *Market vs. Regulatory Responses to Corporate Fraud: A Critique of
    the Sarbanes-Oxley Act of 2002*, 28 IOWA J. CORP. L. 1, 22–23 (2002).
35. Lynn A. Stout, *The Unimportance of Being Efficient: An Economic Analysis of Stock
    Market Pricing and Securities Regulation*, 87 MICH. L. REV. 613, 647 (1988).
36. *See* Riva D. Atlas, *Even the Smart Money Can Slip Up*, N.Y. TIMES, December 30, 2001,
    sec. 3, at 1.
37. *See* Robert A. Prentice, *Chicago Man, K-T Man, and the Future of Behavioral Law and
    Economics*, 56 VANDERBILT LAW REVIEW 1663, 1728–29 (2004).
38. Hersh Shefrin, BEYOND GREED AND FEAR: UNDERSTANDING BEHAV-
    IORAL FINANCE AND THE PSYCHOLOGY OF INVESTING 58 (2000).
39. Jacob Jacoby, *Is It Rational to Assume Consumer Rationality? Some Consumer
    Psychological Perspectives on Rational Choice Theory* 2–3, N.Y. Univ. Ctr. for Law &
    Bus., Working Paper #CLB-00–009, 2000.
40. Robert J. Shiller, IRRATIONAL EXUBERANCE 379–400 (2000).
41. Robert J. Shiller, *Bubbles, Human Judgment, And Expert Opinion* 2–3, 11 Cowles Found.,
    Discussion Paper No. 1303 (May 2001).
42. Werner de Bondt, EARNINGS FORECASTS AND SHARE PRICE REVERSALS
    (1992).
43. Henry Hu, *Misunderstood Derivatives: The Causes of Informational Failure and the
    Promise of Regulatory Incrementalism*, 102 YALE L. J. 1457, 1489 (1993).
44. Ronald Coase, *The Problem of Social Cost*, 3 J. L. & ECON. 1 (1960).
45. Cass R. Sunstein, *Looking Forward: Behavioral Analysis of Law*, 64 U. CHI. L. REV.
    1175, 1179 (1997) ("The [Coase] theory is wrong because the allocation of the legal enti-
    tlement may well matter, in the sense that those who are initially allocated an entitlement
    are likely to value it more than those without the legal entitlement.").

46. *See* Cass R. Sunstein, *Switching the Default Rule*, 77 N.Y.U. L. REV. 106, 112 (2002) (making this point).
47. Most people have a strong preference for the status quo. *See e.g.,* Colin Camerer, *Prospect Theory in the Wild*, in CHOICES, VALUES, AND FRAMES 295 (Daniel Kahneman & Amos Tversky eds. 2000) (finding that motorists' choices of insurance coverage were significantly affected by default legislative rules); Raymond S. Hartman, et al., *Consumer Rationality and the Status Quo*, 106 Q. J. ECON. 141, 160 (1991) (finding that electricity consumers given a choice between higher rates with higher reliability service and lower rates with lower reliability tended to choose whichever choice was presented as representing the status quo); William F. Samuelson & Richard Zeckhauser, *Status Quo Bias in Decision Making*, 1 J. RISK & UNCERTAINTY 7, 26–33 (1988) (finding that people tend to select whichever investment alternative or health plan is presented as the status quo); Maurice Schweitzer, *Disentangling Status Quo and Omission Effects: An Experimental Analysis*, 58 ORG. BEHAV. & HUM. DECISION PROCESSES 457, 472–73 (1994) (reporting experiments finding that people prefer both the status quo and inaction and that these preferences can be additive).
48. Robert A. Prentice & Jonathan J. Koehler, *A Normality Bias in Legal Decision Making*, 88 CORNELL L. REV. 583 (2003); John S. Hammond, Ralph L. Keeney, & Howard Raiffa, *The Hidden Traps in Decision Making*, HARVARD BUSINESS REVIEW 47 (September–October 1998).
49. *See* David Cohen & Jack L. Knetsch, *Judicial Choice and Disparities Between Measures of Economic Values*, 30 OSGOODE HALL L.J. 737 (1992).
50. *See* Russell Korobkin, *The Status Quo Bias and Contract Default Rules*, 83 CORNELL L. REV. 608 (1998).
51. *See* G. Richard Shell, *Fair Play, Consent and Securities Arbitration: A Comment on Speidel*, 62 BROOK. L. REV. 1365, 1367–69 (1996).
52. Francesco Parisi & Vernon Smith, THE LAW AND ECONOMICS OF IRRATIONAL BEHAVIOR: AN INTRODUCTION 5 (2004), *available at* http://ssrn.com/abstract=537784.
53. *See* Ernst Fehr & Simon Gachter, *Fairness and Retaliation: The Economics of Reciprocity*, J. ECON. PERSP. 159 Summer 2000.
54. E. Allan Farnsworth, CONTRACTS 2, 13–14 (1982).
55. *Id.* at 326.
56. *Id.* at 232.
57. *See* Evelin Sullivan, THE CONCISE BOOK OF LYING 206 (2001).
58. DiLeo v. Ernst & Young, 901 F.2d 624 (7th Cir. 1990).
59. Patricia M. Dechow, et al., *Causes and Consequences of Earnings Manipulation: An Analysis of Firms Subject to Enforcement Actions by the SEC*, 13 CONTEMP. ACCT. RES. 1, 31 (1996).
60. Tom Lauricella, *For Staid Mutual-Fund Industry, Growing Probe Signals Shake-Up*, WALL ST. J., October 20, 2003, at A1 (quoting Levitt).
61. *See* Tom Lauricella & Deborah Solomon, *Scrutiny of Mutual Funds Grows as SEC Probes Deals With Brokers*, WALL ST. J., October 23, 2003, at A1 (quoting Bogle).
62. All examples in the following laundry list are explicated in detail and documented fully in Robert A. Prentice, *The Case of the Irrational Auditor: A Behavioral Insight into Securities Fraud Litigation*, 95 NW. U. L. REV. 133 (2000).
63. George Loewenstein, *Behavioral Decision Theory and Business Ethics: Skewed Trade-Offs Between Self and Others*, in CODES OF CONDUCT: BEHAVIORAL RESEARCH INTO BUSINESS ETHICS 214, 226 (David M. Missick & Ann E. Tenbrunsel eds. 1996).
64. George M. Cohen, *When Law and Economics Met Professional Responsibility*, 67 FORDHAM L. REV. 273, 288 (1998).
65. William M. Landes & Richard A. Posner, THE ECONOMIC STRUCTURE OF TORT LAW 280–81 (1987). Some game theorists have posited that it is, in many factual scenarios, rational for buyers to decide not to read seller-provided form contracts. *See e.g.,* Avery Katz, *The Strategic Structure of Offer and Acceptance: Game Theory and the Law of*

Contract Formation, 89 MICH. L. REV. 215, 282–93 (1990) (noting "the fact that the decision to spend resources becoming informed must precede the information that reveals whether it is worth doing so, and that the drafters of form contracts have the incentive to take advantage of this . . . [And] it is just this fact that makes reading irrational.").

66. Margaret M. Blair & Lynn A. Stout, *Trust, Trustworthiness, and the Behavioral Foundations of Corporate Law*, 149 U. PA. L. REV. 1735 (2001).

67. *See* Thomas Donaldson & Thomas W. Dunfee, TIES THAT BIND: A SOCIAL CON-TRACTS APPROACH TO BUSINESS ETHICS 95–96 (1999): "Outside sources may influence the development of norms. Law, particularly when it is perceived as legitimate by members of a community, may have a major impact on what is considered to be correct behavior. Thus, the U.S. Corporate Sentencing Guidelines may be expected to influence perceptions of appropriate structures and policies for assigning managerial responsibility pertaining to corporate social responsibility. Conventional wisdom holds that U.S. law has influenced changes in ethical norms pertaining to racial or gender-based discrimination and also as to the legitimacy of insider trading." *See also* Mark Kelman, *Consumption Theory, Production Theory, and Ideology in the Coase Theorem*, 52 S. CAL. L. REV. 669, 695 (1979) (noting that "perhaps society learns what to value in part through the legal system's descriptions of our protected spheres"); Eric A. Posner, *Law, Economics, and Inefficient Norms*, 144 U. PA. L. REV. 1697, 1731 (1996) ("laws inevitably strengthen or weaken social norms by signaling an official stance toward them").

68. Blair & Stout, *supra* note 66, at 1809.

69. *Id.* at 1785–86.

70. *Id.* at 1787.

71. Iman Anabtawi, *Secret Compensation*, 82 N.C. L. REV. 835, 837 (2004).

72. Michael B. Dorff, *Softening Pharaoh's Heart: Harnessing Altruistic Theory and Behavioral Law and Economics to Rein in Executive Salaries*, 51 BUFF. L. REV. 811, 828–29 (2003).

73. Donald C. Langevoort, *Organized Illusions: A Behavioral Theory of Why Corporations Mislead Stock Market Investors (and Cause Other Social Harms)*, 146 U. PA. L. REV. 101 (1997).

74. Frank H. Easterbrook & Daniel R. Fischel, THE ECONOMIC STRUCTURE OF CORPORATE LAW 93–100 (1991).

75. *See* Hal R. Arkes & Cindy Schipani, *Medical Malpractice v. the Business Judgment Rule: Differences in the Hindsight Bias*, 73 OR. L. REV. 587 (1994).

76. This discussion largely tracks a discussion contained in Robert A. Prentice, *Whither Securities Regulation? Some Behavioral Observations Regarding Proposals for its Future*, 51 DUKE L.J. 1397 (2002).

77. Abolafia, *infra* note 80, at 187.

78. Frank Partnoy, F.I.A.S.C.O.: BLOOD IN THE WATER ON WALL STREET (1997), at 60–61.

79. Michael Lewis, LIAR'S POKER: RISING THROUGH THE WRECKAGE OF WALL STREET 164–70 (1989).

80. *See Dean Witter, Officials Face NASDR Charges Over Sales of Risky Bond Trust Investments*, BNA SEC. L. DAILY, Nov. 21, 2000. [*See also* Mitchel Y. Abolafia, MAKING MARKETS: OPPORTUNISM AND RESTRAINT ON WALL STREET 4 (1996) (noting "a seemingly unending stream of recent scandals" involving profes-sional stock traders).

81. *See* Ellen Kelleher, *Brokers Face Action Over Annuity Advice*, FINANCIAL TIMES, June 10, 2004, at 20.

82. Mitchell Pacelle, *Republic New York Pleads Guilty to Fraud, Agrees to Pay Restitution*, WALL ST. J., December 18, 2001, at C10.

83. Hersh. M. Shefrin & Meir Statman, *Explaining Investor Preference for Cash Dividends*, in ADVANCES IN BEHAVIORAL FINANCE 393, 408 (Richard Thaler, ed. 1993).

84. G. Richard Shell, *Opportunism and Trust in the Negotiation of Commercial Contracts: Toward a New Cause of Action*, 44 VAND. L. REV 221, 269 (1991) at 269.

85. Thus, one prominent study shows evidence of a reputational constraint, but also evidence that the constraint is hardly a strong one. *See* Willard T. Carleton, et al., *Optimism Biases Among Brokerage and Non-Brokerage Firms' Equity Recommendations: Agency Costs in the Investment Industry*, 27 FIN. MGMT. 17 (Spring 1998). Carleton, Chen, and Steiner studied thousands of stock recommendations made by national brokerage firms, regional brokerage firms, and nonbrokerage firms. The brokerage firms have an incentive to give more positive recommendations than nonbrokerage firms because they want to stay on good terms with the issuers whose business they would like to cultivate. And, indeed, the study's findings were that brokerage firms' recommendations were more optimistic than those of nonbrokerage firms. *Id.* at 19. On the other hand, they found that "regional brokerage firms, which have less reputational capital to protect, tend to inflate their recommendations as compared to national brokerage firms." *Id.* at 19–20. Thus, the nonbrokerage firms which had less self-interest at stake had more accurate recommendations than the brokerage firms. *Id.* at 20. But among the brokerage firms, the national firms with more reputational capital to protect proffered more accurate recommendations than the regional firms. *Id.*

86. Stephen M. Bainbridge, *Mandatory Disclosure: A Behavioral Analysis*, 68 U. CIN. L. REV. 1023 (2000).

87. *Id.* at 1026.

88. *Id.* at 1037–41.

89. *Id.* at 1041–43.

90. William Samuelson & Richard Zeckhauser, *Status Quo Bias in Decision Making*, 1 J. RISK & UNCERTAINTY 7 (1988).

91. *See* Jean C. Bedard, *An Archival Investigation of Audit Program Planning*, AUDITING: A J. OF PRAC & THEORY 57, 57–58 (Fall 1989).

92. Bainbridge, *supra* note 86, at 1049–53.

93. *See* Robyn M. Dawes, *Social Dilemmas*, 31 ANN. REV. PSYCHOL. 169, 187 (1980).

94. The following material is summarized from a much longer treatment contained in Robert A. Prentice, *Contract-Based Defenses in Securities Fraud Litigation: A Behavioral Analysis*, U. ILL. L. REV. 337 (2003).

95. William M. Landes & Richard A. Posner, THE ECONOMIC STRUCTURE OF TORT LAW 280–81 (1987).

96. Larry E. Ribstein, *Market vs. Regulatory Responses to Corporate Fraud: A Critique of the Sarbanes-Oxley Act of 2002*, 28 IOWA J. CORP. L. 1, 22–23 (2002).

97. *Nothing But the Truth About Why We Tell Lies*, FINANCIAL TIMES, May 28, 2004 (citing Michael Berry, a senior lecturer in forensic psychology at Manchester Metropolitan University who notes that people who lie in business "have no emotional attachment to the business lie, so most lie detection systems would not discover them.").

98. *See* G. Richard Shell, *Fair Play, Consent and Securities Arbitration: A Comment on Speidel*, 62 BROOK. L. REV. 1365, 1368 (1996).

99. *See* Stephen Choi & Mitu Gulati, *Innovation in Boilerplate Contracts: An Empirical Examination of Sovereign Bonds*, 53 EMORY L.J. 929 (2004).

100. Hillary A. Sale, *Gatekeepers, Disclosure, and Issuer Choice*, 81 WASH. U. L. Q. 403, 406 (2003) (noting that the market did not adequately discount even for risks that were fully disclosed and questioning whether investors could accurately process information about which issuers chose pro-investor regimes and which chose anti-investor regimes).

101. Stephen J. Choi, *Promoting Issuer Choice in Securities Regulation*, 41 VA. J. INT'L. L. 815, 825 (2001).

102. *See generally* Stephen C. Choi & A.C. Pritchard, *Behavioral Economics and the SEC*, 56 STAN. L. REV. 1 (2003).

103. Richard H. McAdams, *An Attitudinal Theory of Expressive Law*, 79 OR. L. REV. 339, 389 (2000).

104. Joel Seligman, THE TRANSFORMATION OF WALL STREET 178–79 (rev. ed. 1995) (noting long-term impact of the SEC's "revolution in financial morality" accomplished in the 1930s).

105. Elaine Welle, *Freedom of Contract and the Securities Laws: Opting Out of Securities Regulation by Private Agreement*, 56 WASH. & LEE L. REV. 519, 541 (1999).
106. *See id.* at 561–62. *See also* Jeffrey J. Rachlinski, *The Limits of Social Norms*, 74 CHI.–KENT L. REV. 1537, 1544 (2000) ("even in the absence of enforcement the mere act of criminalizing conduct can reduce its prevalence").
107. Robert A. Prentice, *Enroll: A Brief Behavioral Autopsy*, 40 AM. BUS. L. REV. 417, 443–44 (2003).

4. History of law and corporate finance

An historical analysis of basic law, corporate law, and securities regulation highlights their importance in the evolution of modern economies, complementing the foregoing economic and behavioral analyses. Organic evolution creates life of greater and greater complexity. Customs and norms are perhaps sufficient to organize commerce in small groups, but greater size requires the "conscious formality" of law to facilitate trade and other economic relationships in a highly interdependent and culturally diverse world.[1] This chapter sets out a necessarily abbreviated history of the development of the law governing corporate finance.

Complex societies require government enforcement of economic transactions. As Nobel prize winner Douglass North has noted, "[t]he move . . . from unwritten traditions and customs to written laws has been unidirectional as we have moved from less to more complex societies and is clearly related to the increasing specialization and division of labor associated with more complex societies."[2] North and other prominent figures in institutional economics have used historical analysis to demonstrate the critical role that legal institutions play in economic development.

Thus, in the early 1600s, the Attorney General of Ireland, John Davis, noted that "[t]he first and principal cause of making kings was to maintain property and contracts, and traffic and commerce among men."[3] Fostering economic development by providing a legal framework that facilitates business development remains a primary purpose of every form of government. History teaches that governments that do it well, encourage economic growth. Governments that cannot foster such an environment, whether they are monarchies or democracies, stunt growth because efficient markets require the rule of law. This chapter reviews the history of the development of the underlying basic law and then the securities laws. The history illustrates the theoretical arguments in the prior chapters about the value of such laws to the economy.

BASIC LAW

There is little controversy regarding the importance for an economy's prosperity of respect for the rule of law, a reliable court system, and basic contract, property, and tort law. As early as the twelfth century, monarchs in parts of Europe began providing security and dispute resolution to their subjects, thereby paving the way for predictability and trust in commercial relationships. Over time, development of the basic bodies of law preceded and paved the way for economic growth.

Contract Law

Certainly familiarity and trust facilitate commercial relationships. But without some governmental enforcement mechanism, historically people trusted and dealt with few beyond friends and family. True, in the eleventh century, the Maghribi, Moroccan traders, built a trading system in the Mediterranean area by creating a system of collective sanctions that it applied to entire groups. If one trader from Genoa breached an agreement with a trader from Morocco, all Genoans were punished.[4] This created an incentive for all Genoan traders to band together and self-police their members' conduct. While this system created an atmosphere that extended trade beyond friends and relatives, it was not as effective as modern government-enforced rules carrying surer enforcement mechanisms and more targeted remedies.

From a modern vantage point in a developed nation, it is difficult to fathom why legal systems all over the world had difficulty developing theoretical bases for enforcing commercial promises, even though rudimentary contractual arrangements date back at least 5000 years to Mesopotamia. In the Western tradition, Roman law initially developed the notion that a promise may give rise to an enforceable duty, but never advanced sufficiently to broadly enforce executory promises.[5] Written codes promulgated by European rulers before 1100 A.D. or so seldom contained any but the most fleeting reference to commercial law. The English common law of contracts emerged in the twelfth century, borrowing heavily from Roman law, especially Justinian's *Corpus Juris Civilis*. Common law courts initially enforced only formal promises known as covenants that were made in writing and sealed with wax. These formalities stultified development as commercial arrangements became more numerous and complex. Economic actors required a method of enforcing informal promises without resorting to the time-consuming and expensive process of putting all arrangements in writing and sealing them with wax.

Through the tort of *assumpsit*, the English common law courts slowly began to allow recovery against parties who failed to carry out a formal contractual promise. However, for a long time even this promising new avenue allowed no remedy for a party who simply failed to perform an informal promise. Then, the common law courts extended their willingness to enforce a contract under *assumpsit* to a situation where the other side had affirmatively relied upon an informal promise. The courts were simultaneously attempting to accommodate merchants and others in order to facilitate commerce, yet searching for a limiting principle because they believed, as courts do today, that it is impractical to enforce every single commercial promise.

Finally, around the dawn of the sixteenth century, English common law courts began enforcing exchanges of promise where no performance had been rendered on either side on grounds that the promisee had limited his own freedom by making a promise. In other words, the doctrine of mutuality of consideration provided the limiting principle that finally induced common law courts to enforce executory promises without going so far as to enforce every single promise any commercial actor made.[6]

Civil law countries took a different route to arrive at much the same location. France, for example, also borrowed heavily from early Roman law, unsurprising given the Roman occupation of Gaul. In delimiting the promises which should be enforceable, French jurists, after some legal evolution, ultimately returned to Roman law's concept of *causa*, examining the motive of the parties. They converted this Roman idea into the French *la cause*, focusing on the volition of the parties, perhaps emphasizing autonomy of the parties even more than the common law.[7] Only with easily enforceable contracts do merchants dare to sell on credit to strangers, can strangers pool resources to form businesses, can banks and other lenders broadly extend credit.

As noted in earlier chapters, law not only embodies customs and norms, it shapes them. English common law emphasized individual responsibility for agreements and that became an accepted norm among businesspeople.[8] Effective contract law thus provides not only remedies for breach of specific agreements but an influential guide for all economic actors as to proper commercial conduct. In this way, contract law institutionalized trust and made the rapid development of capitalism possible. Trust between strangers seldom exists without the institutional and legal framework supporting modern contract law in modern capitalist societies.[9]

Property Law

Without contract law, most exchanges of property could not comfortably take place. And without property law, the existence of private property in its modern conception would itself be in doubt. Property law identifies ownership of resources, making possible commercial trading and accumulation of capital. In nations with formal property law, homeowners can establish that they own their houses, can borrow against the house to start businesses, and banks are willing to make such loans because they know that they can gain legal ownership of the house if the loan is not repaid. In this way, homes and other possessions are used to finance most small businesses, which are the engines driving a substantial portion of economic growth even in economies apparently dominated by large multinational corporations.

By contrast, in developing nations that lack a property rights system, aspiring entrepreneurs cannot prove they own their homes, cannot bind themselves to transfer title, and therefore cannot induce potential lenders to take a chance on making a loan. At America's birth, a sophisticated modern property rights system was not yet in place, but soon thereafter Americans and Europeans established widespread formal property law that allowed owners to convert their property into capital, launching capitalism on a rapidly rising trajectory.[10] Simply put, for developing nations weak property rights are a bigger problem than limited access to external finance because they discourage entrepreneurs from reinvesting their retained earnings.[11] Capitalism triumphed in Western nations in large part because property law allowed people to cooperate and produce under a single integrated system in an expanded market.[12] Even among Western nations, differences in legal systems caused differential economic growth. In the seventeenth century England and the Netherlands surpassed France and Spain in part because they did the better job of establishing and securing property rights.[13] Since the fall of the Berlin Wall, one of the most significant impediments to many formerly communist nations' economic revival has been an absence of doctrines, institutions, and traditions needed to adequately protect property rights. As Nobel laureate Mancur Olson notes, "secure and well-defined rights for all to private property and impartial enforcement of contracts"[14] is essential to economic success.

Ronald Coase's famous theorem assumes zero transaction costs and concludes that in such a world, rational self-interested parties will inevitably bargain to the most efficient solution. In addition to the errors inherent in an assumption of rationality pointed out in the previous chapter, there is no world without transaction costs, as Coase conceded when he gave his Nobel laureate address:

> If we move from a regime of zero transaction costs to one of positive transaction costs, what becomes immediately clear is the crucial importance of the legal system in this new world . . . While we can imagine in the hypothetical world of zero transaction costs that the parties to an exchange would negotiate to change any provision of the law which prevents them from taking whatever steps are required to increase the value of production, in the real world of positive transaction costs such a procedure would be extremely costly, and would make unprofitable, even when it was allowed, such a contracting around the law. Because of this, the rights which individuals possess, with their duties and

privileges, will be to a large extent what the law determines. As a result the legal system will have a profound effect on the working of the economic system and may in certain respects be said to control it.[15]

In short, property law protects property, which is the most significant incentive that exists to motivate people to generate wealth and prosperity.

Most empirical studies indicate that countries with legal systems that protect property rights have economies that regularly outperform the economies of countries that do not.[16] In today's information age, a particular form of property law—that protecting intellectual property—is arguably the single most important factor in the transition to modern growth because it increases the fraction of output paid to compensate creative minds for the fruits of their labor.[17] The first known patent law was passed in Venice in 1474, and some have linked the beginning of the Industrial Revolution to the fact that England and France concluded in the 1700s that patent rights were protectable property rights. There is evidence that during the 1800s America's economic development outstripped England's because America had more advanced patent law and thereby granted more patents and encouraged more inventiveness by its citizens.

Tort Law

In addition to efficient enforcement of contracts and protection of property rights, one other foundational feature of an efficient economy is needed —promotion of fair play. "Capitalism, it turns out, is not a naturally occurring system. It requires rules, laws and customs to protect private property, enforce contracts and *ensure fair play*. Until those are in place you don't get a free market but a free-for-all, which quickly becomes the rule of the strong."[18] Fraud leads to inefficient allocation of resources and discourages economic actors from participating in markets, so the legal systems of all nations attempt to provide remedies for defrauded buyers and sellers. Simple fairness is valued by humans in every society. Rules that punish deceit not only provide remedies for unacceptable conduct but also signal commercial actors as to what standards they will be held to. In so doing, tort rules beneficially shape nations' commercial atmospheres.

The basic law of deceit in common law nations is grounded in the earliest English law. As early as 1201, English common law recognized a very limited writ of deceit, which slowly evolved from what today we would consider breaches of contract into an independent tort. Both civil and criminal remedies for fraud in commercial transactions have been staples of the common law for centuries. Similarly, civil law nations have long punished fraud. For example, the Napoleonic Code from early on contained several provisions punishing fraud, deceit, and stellionate (fraud in the form of selling mortgaged property without revealing the mortgage to the buyer).[19] The French word *dol* used in the original Code technically carries a wider meaning than the English "fraud."

As the securities markets developed in both England and the United States, established property law concepts from real estate and goods were easily applied to this new form of property. Thus, by the late 1700s, common law courts in England were applying fraud rules to the sale of securities in the same manner that they applied them to sale of any other property.[20] And American courts were similarly protecting defrauded parties in securities transactions by at least 1790.[21]

An important development in the common law of fraud and deceit occurred when the courts addressed cases where the deceivers were not parties to the transaction. Courts commonly handled situations where a seller of a horse lied to the buyer about the horse's state of health. But then they had to decide whether the law of deceit should be expanded to cover lies by nonparties? In the 1789 case, *Pasley* v. *Freeman*,[22] English courts held that a defendant who had no contract with the plaintiff could be liable for misleading the plaintiff into contracting with a third person.[23] So, suppose a shareholder of ABC Co. sells ABC stock to an investor, both believing that ABC is a sound company and that its share price is representative of the shares' true value. Assume further that their belief is based upon the statements of a promoter or officer of ABC Co., who is not a party to the transaction. Should the buyer be able to recover damages in common law fraud from the deceitful promoter or officer? *Pasley* v. *Freeman* set an adequate precedent, and early in the 1800s, American judges began to allow recovery in such situations, which clearly paved the way for fairer and more efficient stock markets.[24] The development of public companies would later require invention of an extended liability, the securities law "fraud on the market" theory (discussed in economic terms in Chapter 2 and revisited later in this chapter), but this was an important first step.

Thus, developments in the basic law of contracts, property, and the tort of fraud and deceit have provided important foundations for the growth of economies in general and of corporate activity and securities markets specifically. Only the most ardent opponents of government interference with free enterprise would doubt the value of these legal rules as enablers of commercial development.

Before leaving the discussion of basic law, it is relevant to note that statutes and judicial decisions are merely words on a page. There must exist enforcement mechanisms, legal institutions, and cultural norms to give these words real meaning in the marketplace. Without institutions to enforce them or the right of injured individuals to sue for their breach, and without effective legal processes to reach fair results in these actions, the substantive rights themselves mean little. The quality of courts is important, as is the substance of the law. The US common law judge-made system derives from English tradition, while most continental European nations use a civil law system of statutory codes.

CORPORATE LAW

Although the first semi-comprehensive corporate codes date back less than two hundred years, the roots of business organizations can be traced back at least to Mesopotamia in 3000 BC. Ancient Phoenicians and Athenians developed early forms of partnership. In medieval times, shipping businesses aggregated capital and distributed shares in a form closely resembling modern partnerships. Although some trace the origin of corporations to the ancient Greeks,[25] Blackstone concluded long ago that the honor of inventing companies belonged to the Romans, for they devised the notion of a corporation having an identity separate and apart from that of its owners and the concept of limited liability.

The development of the corporation was critically important. Around 1000 AD both the Chinese and the Arabs had important trading and commercial advantages over the West, but many suggest that because their legal systems were not conducive to developing companies,[26] they lost the commercial advantage that they enjoyed.[27] Rather, in the twelfth century in Venice and Florence, in the sixteenth century in England and soon thereafter in France, in the early seventeenth century in Holland, and in the late 1700s in America, the modern legal notion of a corporation began to evolve and flourish, sparking economic development that outstripped that of nations without the legal structures to create such entities.

These proto-corporations initially took two basic forms. One was the unincorporated joint-stock company that slowly evolved to contain more and more corporate-like features and to resemble less and less the partnership form. The other was the specially-chartered corporation that was often privately financed but featured government participation and was often a government-sheltered monopoly. In the late 1700s and early 1800s in England, France, and America, such special charters were often granted to corporations formed for public works projects that governments did not wish to undertake via tax revenues, such as canals and roads.

Until the nineteenth century, governments in these nations required promoters to receive special government permission for their enterprises to assume the corporate form. During the 1800s, however, today's developed nations gradually began allowing free registration of corporations that met given criteria rather than requiring promoters to secure governmental permission for each charter. France was one of the first nations to do so, but then changed course with its Code de Commerce in 1807 and went back to requiring special legislative concession. When England began allowing free registration (first without limited liability in 1844 and then with limited liability in 1855), France was forced to follow (in 1867) because of French resources migrating to England and increased activity of English companies on the continent. Germany then followed suit in 1870. Meanwhile, beginning in the 1830s a substantial shift among American states to free registration began.

Provisions dispensing with the requirement of special legislative act as a prerequisite for forming a corporation were often part of broader corporate codes that addressed many issues necessarily raised by a proliferation of private business corporations. In the United States, New York passed one of the first broad state corporate statutes in 1811. England, which had a fairly well-developed common law in the area, did not begin its codification process until 1844. In Prussia, a corporate law was enacted in 1843. With the creation of these codes, both the specially-chartered corporation and the unincorporated joint-stock company faded away to be replaced by a corporate form that quickly evolved to contain modern features.

The speed of the evolution varied from country to country and was not always steady, but most developed European and North American nations moved slowly at first, then quickly during the late nineteenth century, toward promoting and enabling corporate entities sporting these key features: (a) separateness of identity, (b) perpetuity of existence, (c) limited liability, (d) centralized control, (e) fiduciary duties for managers, (f) protection for minority shareholders, and (g) the ability to amass "bonded capital." The importance of these modern companies for economic development cannot be gainsaid. Corporations increase the pool of available capital, enable investors to spread risk, provide an avenue for effectively managing large organizational structures, and provide a strong incentive for organizations to be efficient by allowing investors to move their money elsewhere.[28]

Nicholas Butler, a former president of Columbia University, concluded that "[t]he limited liability corporation is the greatest single discovery of modern times; even steam and electricity would be reduced to comparative impotence without it."[29] The first enterprises requiring huge accumulations of capital—railroads—were universally formed as corporations, as are virtually all large enterprises today. Indeed, the corporation may be the most important of all the institutions that enable the modern market economy.[30] Today, these engines of economic power produce 90 percent of the sales and receipts reported by American businesses. Across the globe there appears to be a broad correlation between economic progress and the embracing of the corporate form. While some partnerships and even sole proprietorships have reached a large size and lasted for lengthy periods, it is the corporate form that has overwhelmingly accounted for the size and scope of modern enterprises. And it is modern corporate law that has facilitated and enabled those enterprises in a way that private contracting among individuals could never accomplish alone.

Separate Legal Identity

The most obvious contribution of corporate law to the creation of the modern corporate enterprise is simply that corporations cannot exist without legal sanction. Corporations are artificial creatures of the state. While theoretically people could contract for all of the relationships that make up a corporation, in reality such organizations simply do not exist in the absence of legal sanction beyond simple contract enforcement. As Peter Drucker has noted, "[t]his new 'corporation,' this new Société Anonyme, this new Aktiengesellschaft, . . . clearly was an innovation . . . It was the first autonomous institution in hundreds of years, the first to create a power center that was within society yet independent of the central government of the nation state."[31]

In his 1937 article "The Nature of the Firm," Coase contended that the corporate form allows minimization of the transaction costs of coordinating economic activity and thereby provides a competitive advantage when compared to buyers and sellers making new contracts at every stage of production. More recently, Blair and Stout have made the same point, viewing the corporation as a mechanism for solving "team production problems" that in today's large modern enterprises are simply too complicated to handle via individual contracting alone.[32]

> The essence of the team production problem is that varied inputs from a number of individuals are needed, these inputs are difficult or impossible to monitor or specify contractually, and the output is a joint output, not readily divisible or attributable to individual inputs. These inputs and investments are often enterprise-specific, because their value, once they have been sunk into the enterprise, is tied to the overall success of the enterprise. The specificity, or "sunk" quality of the investments, increases the difficulty of writing simple contracts among individuals that could elicit and coordinate the use of such inputs.[33]

While it is possible for large organizations to be operated in the partnership form, as large accounting firms proved for a time, it was exceedingly rare for businesses to amass huge quantities of assets, to employ thousands of workers, or to take on truly large projects before the modern corporation began to evolve.

As noted, because of the very novelty of the corporate form, fear of great accumulations of assets, sovereign worry about loss of control, and even undue greed by government officials, for quite a time in most nations the law required a specific act of government to create a corporation. Placed in historical context, it is not surprising that governments imposed these requirements, but it is also clear that such requirements retarded corporate formation, presented opportunities for corruption when promoters were tempted to bribe government officials, and even enabled fraud by promoters who collected assets while promising to form a corporation that they knew the government would likely not approve. The need for government approval also restrained economic development by sometimes requiring intrepid entrepreneurs to accomplish their goals through less satisfactory forms of business organization including partnerships and unincorporated joint-stock companies. For example, although England's "Bubble Act" of 1720 is typically referred to as one of the earliest securities regulations, its most significant provision made it illegal to sell shares in joint-stock companies that had not received Parliamentary permission to form. Until it was repealed in 1825, this Act may have inhibited evolution of the modern corporate form in England (although the Act did not apply to Scotland, and joint-stock companies did not flourish there either).[34] Many believe that a turning point in American corporate development occurred with the post-Revolution formation of a strong federal government which made it clear that the Bubble Act no longer applied in America. Formation of corporations exploded thereafter in the former colonies.[35]

With the decision in *Fletcher* v. *Peck*[36] that a legislative grant to a private company was a contract under the American Constitution's Contract Clause, and in *Dartmouth College*[37] that a corporation's state charter was also a contract that could not be altered by the legislature unless the right to do so had been specifically reserved in the charter, the safe existence of the corporation relatively free from legislative interference was affirmed and capital flowed to corporations in amounts ensuring that they would be the preeminent vehicles for economic growth in America.[38]

Only as the laws of England, France, Germany, and the United States (which have served as a model for the corporate laws of most other nations around the world) dispensed with the requirement of special governmental approval for corporate formation did the modern corporation begin to flower. Allowing large numbers of artificial corporate entities to enjoy corporate personhood, to own property, to sue in their own name, to (in America) enjoy substantial Constitutional rights, provided flexibility and continuity unmatched by other forms of business enterprise.

Perpetuity

An important aspect of the new corporate form was the potential perpetuity of its existence. Sole proprietorships obviously ended with the death of their owner (although an heir or another might take up the burdens of the business). The default common law position was that partnerships also dissolved upon the death or other departure of any of the partners. Early joint-stock companies, such as those in England, often were formed for the purpose of collecting capital to stock a ship for trading in newly discovered lands. Typically, the merchants who chartered the ship with their pooled capital would have an accounting after each journey. The next trade mission would involve an entirely new enterprise.

Thus, the notion of a truly long-term business enterprise was rare in private business ventures. The concept of perpetual existence of a corporate form may have evolved in ecclesiastical organizations as a way to enable churches to own property over time even as parishioners, priests, and others came and went. Obviously, such an ability could be useful to private business enterprises as well.

In 1623 the Dutch East India Company was granted the right of perpetuity. It collected capital to fund not just one voyage, but a potentially endless series of voyages. In 1654 the British East India Company followed suit. These entities paved the way for creation of large accumulations of capital that could be used to advance business endeavors over long periods of time. Owners could come and go. Managers could come and go. But the enterprise would continue, making binding commitments to employees, to suppliers, to customers, and to creditors of a character that sole proprietorships and partnerships could not make. The corporate form could more easily undertake long-term endeavors than any preexisting form of enterprise. And the corporate entity itself could establish a reputation in the economic community—separate and apart from that of its individual owners or managers—that would assist it in achieving commercial success. Simple contract law could never accomplish such progress.

Limited Liability

Many believe that corporate law's most significant contribution to the development of capitalism is limited liability. More than any other single concept, limited liability encourages people to invest in enterprises operated by strangers, enabling business enterprises to grow to substantial size and enjoy economies of scale, the benefits of perpetuity, and other advantages of size. In earlier times, sole proprietorships tended to employ family members and neighbors. Partnerships were necessarily small because partners needed to know much about the reliability of their fellow investors/partners for the simple reason that if other partners defaulted, then the personal liability of the nondefaulters could skyrocket. For many years, partners who were unable to pay their obligations faced debtors' prison or even the prospect of being sold into slavery. Such a state certainly discouraged any person from casting his economic lot with strangers.

While it is perhaps theoretically possible for partnerships to contract for limited liability for their partners when negotiating contracts (just as it is possible for shareholders to contractually forfeit their limited liability as they often do in close corporations), in matters of tort law such is not possible. The owners of a company could not contract for limited liability with unknown and possibly unforeseeable victims of the tortious actions of their companies' managers and employees. The corporate form can provide such protection for liabilities in tort as well as contract, thereby facilitating investment because a shareholder's total potential liability is generally unaffected by the personal reliability or solvency of other shareholders. Limited liability solves an agency problem. Without it, shareholders would have to monitor much more closely and expensively their corporate managers. Limited liability protects shareholders from liability, shifting the risk to the corporate entities' creditors who often are better equipped and more intensely motivated to monitor than shareholders of a corporation whose ownership is widely dispersed.[39]

Limited liability was initially recognized for government-sponsored corporations, such as the Dutch East India Company. Slowly, it began to become a more common feature of private corporations, especially as general corporation statutes spread. Britain in 1855 formally recognized limited liability; Germany did so in 1861 and France in 1863. Over the course of the nineteenth century, limited liability became the default rule in American jurisdictions as well (although not in California until 1931).

Limited liability came in stages and was likely not as important to shareholders in the early 1800s as it later became, but virtually every relevant legislative change in the developed countries during the nineteenth century strengthened and broadened the shield of limited liability and thereby gave added incentive to the investment that is critical to economic development. Limited liability is arguably a near prerequisite for broad investor participation in company ownership.[40] With the advent of modern tort liability for on-the-job injuries, for automobile crashes, and for product defects, limited liability has become so important that even the law governing small entities stresses its importance. In America in recent years state legislatures have created all manner of new organizational forms (limited liability partnerships, limited liability companies, and limited liability limited partnerships, for example) to provide limited liability for almost all entrepreneurs.

Centralized Control by Managers

The separate corporate entity, the perpetuity of existence, and the limited liability of investors all led to a formal separation of ownership from control in larger corporations. Although partners in a partnership can hire managers to operate the business for them and thereby evade the default rule that important decisions require the majority vote of all partners, this typically is not the practice. And it would be very difficult in the partnership form to do this in an enterprise for a lengthy period of time. Before the corporate form blossomed among private business enterprises, they tended to be small and often family-managed.

The corporate form with its perpetual existence, however, facilitates delegation of control and, indeed, creates a presumption in a firm of any size that such delegation will occur. The Dutch East India Company was one of the first to formalize and take advantage of this separation by creating a layer of professional managers separate and apart from the firm's investors. Providing monitoring by a board of directors, this structure commits to the discretion of managers the day-to-day decisions necessary for operation of the business. Managers not only make the daily decisions necessary to operate the firm, they initiate the long-term strategies that are monitored by the board and the organic changes that must be approved by both directors and shareholders.

It was the development of the corporate form in private business enterprises that created a framework wherein despite the coming and going of owners, of specific managers, of rafts of employees, of assets in various forms, a team of professional managers can continue to coordinate the enterprise using the principles of Chandler, Sloan, Deming, Drucker, Porter, and others (primarily Americans).[41] Utilization of the corporate form promoted the development of hierarchical management structures that led, in turn, to the creation of a class of middle managers and technical specialists who could have long careers with their employers. It also facilitated the creation of brands for both corporate entities and their products.[42]

America was quicker to adopt professional managers than England, and it made a difference in economic development.[43] Hiring the best managers available rather than the best family members available, as was the British custom for so long, facilitates efficient operation of modern economic enterprises. France also suffered under a family-dominated approach, leading to a general weakness of its capital markets. Only after World War II did France produce large, vertically-integrated companies capable of making use of sophisticated management techniques.

Fiduciary Duty of Managers

Separation of ownership from control, though creating some obvious advantages, also creates a potential agency problem. According to Adam Smith, an agent watching over someone else's assets would never be as careful as a principal guarding his own.[44] More than a hundred years after Smith, Berle and Means famously echoed this concern about the problems stemming from a division between ownership and control.[45] Again, theoretically it would be possible for investors to contract for a proper level of protection from the potential misdeeds of corporate managers and employees. In real life, especially given the behavioral considerations outlined in the previous chapter, it is exceedingly difficult to truly manage this problem contractually.

Modern corporate law has evolved to address this problem in at least two fundamental ways. First, it sets up a system of monitoring. In America, for example, shareholders have the right to vote and therefore to have direct input into how their assets are being used. They may typically vote regarding important corporate matters such as mergers and liquidations. They may also vote for directors who will monitor the managers who run the company day-to-day, thus giving them indirect input into broad policy decisions as well.

Similar monitoring systems have evolved in other nations as well.[46] UK corporations have long had a board of directors that operated in similar fashion to those in America and as early as 1862 provided for modest independent monitoring of public companies by a government agency. Since 1870, Germany has required a supervisory or first-tier board (*Aufsichtsrat*) that has acted much as an American board of directors, choosing and broadly supervising managers. Today, in the Aktiengesellschaften (AG), the corporations most comparable to American public companies, the *Aufsichtsrat* usually contains representatives of powerful German banks, as well as labor representatives. The supervising board has substantial paper authority to choose the members of and supervise and investigate the second-tier or "managing" board (*Vorstand*) that is composed substantially of company insiders. In reality, the *Aufsichtsrat*'s exercise of authority is often not impressive. It frequently has trouble getting the information required for effective monitoring, and under law its members need meet no more than twice a year. The monitoring role of the powerful German banks is significant, but tends to protect creditors more than shareholders. There is some evidence that German citizens are less willing to invest in corporations than Americans because the boards do not view their primary goal as protecting the interests of shareholders. Recently there have been many suggestions by German scholars that German practice migrate more toward an Anglo-Saxon model of corporate governance and there has been movement toward that model.

France introduced supervision of managers via *commissaries* in 1863. They came to be charged with a wide range of responsibilities, including ensuring the accuracy of information supplied to shareholders, ensuring equal treatment of shareholders, and notifying shareholders of "irregularities." On the whole, however, directors in France have often been disappointing monitors,[47] in large part because of a lack of independence. As with Germany, most scholars have recommended a move toward the Anglo-American model and France has taken steps in that direction.

For both economic reasons (diversified shareholders have no strong reason to pay attention to the performance of any particular company, given the associated costs) and behavioral reasons (investors have a tendency to overtrust their directors), shareholders usually do not pay sufficient attention to either their decisions regarding which directors to vote for or the job those directors and the managers they monitor are doing. Similarly, officers have traditionally had substantial influence in selecting the directors who would monitor them, thus substantially undermining the efficacy of that monitoring.

Therefore, the second thing that corporation law does, more so in common law jurisdictions, that cannot be effectively done contractually, is to impose fiduciary duties upon officers and directors. These duties not only impose legal responsibilities upon the officers and directors, but also create a model, a norm for directors. In America, this fiduciary duty generally cannot be contractually escaped. As the Enron and related scandals demonstrated at the beginning of the current century, these provisions certainly do not work perfectly, but they are better than a mere contractual alternative and improvements continue. The continuing struggle involves the need to create effective monitoring by the directors on the one hand, but to avoid unduly hamstringing managers' decisionmaking on the other.

Early on, common law judges imposed a fiduciary duty on officers and directors, while civil law nations allowed more freedom of contract for fiduciary responsibilities. In broad outline it is fair to say that investors fare better in America and the United Kingdom, where managers owe their primary fiduciary duty to shareholders, than in France and Germany where equal loyalty is owed to creditors and employees. Germany has recognized the rudiments of a fiduciary duty, but lacks an efficient enforcement mechanism.[48]

Admittedly, the role of the directors as protectors of shareholders is not as critical in jurisdictions such as Germany and Japan, where financial institutions provide more of the financing and play a bigger role as intermediary and monitor of corporate management. Until recently, state ownership and control of private enterprise was a central phenomenon of the French economy, so government monitoring of corporations played an important role. That is now fading away substantially, making board-style monitoring and attendant fiduciary duties more important.

Even in America's common law system, the law tends to draw a stark distinction between a breach of the duty of loyalty and a breach of the duty of care, being much more reluctant to impose liability upon directors, especially outside directors, in the latter case. Indeed, around the world it seems rare for liability to be imposed upon outside directors for anything other than clear breaches of the duty of loyalty.[49] Whatever the faults of the Anglo-American system exposed by the Enron scandals, the clear trend around the world is toward models that promise better and more independent board monitoring and increased fiduciary duties imposed by law. The historical experience of the past two hundred years is not leading any nation to conclude that less vigorous board monitoring and less rigorous fiduciary obligations are a good idea.

Protection of Minority Shareholders

Just as passive shareholders can be exploited by those who manage their assets, minority shareholders can be exploited by controlling shareholders. This possibility, of course, discourages investment. So, over time, corporate laws have been developed to protect minority shareholders from such exploitation. As corporate law evolved in this area, there remained a continuing tension between the need to protect minority shareholders from exploitation by majority shareholders on the one hand, and the need to avoid giving minority shareholders an undue ability to "hold up" the company when a transaction beneficial to the corporate enterprise but perhaps detrimental to a minority shareholder was at stake.

Consider the right to vote on major organic changes in corporate form mentioned in the previous section. Under most modern corporate codes shareholders have the right of "voice" (to vote on major transactions) and "exit" (to have their shares purchased should a major corporate change with which they disagree occur). But all modern legal regimes struggle with striking the proper balance between protecting minority shareholder factions from abuse and awarding them the power to shakedown the majority in such transactions. Regarding a merger, certainly shareholders should have the right to vote. But should majority approval be sufficient? Would a super-majority provision allow minority shareholders undue power to block the majority's wishes? The trend in America has been to do what Delaware did in 1929 and reduce the merger approval requirement to a simple majority.

Until relatively recently, in France the right to vote seemed to be used more to regulate relationships between management and the largest share-holders.[50] However, in the last 15 years or so, France's regulations have evolved to more generally resemble American rules that protect capital market investors more fully by, in part, giving them the right to vote on important matters of corporate change, such as mergers.

Another protection for minority shareholders is appraisal rights—the right to have their shares bought at a court-determined fair price if they oppose a major organic change. Of course, if too many shareholders exercise their appraisal rights, the organic change often becomes infeasible even if supported by a large majority of shareholders. Does this allow minority shareholders to hold up the company? American shareholders who oppose a merger but are outvoted generally have the right to demand that their shares be purchased at a fairly appraised price. The expense of actually pursuing these appraisal rights may render them somewhat hollow, minimizing the likelihood of holdup.

Another mechanism for minority protection is inspection rights. The common law of England recognized shareholders' rights to access corporate books and records in the early 1700s.[51] At first, the right stemmed from the fact that the corporation was viewed as a trustee holding property for the benefit of stockholders. Later, the view was that shareholders needed the inspection right in order to protect their property interests.[52] Throughout the 1800s, as corporations grew in size, statutes were enacted in England and America to supplement the common law inspection right. Generally, shareholders in common law nations have the right to inspect relevant corporate records at a proper time, in a proper place, for a proper purpose. On paper, French shareholders have substantial inspection rights but, as elsewhere, these rights benefit mostly shareholders in closely held corporations and major shareholders of public corporations. The situation is comparable in Japan where inspection rights on paper are roughly analogous to those accorded shareholders in the United States, but shareholders have difficulty enforcing those rights in court.

The right to sue derivatively on behalf of the corporation is another means of protecting minority shareholders. This right to sue has been recognized in America for 120 years, and despite procedural obstacles, remains a potent weapon for shareholders. The United Kingdom, on the other hand, does not have a strong derivative right for shareholders. Nor does Germany, which relied more on its supervisory boards to protect the interests of minority shareholders. France has procedures that are in some respects even more pro-plaintiff than those in the United States, but they are typically not used much, in part because shareholders must own a substantial block of stock to be able to sue. Whether because of these problems or a lack of litigious culture or absence of an active plaintiffs' bar, there have been relatively few such suits. The derivative suit was rarely used in Japan until some 1993 legal reforms; it is used more now, but the Japanese system, like Germany's, still relies substantially upon monitoring by companies' "main banks."[53] Such lawsuits have been brought so seldom that directors and officers (D&O) insurance was not even offered in Japan until 1994, and then it was introduced to respond to lawsuit exposure overseas.

In general, common law nations appear to provide more protection to minority shareholders than do civil law nations (particularly those in the French tradition), and there is recent empirical support for the notion that these protections aid investment, encourage ownership dispersion, facilitate capital markets, and allow companies to access external finance more easily. In Germany, Belgium, Holland, and elsewhere, it is common to have employee voice in manager supervision. Although no major changes are likely in the immediate future, many scholars and businesspeople even in those nations seem to believe that to improve capital markets, protections for shareholders will likely have to be strengthened relative to the interests of workers and creditors.

Bonding Assets

Importantly, the corporate form enables a commitment of resources to a venture that no earlier form of organization provided. By partitioning the assets of the separate corporate entity from the individual assets of its owners, the corporate form ensures not only that owners will enjoy limited liability for corporate debts, but also that assets committed by the shareholders to the corporate purpose cannot easily be reached (a) by the creditors[54] or heirs[55] of individual shareholders or managers, or (b) by those shareholders and managers themselves. These assets are to remain devoted to the corporate purpose. They become "bonded" to the corporate enterprise, theoretically in perpetuity, although that is not truly required to make it easier to entice investment from others and to borrow money from banks and to purchase on credit from suppliers. These two results could not be achieved contractually in the absence of corporate law because a business's owners cannot by contractual arrangements among themselves bind their individual creditors.[56]

Partnership law and the law of other forms of business organization that predated the company gave investors substantial leeway to remove their investment, even if the business's affairs were substantially disrupted. This ability not only disrupted the partnership's business, it also enabled one partner to hold up the others. Even a partner's death or mental disability traditionally dissolved the enterprise. But corporate law commits capital so that it cannot be easily withdrawn. Over the course of the twentieth century in America, repeated changes in the law aimed at tightening this connection, which was recognized as early as 1824 in *Wood* v. *Dummer*[57] where Judge Story explicated the "trust fund" doctrine.

Corporate law works comparably in other nations, facilitating large accumulations of capital that can be held in place for long periods of time and applied by professional managers. By providing limited liability and protecting investors from exploitation by managers and majority shareholders, the corporate form should also encourage investment.

Conclusion

While the history of corporate law certainly highlights important differences among the various nations in addressing very basic issues such as stakeholder rights, shareholder remedies like derivative suits, and other issues, there has been substantial convergence toward the common law model as evolved in England, and especially America. Even before 2002, experts had pointed to the substantial convergence toward the American model in terms of black letter law around the world.[58] Whether nations had the will, resources, and institutions necessary to effectuate the protection of minority shareholders deemed a critical priority in every nation was another matter, of course. Those that succeeded in producing those institutions seemed to prosper more than those that did not.

After the 2002 enactment of the Sarbanes-Oxley Act, in which the American Congress largely mandated that corporations formed in other nations but accessing American capital markets must adopt important aspects of American-style corporate governance, that convergence was hastened. Although there was immediate resistance by European and Japanese companies, there is now increasing acceptance that Sarbanes-Oxley's requirements of independent directors, strong audit committees, stringent enforcement of disclosure and antifraud requirements, and the rest, constitute worldwide "best practices" insofar as the current state of knowledge goes.

Although the EU will not adopt the Sarbanes-Oxley Act's requirements *in toto*, many European commentators have recognized the wisdom of emulating the core Sarbanes-Oxley requirements. Germany, France, the United Kingdom, and other EU nations on their own impetus have for the past decade moved toward more independent boards, greater use of audit committees, more vigilant auditors, and more realistic and uniform accounting standards. While some argue that governance reforms of this type should not be imposed from the top down, but should be "evolutionary and market-driven,"[59] they admit the desirability and inevitability of such changes.

This convergence is not limited to the EU. In recent amendments to its Commercial Code, Japan moved toward greater concern for shareholder welfare in corporate governance and facilitated adoption of independent audit committees and formal separation of inside and outside directors. Other Asian nations have followed suit in a belief that emulation of American-style corporate governance would pay dividends.

SECURITIES REGULATION

Having corporate and other efficient forms of business organization will have little impact if those organizations cannot raise the funds necessary to pursue entrepreneurial ventures. The three basic business inputs are, after all, land, labor, and *capital*. As noted in the previous discussion, corporate law can induce investment by offering limited liability and can bond those funds to the corporate purpose. But perhaps other legal features can help as well, especially those offered by securities regulation.

William Bernstein pointed out in his recent book *The Birth of Plenty: How the Prosperity of the Modern World was Created*, that world economic growth was essentially flat from as far back as we can measure until around 1820, when sustained growth began in some parts of what we now consider the developed world. Based on the preceding thousand years, one would have projected perhaps a doubling of per capita GDP in the 172 years following 1820. Instead, England's increased tenfold and America's twentyfold.[60] What accounts for this recent, sustained development? Bernstein maintains that such rapid development requires the coalescence of four factors. Two have little to do with our story: scientific rationalism (so that ideas can be created for eventual commercialization and development), and fast and efficient communications and transportation (as Stephen Ambrose pointed out, in Thomas Jefferson's time, no goods or information could move faster than the fastest horse).[61] Bernstein's third factor was discussed above—the development of property rights that encourage men and women to work hard and to create by allowing them to keep a fair portion of the fruits of their labor and not worry about arbitrary confiscation by the government or others.

The fourth and final factor necessary for economic progress, Bernstein maintains, is capital markets. Before 1820 or so, few of even the most entrepreneurial minds with the best business ideas had access to the amounts of money needed to bring their ideas to market.[62] This section traces the historical development of modern securities regulation and explores the ways in which it may have assisted the development of efficient modern capital markets, focusing on four areas of law: (a) disclosure requirements,

(b) misrepresentation provisions, (c) insider trading rules, and (d) tender offer rules.

The discussion necessarily draws artificial distinctions between securities regulation and corporate law. As noted earlier, had England's Bubble Act simply stated that no corporation could be formed without the special authorization of Parliament, it would have been viewed as a corporation law. But by providing that no one could sell securities of corporations formed without such authority, the Act appeared more like a securities law. Insider trading rules similarly address an agency problem at the heart of corporate law and tender offers are one of a variety of forms of corporate organic change that are central to many corporate law concerns. Proxy rules embedded in US securities laws represent an attempt to give meaning to an important corporate law right—the shareholder right to vote. Even England's original securities disclosure rules were embedded within its corporate law in the Company Acts, and America's recent Sarbanes-Oxley Act took dead aim at corporate governance practices even though it is viewed essentially as a securities law. So, clearly, these bodies of law are closely related and any distinction between them is necessarily arbitrary.

The history of capital market development is largely a Western story rather than a Middle Eastern story, for Islamic law eventually came to be interpreted as largely prohibiting the charging of interest (although it was not so interpreted originally). With no interest there are few loans. Without loans there is little investment. And, of course, without investment there can be no capital markets.[63] Additionally, these nations lacked clearly defined property rights. Only in 2004 did financiers in the Muslim world receive Koranic permission to form the first Islamic hedge fund, for example. Nor, until quite recently, is this a story of the Far East, for Japan, China, Korea, and other nations had the resources but lacked the institutions (especially property rights) necessary to create capital markets until they began to adopt Western ideas. Their emulation of Western laws over the past century is a testament to a broad worldwide consensus that Western nations have generally the correct approach to stimulating broad capital investment.

General Background

For many centuries and in many parts of the world, commercial instruments that meet modern definitions of "securities" have been sold and traded. Venice had a secondary market in securities as early as the fourteenth century. The Amsterdam Bourse was created in 1530, though it is largely famous today for the Tulip Mania of 1636–37. The Dutch also invented investment banking, allowing the risk of loans to be distributed among thousands of investors in the seventeenth century.

But the roots of modern securities regulation can be traced to England, where securities trading in secondary markets arrived around 1694 when the Bank of England was formed. In these early days of Western securities markets, the securities that were traded were primarily governmental debt instruments, which became prominent when the monarchs of England and France began issuing long-term, transferable debt instruments to finance their wars and other national projects. As early as 1695 there were 150 or so English companies whose shares were trading sufficiently to justify creation of an informal stock exchange in the coffee houses lining what came to be known as London's "Exchange Alley." Still, corporate securities were relatively unimportant in these early days for the simple reason that few corporations existed until general corporation statutes were enacted during the 1800s. As the number of corporations exploded during the nineteenth century, corporate-issued securities rapidly came to the fore.

As noted earlier, Western courts quickly recognized that securities were just another form of property and readily applied the common law of contracts, torts, and property to securities transactions. Thus was born securities regulation, which even today is in substantial part just a body of contract and tort law specifically adapted to the needs of public corporations, capital market investors, securities professionals, and their special transactions. Because the first comprehensive body of securities law was not enacted until 1933 and 1934 in the United States, many have the impression that securities transactions were largely unregulated until that time. However, a leading securities law historian reminds us that from their beginnings English and American securities markets were substantially regulated.[64]

This early regulation was prompted by early abuses. Rapscallions quickly realized that it was easier to fool another regarding the value of a security than regarding the value of a horse, and that it was easier to artificially manipulate the price of stocks than the price of real estate. And then there were the bubbles. The Dutch stock exchange, founded around 1611 primarily to trade Dutch East India Company stock, suffered a crash with the Tulip Mania of 1636 and 1637.[65] In 1720, some legitimate success of the British South Sea Company, coupled with a fair measure of fraud and manipulation, created an irrational market bubble that set the pattern for later bubbles such as that involving American dot.com stocks in the late 1990s. Nearly simultaneously France's largest early securities endeavor (John Law's Mississippi Company) created a similar boom and bust.[66]

These bubbles and their bursting did inestimable damage to burgeoning capital markets. Impersonal capital markets require investor confidence, and that is often a fragile commodity that is easily undermined. In France, for example, John Law's debacle created such distrust that impersonal securities markets did not develop until more than a hundred years later.[67]

Perhaps unsurprisingly, it is the bursting of bubbles and the disclosure of financial scandals that simultaneously subvert investor confidence and virtually require government intervention to bolster market confidence. Therefore, frauds and bubbles provided an early impetus to government consideration of securities regulation. No sooner had a stock exchange organized itself in London around 1695 than Parliament passed "An act to restrain the number and ill practices of brokers and stockjobbers,"[68] and such fraud and manipulation followed an English commission's conclusion in 1696 that "[T]he pernicious art of stockjobbing [has] perverted the end and design of companies . . . to the private profit of the first projectors, [who sell worthless stock to] ignorant men, drawn in by the reputation, falsely raised and artfully spread, concerning the thriving state of their stock."[69]

The law did little more than forbid brokers from trading for their own account, capped their fees, limited their number to 100, and put some restrictions upon options trading (then known as "time bargains"). The Act expired in 1708, but then the City of London stepped in and licensed brokers, primarily as a revenue raising measure. In 1711, Parliament reinstated a ceiling on brokers' fees, but the next relevant law was passed near the height of the 1720 South Sea Bubble.

The South Sea Bubble which soared in the first half of 1720 and crashed to earth in the second half, created numerous concerns for Parliament and others. The irrational exuberance of investors prompted charlatans to form many bogus companies offering securities for all manner of unrealistic enterprises. Additionally, there was a broad and perhaps exaggerated fear that insiders could easily manipulate the price of securities and thereby defraud outsiders. Because very little disclosure regarding the financial or commercial status of companies was required or practiced, the stock price of companies and the amount of dividends they issued were the market's best signals as to the status of a company and the easy manipulability of those two signals by insiders justifiably led to some concern.

Parliament passed the "Bubble Act" before the South Sea bubble burst, barring the selling of securities of companies other than those formed with Parliament's permission. This was likely already the common law rule, so the Act's main impact was to provide remedies for violation of preexisting rules. Many believe that the primary motivation for the Bubble Act's passage was a desire to funnel financing to those ventures that Parliament favored such as the South Sea Company, although there is little doubt that during the South Sea Bubble many unapproved companies were formed with seriously fraudulent intent. The Act was also aimed in part at stopping the practice of buying lapsed charters and starting businesses under their umbrella. Repealed a century later in 1825, the Bubble Act generated only one known case in the entire eighteenth century and therefore had minimal impact on the practice of securities trading,[70] although it likely discouraged to at least a minor degree the evolution of joint-stock companies.

Although Parliament often debated serious reforms over the following century, with the exception of a 1722 law that harshly punished (by death) the forging or counterfeiting of a power to transfer securities, the only securities measure enacted in England during this time was Sir John Barnard's Act in 1834. Barnard's Act was entitled "An act to prevent the infamous practice of stockjobbing," and aimed primarily at the more speculative forms of securities trading, those involving "time bargains" (options). Its primary remedy was to make such deals unenforceable. Because of the general benefit of options trading, Barnard's Act's primary effect was not to eliminate such trading, which apparently continued apace, but to impose upon legitimate dealers losses caused by others who occasionally chose to refuse to live up to their contracts. The evidence indicates that Barnard's Act had little impact on actual market practices, especially because courts generally construed its application narrowly.[71] Whatever impact it did have was probably negative, restricting the ability of investors and others to manage risk. By the 1770s, there was little or no active regulation of the British financial markets, as a philosophy of self-regulation took hold. Markets did not flourish in this regulatory vacuum. Because of the high risk and lack of information regarding private companies, investors preferred to put their money in government debt instruments.[72]

After more than a century of ineffective regulation, Barnard's Act was repealed in 1860 at a time when large corporations were finally becoming common, especially those building railroads. For the first time, corporate securities were becoming the most important investment instrument and the need for a body of securities law was becoming evident. The United Kingdom led the way. Other nations eventually followed, with the United States adopting the first fully comprehensive body of securities law in the 1930s. That body of law addressed issues of disclosure, fraud prevention, insider trading, and, as amended 35 years later, tender offers.

Disclosure

Mandatory disclosure is a critical part of the securities laws of most developed nations. Before securities laws began requiring disclosure by corporations, corporate promoters and managers typically disclosed relatively little information to either potential investors or current shareholders.[73] Mahoney makes a persuasive case that the earliest forms of disclosure rules were aimed at protecting investors from the multitude of ways in which promoters and managers could exploit information asymmetries to profit unfairly. This lack of reliable and timely disclosure undoubtedly discouraged investment and thereby retarded development of broad capital markets.[74] Institution of mandatory disclosure has simultaneously mitigated this agency problem and created the conditions for the evolution of large, efficient capital markets.

While the Italians invented double-entry bookkeeping, the British are most responsible for modern financial reporting. After the Bubble Act of 1720 was rescinded in 1825, joint-stock companies in England proliferated. Unfortunately, these unregulated entities committed a noticeable amount of fraud, so via the Joint-Stock Companies Registration, Incorporation and Regulation Act of 1844, Parliament sought to minimize abuses by requiring certain minimal disclosures and the filing of semi-annual audited balance sheets with the Board of Trade. The Companies Clauses Consolidation Act of 1845 further required firms to prepare a balance sheet 14 days prior to any ordinary meeting of shareholders. However, these requirements were soon allowed to lapse and were replaced by exhortations that companies voluntarily make similar disclosures. This experiment with a system of voluntary disclosure, unfortunately, soon proved inadequate to protect investors.[75]

The Overend Gurney bank collapse, which led to the Panic of 1866, made it clear that corporate law's imposition of fiduciary duties upon promoters was insufficient to protect investors. Parliament reacted in 1868 by requiring promoters to disclose in their prospectuses information about prior contracts entered into by the company, its promoters, directors, or trustees. The Overend Gurney debacle ignited a debate over the mandatory disclosure issue that lasted for 35 years. Parliament enacted laws that required disclosure by railroads (1868), utilities (1871, 1882), and banks (1879). Ultimately, this trend culminated in passage of the Companies Act of 1900 that for the first time required most public corporations to provide audited financial statements to their shareholders. A 1908 revision required the statements to be filed with the Board of Trade, but not until the Companies Act of 1928 were requirements for the form and content of financial statements and for distribution to shareholders prior to meetings fully in place.

As in England, American corporations made minimal disclosure in the early 1800s.[76] One observer wrote in 1840 that directors "endeavor to keep the stockholders and the public in the dark respecting the condition of the corporation, while they are themselves in the light . . . They make no exhibit to the stockholders of the actual condition of the market."[77] The reasons were quite clear and very self-serving. Because corporations made no disclosures, their declarations of dividends were the clearest signal they sent to the market regarding their progress.[78] If a company was progressing well, its directors could declare a small dividend, sending a negative signal to the market. The stock price would drop and they could buy the shares up, becoming major owners of a successful corporation. If the company was struggling, the directors could declare a large dividend. The stock price would rise, and they could sell their shares on favorable terms and thereby bail out of a failing enterprise.[79]

Although in the late 1800s regulators required railroads and utilities to make regular reports of their financial condition, most of America's other leading corporations maintained "the utmost secrecy, either as a matter of tradition, or on the grounds of competition."[80] The prevailing corporate philosophy was publicly displayed in testimony before the Industrial Commission in 1899 by Henry O. Havemeyer, president of the American Sugar Refining Company, who was asked whether he believed that the public had no right to know what his company's earning power was and no right to inspect its books before blindly buying his company's stock. His response was:

> Yes; that is my theory. Let the buyer beware; that covers the whole business. You cannot wet-nurse people from the time they are born until the day they die. They have got to wade in and get stuck and that is the way men are educated and cultivated.[81]

Between the turn of the century and 1933, some companies began to disclose more information, largely because they faced being compelled to do so if they did not do so voluntarily. Indeed, in 1905, the Equitable Life Assurance Society announced that it was adopting a new policy of having its financial statements audited, giving as reasons a desire to restore investors' confidence *and* to avoid restrictive regulation.[82]

While "voluntary" disclosure improved somewhat and the New York Stock Exchange (NYSE) started to impose disclosure requirements on its listing companies before the federal securities laws were passed,[83] these changes were motivated by a series of state and federal investigations and proposals for legislation that the companies and the NYSE were attempting to forestall. Absent credible threats of government regulation, it is not clear at all that companies' disclosure practices would have improved or that the NYSE would have increased its disclosure requirements for listed companies.

Unfortunately, the NYSE indifferently enforced the disclosure rules that it did adopt.[84] For example, one of the most infamous scandals of the time —involving Ivar (the "Match King") Kreuger that began before and ended after the great crash of 1929—was made possible by Kreuger's total secrecy.[85] When auditors questioned him, he simply refused to answer any

of the questions or provide any of the information that would have disclosed his Ponzi scheme. Kreuger, Samuel Insull, and other great fraudsters
of the time "had no fear that independent auditors would be called in."[86]
The NYSE was not keen to delist some of its most popular companies.

Notwithstanding the "voluntary" efforts of companies and the
"requirements" of the NYSE, Laurence Sloan's exhaustive study of the
financial disclosures of major American corporations right before the 1929
crash concluded that industrial financial reports were "woefully inadequate," lacking uniformity and meaningful explanation.[87] Indeed, he concluded that "[i]n several important respects, no criticism of the abuses that
exist can be too harsh."[88] The typical offering circular before passage of the
1933 Act contained "get rich quick" promises, but very little useful information about the securities, the planned use of proceeds, or even the background of the issuer itself.[89]

After the 1929 stock market crash, Congress held hearings which indicated that various state efforts at securities regulation, dating back to
Kansas's 1911 adoption of the first "blue sky" law, had been truly inadequate. In response, Congress passed six major securities laws, two of which
—the Securities Act of 1933 and the Securities Exchange Act of 1934—
contained particularly important disclosure requirements that laid the
predicate for much of today's regulatory philosophy. As noted, these two
Acts together constitute the first truly comprehensive securities regulation
scheme ever enacted.

As noted earlier, the 1933 Securities Act regulated the initial offering
process. When corporations issued securities to the public, they were
required by the Act to either fit the transaction within one of several available exemptions or to file a registration statement with the SEC. The contents of the registration statement would be distributed to potential
investors in preliminary and final prospectuses that would contain more
useful information than those used before. The required contents of the
new prospectuses were patterned on the United Kingdom's Companies
Acts of 1928 and 1929 and focused on the nature of the company, its
financial status, the background of its principals, the characteristics of the
instruments to be issued, and other relevant information.

Next, Congress enacted the 1934 Securities Exchange Act which, among
many other provisions, regulated disclosure in the secondary securities
markets. The 1934 Act came to require periodic disclosure in the form of
annual, quarterly, and interim reports. It also required disclosure at the
time of corporate directors' elections and votes regarding significant
organic changes to the corporate form. In 1968, it was amended to require
further disclosure in the event of a tender offer. In 2002, Congress passed
the Sarbanes-Oxley Act that had several provisions aimed at ensuring the

accuracy of financial disclosures made in the 1934 Act's required periodic reports. Although Mahoney may be correct that the 1933 Act focused narrowly upon the agency problem presented by information asymmetry between promoters and investors, it seems clear that the 1934 Act, especially given its evolution over the years, focuses upon providing shareholders with the means to accurately price shares when making investment decisions. These Acts helped restore investor confidence. As noted in Chapter 2, there is substantial empirical evidence that these disclosure provisions also improved stock market efficiency.

Although the Enron debacle made many question the US approach to disclosure and other securities issues, Congress passed the Sarbanes-Oxley Act in June 2002 to reaffirm and extend this commitment to disclosure. More disclosure rather than less was the prescription, just as a crime wave leads to more streetlights and more cops on the beat, not fewer. The effects of Sarbanes-Oxley are discussed in greater detail in Chapter 6.

The civil law nations have had a different tradition than England and the United States. With more government involvement in corporate ownership (in France) or more central bank involvement (in Germany and Japan), there has been less focus on creating the conditions for broad and deep capital markets. In France, for example, there was no identifiable body of securities law until 1967 or so. Since that time, however, its disclosure rules have gradually developed as French lawmakers sought to facilitate development of French capital markets. Particularly important to this evolution was creation of government agencies (such as the Commission des Operations de Bourse—COB) that, like the SEC in America, have increasingly been given authority to require disclosure and monitor disclosure practices. Disclosure practices are still spottier than in the United States and United Kingdom, but are increasingly comprehensive.

As early as the Stock Exchange Act of 1896, Germany had disclosure requirements and liability for fraud in prospectuses. However, overall it is fair to say that enforcement of German disclosure rules has been inconsistent and the Frankfurt Stock Exchange's disclosure rules have traditionally been lax. Large banks with bargaining power to gain the information they needed have dominated the capital-providing process. Given the relatively minor role played by individual investors, mandatory disclosure was traditionally give short shrift. Recently, however, Germany has undertaken disclosure reforms in an attempt to broaden the base of investors in German companies. For example, the Frankfurt exchange established a new stock market for high tech stocks, the *Neuer Markt*. To make investors comfortable, the *Neuer Markt* featured more rigorous disclosure requirements than the Frankfurt Exchange. For a time the new market flew very high, but good intentions were insufficient and a failure to enforce the disclosure and antifraud rules led the *Neuer Markt* to collapse in a wave of scandals and go out of business.

Although European companies and countries (particularly Germany) have complained about the Sarbanes-Oxley Act's international applications, in their own EU studies and decisions they have been moving in the same direction. For example, the recently-promulgated Organization for Economic Co-operation and Development's (OECD's) Principles of Corporate Governance recommend a US-style system of mandatory disclosure.[90] In Asia, Japan and China have both increased mandatory disclosure in recent years as they have sought to move toward the transparency of Western markets. Korea as well has adopted disclosure provisions patterned after both the 1933 Act and the 1934 Act.

While it is certainly possible to require inefficiently comprehensive corporate disclosures, the trend in all successful modern capital economies has been toward more and prompter required disclosure by corporations. Experience has taught all sensible governments that voluntary disclosure will generally be inadequate. Less successful capital markets have emulated more successful capital markets by moving in the direction of requiring substantial corporate disclosure.

While some academics have been engaged in an ideological debate regarding whether mandatory disclosure is really needed, governments worldwide have uniformly concluded that comprehensive and comparable corporate disclosure facilitates international capital flows. For example, an important part of disclosure is accounting. It is costly for companies that sell their securities in several nations to have to disclose their financial situation in several different accounting formats. It is also inefficient for investors to have to compare statements that are presented in different formats. Therefore, by 2005, all European-listed companies must use the international accounting standards (IAS) and the SEC and EU are working toward accounting convergence between these international standards and American GAAP.

Misrepresentations

Both common law nations and civil law nations punished fraud in commercial transactions well before the creation of modern securities laws. Nonetheless, a major feature of modern securities regulation has been an increased emphasis on preventing and punishing fraud and misrepresentation in securities transactions. The Dutch may well have lost their preeminent position as financiers of capital markets that they enjoyed during the 1600s and much of the 1700s by failing to create regulatory bodies or otherwise to protect investors from securities fraud and unfair dealing.[91] Other nations have learned from this apparent historical lesson. Again, the United Kingdom and the United States, which have been the leaders in developing deep and fluid capital markets, were also the first to put in the legal infrastructure needed to accomplish that task.

After the 1825 repeal of the Bubble Act, joint-stock companies flourished in England. Unfortunately, unscrupulous promoters used joint-stock companies to launch fraudulent business enterprises.[92] English common law provided two basic remedies for a purchaser of securities who relied upon an inaccurate representation[93]—a suit for deceit or one for rescission. In *Derry* v. *Peek*,[94] the House of Lords held that directors could be liable for false statements in a prospectus only if the purchaser could show their bad intent. Parliament thereafter enacted the Directors Liability Act of 1890 which created liability for such misstatements even absent *scienter*. However, investors were protected only by their own civil actions, as the Board of Trade and its subsidiary, the Registrar of Companies, were essentially sunshine agencies that could require the filing of periodic financial reports but had little enforcement power to cope with fraud.[95]

America's common law remedies were similar to England's. In part because of the perceived inadequacy of the common law fraud remedy as applied to securities transactions, in 1911 American states began to enact civil and criminal provisions in their blue sky laws in order to target fraud involving securities specifically. However, these state provisions were generally ineffectively enforced for several reasons, including that the statutes were typically riddled with exceptions, the state regulators lacked adequate budgets and enforcement sophistication, and defendants knew that they could usually evade the proscriptions by operating across state lines.

The weakness of the common law and state remedies made enactment of comprehensive federal remedies in the 1930s particularly noteworthy. When Congress passed the 1933 Act, it borrowed from Parliament's Directors Liability Act of 1890 in enacting section 11, which made directors, underwriters, auditors, and others potentially liable on a negligence basis for damages caused by false statements in a prospectus. These defendants have the burden of proving that they acted with due care. The issuing company is liable for misstatements on a strict liability basis, similar to England's common law action for rescission. Section 11 was viewed as potentially so onerous by securities professionals that they predicted in 1933 that it would cause grass to grow on Wall Street. This proved an exaggeration, especially because the first major damages action under the provision did not reach the courts for 30 years. However, after the mid-1960s, section 11 reliably provided injured investors with a damages remedy for false statements, at least in initial public offerings.

The 1933 Securities Act also provided a criminal sanction, enforceable by the Department of Justice, for any person who *intentionally* violated any provision of the Act, including that forbidding false statements in the prospectus. Section 12 and section 17 of the 1933 Act also provided proscriptions against misrepresentations in broader contexts than just the prospectus, and an intentional violation of those provisions was also obviously a crime. Again, until at least the 1960s, there were virtually no criminal actions undertaken pursuant to these provisions.

The 1934 Securities Exchange Act contains the most potent securities fraud provision ever enacted in section 10(b). As noted in earlier chapters, it broadly punishes misstatements made intentionally or recklessly in any context—primary market or secondary market, public company or private company—and by any actor (buyer, seller, issuer, auditor, officer, director, etc.). An intentional violation is also punishable in a criminal action by the Department of Justice. The penalties have always been substantial, but were recently increased significantly by the Sarbanes-Oxley Act (including fines of up to US$5 million and incarceration for as long as 20 years for individuals).

Despite the severity of the criminal punishments under the 1933 and 1934 Acts, the most fearsome and unique feature of American securities fraud law is procedural rather than substantive in nature. It is the civil class action suit for damages. This device's procedural benefits were spelled out in Chapter 2 and evidence of its benefits will be demonstrated in Chapter 5. Suffice it to say here, that evolution of the law of section 10(b) cause of action created a securities fraud remedy many times more potent than any that existed before anywhere in the world.

Obviously, fraud is morally reprehensible and economically inefficient. The bigger question is whether the American class action lawsuit has become an *in terrorem* device that does more harm than good. Does it give plaintiffs' attorneys a club with which to extract settlements in frivolous suits? Does it unnecessarily distort normal corporate disclosure practices? Does it discourage honest people from serving in positions, such as corporate director, that are necessary for economic success? As noted earlier, in 1995, Congress listened to the debate and decided that the class action device was excessive and passed legislation, the Private Securities Litigation Reform Act (PSLRA), that made it more difficult for plaintiffs to win such suits and more difficult for plaintiffs' attorneys to profit from them. A few years later, many argued that the PSLRA had sent a sign to corporate actors that the government was not serious about fraud prevention, helping to give rise to the Enron fiasco. Then Congress heard more testimony and, in passing the Sarbanes-Oxley Act, reached decidedly opposite conclusions on these issues than it had reached in 1995. It strengthened the SEC, added criminal provisions, increased punishments for preexisting criminal provisions, and made it easier for defrauded investors to sue for damages.

While no other nation has as powerful a brace of remedies for securities fraud as does the United States, the irresistible trend around the world for the past several years has been, and remains, toward creating more effective enforcement agencies, enabling injured investors to sue to protect their interests, and stiffening penalties for securities fraud. European nations, for example, tend not to have the tradition of either a strong SEC-like agency to enforce securities laws or a healthy and well-rewarded plaintiffs' bar to bring private civil actions. But after considerable study, the EU nations are moving toward the American model, given its perceived success.

In recent years, every EU member has created a version of the SEC. The United Kingdom has created the Financial Services Authority (FSA), Germany the Bundesanstalt fur Finanzdienstleistungsaufsicht (BAWe), France the Autorites des Marches Financiers, and Spain the Comision Nacional del Mercado de Valores. Some have argued that one European "super-SEC" would be an optimal approach, and few doubt the wisdom of creating agencies to enforce European securities laws. Asian nations have followed suit, as, for example, China has created the China Securities Regulatory Commission (CSRC), Japan the Financial Supervisory Agency (FSA), and Korea the Financial Supervisory Commission (FSC).

Most of these nations have also strengthened antifraud rules and strengthened shareholders' ability to protect their own interests. For example, the EC Public Offer Prospectus Directive of 1989 required member nations to adopt a system of mandatory disclosure for public offerings and punishment for misrepresentations analogous to the 1933 Securities Act. In the last decade or so, Germany has expanded the authority of regulators and reduced roadblocks to the right of defrauded investors to sue on their own behalf. Japan, China, and other Asian nations have also adopted American-style securities fraud statutes and strengthened shareholder rights. The lesson history has taught these regulators is that fraud undermines the development of capital markets and stronger measures to combat it will ultimately pay dividends by making markets more attractive to investors.

Insider Trading

Although insider trading rules seek to remedy an agency problem—the use of corporate information to benefit a few select insiders rather than to benefit all shareholders—such rules are typically treated as securities laws rather than corporate laws. Historically, there existed little regulation of insider trading until passage of federal securities laws in America in the 1930s. The American common law of tort did provide a limited remedy in deceit for insider trading where the buyer and seller met face-to-face, but this remedy was of little use in most market transactions, where both buyer and seller acted through a stockbroker. When evidence adduced at the hearings leading to passage of the 1933 and 1934 Acts led Congress to conclude that insider trading by public company officials was a serious problem, it responded by putting section 16 into the 1934 Exchange Act. This provision, enforceable only by a public company or a shareholder acting on its behalf, essentially prevents officers, directors, or holders of 10 percent of the company's securities from retaining profits on "short-swing" transactions, which are defined as purchases and sales which occur within six months of each other. Six months is presumed to be the limit of the useful life of inside information, and officers, directors, and 10 percent holders are presumed to be the sorts of people who would have access to such information. Therefore, section 16(b) requires a defendant to disgorge to the company any profit made (or loss avoided) when he or she sells company stock within six months of buying the stock and makes a profit (or avoids a loss). Section 16(a) seeks to make the provision easily enforceable by requiring these company insiders to file with the SEC records of their purchases and sales. The Sarbanes-Oxley Act substantially shortened the deadline for filing these reports.

Because neither the SEC nor the Department of Justice can enforce section 16(b) and because its remedy is only disgorgement of profits, the truly significant insider trading provision in America has come to be section 10(b)—the broad antifraud provision of the 1934 Act—as supplemented by various statutory provisions such as the Insider Trading Sanctions Act of 1984 and the Insider Trading Securities Fraud and Enforcement Act of 1988. Section 10(b) was not used to punish insider trading until the late 1960s. During the late 1970s and early 1980s, however, insider trading fraud became a major Congressional and SEC priority, based on the theory that investors would not want to "play the game" if they believed that it was rigged in favor of insiders.

A raft of civil and criminal cases slowly created a distinct body of interpretive case law (neither Congressional statutes nor SEC rules define insider trading for fear of creating a standard that clever defendants could evade via technicalities). As the law now stands, four types of defendants can be held criminally or civilly liable for insider trading:

a.   company insiders (employees of the company who by virtue of their employment owe a fiduciary duty of fairness to shareholders and potential shareholders);

b. temporary insiders (individuals such as outside auditors and attorneys who learn company information for a business purpose and thereby temporarily assume the same fiduciary duty as traditional or company insiders);
c. misappropriators (people who use inside information to trade in breach of a fiduciary duty that they owe to the source of the information); and
d. tippees of any of the first three categories or of other tippees, for the law does not allow insiders to profit by trading indirectly through friends, family members, or others.

Although civil damages actions are occasionally brought by investors against inside traders, the law has evolved so that the primary remedies are civil actions by the SEC (which can force disgorgement of illicit profits and impose fines of up to three times the amount of those profits) and criminal actions by the Department of Justice (now carrying the potential for fines of up to US$5 million for an individual and a term of imprisonment as long as 20 years).

For quite a long time only the United States showed any particular interest in punishing insider trading. During the 1980s and 1990s, as American insider trading defendants often attempted to hide their misdeeds by using foreign brokerages and foreign bank accounts and as foreign investors occasionally used inside information to trade on US stock exchanges and thereby subvert their integrity, the SEC sought to persuade other nations to enact and enforce insider trading laws. In 1989, an EU Council Directive mandated that Member States enact insider trading rules meeting specific standards. Since that time, developed nations across Europe and Asia have virtually all enacted US-style insider trading laws and have even begun enforcing them from time to time. A consensus has developed that insider trading is ethically unfair and that in practical terms it undermines the development of capital markets by discouraging outsiders from "playing the game" that they perceive to be rigged.

Takeovers

When the directors of Company A and Company B decide to merge, American shareholders are protected from the adverse consequences of such a major change by rules that (a) require that the merger be proposed by a majority of directors who, of course, owe a fiduciary duty to the shareholders; (b) require that shareholders be given an opportunity to vote on the transaction and that at least a majority (and in some states a super-majority) of those shareholders approve it; and (c) give dissenting shareholders the right to have their shares bought by their company at a judicially-determined fair price. Shareholders in most other developed nations receive roughly comparable protections.

When the directors of Company B resist the entreaties of Company A's directors by rejecting merger talks and signaling an intent to stay independent, Company A's directors may resolve to pursue a tender offer wherein they bypass Company B's directors and go straight to its shareholders with an offer to buy their shares at a premium over market price. By way of this tender offer, Company A hopes to gain voting control of Company B and, often, to follow with a freeze-out merger in order to eliminate minority shareholders and gain 100 percent ownership of Company B.

Different attitudes toward the economic wisdom of tender offers are reflected in a diversity of takeover rules scattered around the globe. American law has been the most influential. Tender offers are a relatively new phenomenon, unknown for most of corporate history. Until 1968, there was no explicit federal regulation of tender offers in the United States. That changed during a wave of tender offers in the 1960s when Congress decided that tender offers could be unfair and coercive. Therefore, in 1968, Congress passed the Williams Act, which does not attempt to either discourage or encourage tender offers. Nor does it seek to favor offerors seeking to effectuate tender offers nor targets resisting them. The Williams Act:

a. imposes substantive duties, such as the "best price" rule, requiring offerors to pay to all shareholders the best price that they offer to any shareholder in a tender offer;
b. imposes procedural requirements, such as a 20-business-day minimum hold-open period so that all shareholders have the opportunity to seek out and process information about the wisdom of the transaction;
c. creates disclosure requirements to ensure that shareholders will have the information that Congress and the SEC deem critical for their decision; and
d. establishes antifraud rules that punish any party (offeror, target, or third party) who misleads shareholders during a tender offer, supplementing section 10(b) in this regard.

The Williams Act policy foundations are level playing field, equal treatment of target shareholders, full disclosure, and fraud prevention.

Potential target companies, which desired substantive protection from tender offers of the type that the Williams Act refused to grant, petitioned state legislatures for assistance and most of those legislatures initially enacted their own versions of the Williams Act that contained substantive provisions that tilted the scale decidedly toward the target company and made it much harder for offerors to effectuate these takeovers. For example, some of these laws required offerors to warn targets substantially in advance of launching a takeover and to hold the offers open much longer than the federal minimum of 20 business days. Both provisions had the effect of making the takeover more expensive for the offeror and giving the offeree substantial extra time to implement legal defenses. These state laws were declared unconstitutional by the US Supreme Court under the American Constitution's Supremacy Clause because in a clash between federal law and state laws, federal law is to prevail.[96] However, the states passed more rounds of legislation, this time framing their laws as corporate laws rather than securities laws and eliminating provisions that nakedly contradicted Williams Act provisions. Corporate law has always been traditionally within the states' bailiwick in the American system whereas since 1933 federal law has dominated the securities field (although, as noted above, any boundary between the two is necessarily artificial). These "second generation" state takeover laws have passed Constitutional muster.[97]

These new state rules, coupled with preexisting state corporate law rules regarding mergers and other organic corporate changes, clearly affected the takeover landscape. Consider Delaware, as one example of a variety of different state approaches. Delaware law discourages takeovers by imposing several requirements upon an offeror that make it difficult to complete a takeover. For example, any offeror seeking more than a certain percentage of shares cannot complete a freeze-out merger for at least three years. This is cumbersome and discouraging to the offeror. However, the law contains exceptions and allows immediate effectuation of a freeze-out merger if, for example, a high percentage of shares are purchased and all shareholders, including those whose shares are purchased in the freeze-out merger, receive the same premium over market price. This provision advances fair treatment.

Although judicial interpretation of the fiduciary duty owed by target company directors to shareholders currently forbids Delaware directors in a takeover from considering any goal other than attaining the highest price for shareholders once they have decided a change of control of some type should occur, the statutes of many states allow (and of at least one state requires) target directors to consider the interests of other constituencies as well when plotting strategy. Thus, target directors could consider the interests of their employees, their customers, and the communities in which they have operations in deciding whether a tender offer should be accommodated or resisted.

Takeovers were much less frequent in Europe than in the United States, so takeover law there is less developed. However, the Vodafone hostile tender offer for control of Mannesmann in 2001 is symbolic of a new era. Hostile takeovers have come to the Continent and, as in America, few issues have been more controversial among EU rulemakers. EU member nations have traditionally taken very diverse approaches to takeover law. In the United Kingdom, a pro-takeover environment exists and hostile offers are common. The process is regulated by the Panel on Takeovers and Mergers operating pursuant to the City Code on Takeovers and Mergers. Shareholders of the target company must be allowed to decide whether the offer is accepted. Takeover defenses by target boards are generally prohibited. On the other hand, rules encourage equal treatment of minority shareholders by stipulating that no person may cross a defined ownership threshold without making a tender offer for all the target firm's shares.

France has little tradition of hostile takeovers, so its takeover law is nascent. In broad outline it seems slightly more target-protective than US law. Because German managers are given a long-term mandate, German law has generally been more protective of potential target companies than the laws of other European nations. Management supervision comes more from banks than from shareholders. Therefore, a pro-target atmosphere reigns as does a reluctance to impede defense maneuvers. Similarly, Dutch law generally allows target boards to "just say no."

The EU has pursued a 15-year effort to encourage all members to adopt a common approach to takeovers. In general, the favored approach has been an American-style regime that would generally allow the market to decide whether offers should succeed or fail with a minimum of government interference. However, many nations, with Germany leading the way, resisted this free market solution. Ultimately, in December 2003 the European Commission adopted such a tortured compromise as to be "not worth the paper it was written on." Rather than banning poison pills and other takeover defenses, the new takeover code allows each nation to decide whether or not to allow such defenses.

Turning to Asia, Japan has adopted American-style takeover law. However, so few hostile takeovers have occurred in Japan that the subject remains largely academic, though hotly debated. China also has little experience with hostile takeovers, but has recently adopted American-style regulations in an attempt to change an environment that had discouraged the takeover process. As in Japan, the culture of Korea is not inviting to hostile takeovers, and the nation had little experience with takeovers until 1998. Korea's takeover law is patterned heavily after the Williams Act and has been amended in recent years with the purpose of making takeovers easier to execute.

The inability of European nations to harmonize their laws, the inconsistency of approach between the generally neutral US federal government and the generally anti-takeover state governments, and the bitter disputes among academics make it clear that there currently exists no consensus as to whether the capital markets are bettered or undermined by liberal treatment of hostile takeovers. Most interested observers support giving tender offerors a free rein, for hostile bids provide market discipline to managers of corporations. If they do not do a good job, their company's market price will drop, leaving the firm particularly vulnerable to a tender offer. Others believe that waves of takeovers are typically followed by waves of divestitures, because most acquisitions do not work out well. Shareholders of the target corporation prosper; shareholders of the acquiring firm suffer. Investment bankers do well both in the takeover transaction and in the divestiture. There is some evidence that hubris by officers of the acquiring corporation is an important factor in hostile takeovers. In any event, the evidence is inconclusive and the debate is complex and ongoing. The general trend, as with mandatory disclosure, fraud prevention, and insider trading, has been toward the American model that is at least marginally facilitative of hostile takeovers.

CONCLUSION

If a benevolent, enlightened ruler of a developing nation were granted just one wish by a magic *djinn*, he or she should not choose natural resources, or a brace of modern manufacturing plants, or a plethora of Western management consultants. Rather, the enlightened wish would be for the rule of law. History demonstrates that nothing is more important to economic development than a stable legal system that enforces contracts, preserves property rights, and punishes fraud.

Once economic actors are protected by the rule of law, they can begin to realize their dreams. If they dream big, they will need corporations. These are a critical institution for coordinating large economic enterprises. Corporate law authorizes and, if properly drafted, enables corporate formation and growth. Governments constantly tweak their corporate law to strike a proper balance between limited liability for investors and fair protection for creditors, between discretion for managers and control by shareholders, between adequate compensation and incentives for managers and protection from looting for shareholders. History has not written the final chapter on the proper mix of incentives and protections in corporate law, but increasingly, there is a consensus that with substantial cultural variation, "best practices" in corporate governance will include strong protection for minority shareholders, active monitoring of the day-to-day managers by a relatively independent board of directors, and some additional mix of devices that will allow minority shareholders an effective voice in corporate affairs or an efficient and fair means of exit.

Well before Enron or the Sarbanes-Oxley Act, the Vienot Report (1999)[98] in France concluded that French law provided insufficient protection for average investors and that French capital markets could be strengthened by implementing a series of recommendations that resemble Sarbanes-Oxley's prescriptions—more independent directors, a board committee to deal with critical subjects such as audit and compensation, increased information and responsibility for directors, and more disclosure for shareholders to increase their involvement in company decisions.[99] The previous Marini Report also recommended French adoption of Anglo-Saxon style reforms.[100] Various EU studies have recommended European harmonization of prospectus liability, insider trading rules, tender offer rules, and other areas, and that harmonization has almost always converged upon current American legal practice. France can outlaw insider trading and create a French SEC, but when the United States has scores of enforcement actions annually and France has only the occasional one, markets are going to be more inviting to investors in the United States. History shows that the content of the law is not sufficient to stimulate markets, but it certainly is necessary.

NOTES

1. O. Lee Reed, *Law, the Rule of Law, and Property: Foundations for the Private Market and Business Study*, 38 AM. BUS. L. J. 441, 449 (2001).
2. Douglass North, INSTITUTIONS, INSTITUTIONAL CHANGE AND ECONOMIC PERFORMANCE 46 (1990).
3. Reed, *supra* note 1, at 441 (quoting Davis).
4. Avner Greif, *Contract Enforceability and Economic Institutions in Early Trade: The Maghribi Traders' Coalition*, 83 AM. ECON. REV. 525 (1993).
5. E. Allan Farnsworth, CONTRACTS 11–12 (1982).
6. *Id.* at 20–21.
7. Philip M. Nichols, *A Legal Theory of Emerging Economies*, 39 VA. J. INT'L. L. 229, 264–65 (1999).
8. James Surowiecki, THE WISDOM OF CROWDS: WHY THE MANY ARE SMARTER THAN THE FEW AND HOW COLLECTIVE WISDOM SHAPES BUSINESS, ECONOMIES, SOCIETIES, AND NATIONS 121 (2004).
9. *Id.* at 124.
10. Hernando de Soto, THE MYSTERY OF CAPITAL: WHY CAPITALISM TRIUMPHS IN THE WEST AND FAILS EVERYWHERE ELSE 5–10 (2000).
11. Simon H. Johnson, John McMillan, and Christopher Woodruff, *Property Rights and Finance*, Stanford Law and Economics Olin Working Paper No. 231 (March 2002).
12. De Soto, *supra* note 10, at 71.
13. Douglass North, STRUCTURE AND CHANGE IN ECONOMIC HISTORY 147–57 (1981).
14. Charles Cadwell, *Forword* to Mancur Olson, POWER AND PROSPERITY viii (2000).
15. Ronald H. Coase, *The Institutional Structure of Production*, *in* NOBEL LECTURES IN ECONOMIC SCIENCE 11, 17 (Torsten Persson ed. 1997).
16. Reed, *supra* note 1, at 459.

17. Charles I. Jones, *Was an Industrial Revolution Inevitable? Economic Growth Over the Very Long Run*, 1 ADVANCES IN MACROECONOMICS 1028 (No. 2, 2001).
18. Fareed Zakaria, *Lousy Advice Has Its Price*, NEWSWEEK, September 27, 1999, at 40.
19. Jean Domat, I THE CIVIL CODE IN ITS NATURAL ORDERS (1850 William Strahan (trans.), republished Fred B. Rothman & Co., Colorado Springs, CO, 1980).
20. Stuart Banner, ANGLO-AMERICAN SECURITIES REGULATION: CULTURAL AND POLITICAL ROOTS, 1690–860, 117 (1998).
21. *Id.* at 236, *citing* Bacon v. Sanford, 1 Root 164, 165 (Conn. 1790).
22. (1789) 100 Eng. Rep. 450.
23. PROSSER AND KEETON ON TORTS 728 (5th ed. 1984).
24. Banner, *Supra* note 20, at 117.
25. Joseph Angell & Samuel Ames, TREATISE ON THE LAW OF PRIVATE CORPO-RATIONS AGGREGATE (1832, reprint, N.Y. Arno Press, 1972), *cited in* Douglas Arner, *Development of the American Law of Corporations to 1932*, 55 SMU L. REV. 32 (2002).
26. Timur Kuran, WHY THE ISLAMIC MIDDLE EAST DID NOT GENERATE AN INDIGENOUS CORPORATE LAW 30 (2004).
27. John Micklethwait & Adrian Wooldridge, THE COMPANY: A SHORT HISTORY OF A REVOLUTIONARY IDEA 5–6 (2003).
28. *Id.* at xxi.
29. *Id.* at xx (quoting Butler).
30. John Kay, CULTURE AND PROSPERITY: THE TRUTH ABOUT MARKETS: WHY SOME NATIONS ARE RICH BUT MOST REMAIN POOR 322 (2004).
31. *Quoted in* Anthony Sampson, COMPANY MAN: THE RISE AND FALL OF COR-PORATE LIFE 19 (1995).
32. Margaret M. Blari & Lynn A. Stout, *A Team Production Theory of Corporate Law*, 85 VA. L. REV. 247 (1999).
33. Margaret M. Blair, *Locking in Capital: What Corporations Law Achieved for Business Organizers in the 19ᵗʰ Century*, 51 UCLA L. REV. 387, 395 (2003).
34. Ranald C. Michie, THE LONDON STOCK EXCHANGE: A HISTORY 17 (1999).
35. Douglas Arner, *Development of the American Law of Corporations to 1832*, 55 S.M.U. L. REV. 23, 44 (2002).
36. 10 U.S. (6 Cranch) 87 (1810).
37. 17 U.S. (4 Wheat) 518 (1819).
38. Arner, *supra* note 35, at 49, *citing* R. Kent Newmyer, *Justice Joseph Story's Doctrine of "Public and Private Corporations" and the Rise of the American Business Corporation*, 25 DEPAUL L. REV. 825, 828 (1976).
39. Henry Hansmann & Reinier Kraakman, THE ANATOMY OF CORPORATE LAW 10 (2004).
40. William J. Bernstein, THE BIRTH OF PLENTY: HOW THE PROSPERITY OF THE MODERN WORLD WAS CREATED 150 (2004).
41. Blair, *supra* note 33, at 393.
42. *Id.* at 441.
43. Micklethwait & Wooldridge, *supra* note 27, at 82.
44. Adam Smith, 2 AN INQUIRY INTO THE NATURE AND CAUSES OF THE WEALTH OF NATIONS 733 (Oxford University Press, 1976).
45. Adolph A. Berle, Jr. & Gardiner C. Means, THE MODERN CORPORATION AND PRIVATE PROPERTY (1932).
46. Alfred F. Conard, *The Supervision of Comparative Management: A Comparison of Developments in European and United States Law*, 82 MICH. L. REV. 1459 (1984).
47. James A. Fanto, *The Role of Corporate Law in French Corporate Governance*, 31 CORNELL INT'L L.J. 31, 53 (1998).
48. John C. Coffee, Jr., *Privatization and Corporate Governance: The Lessons from Securities Market Failure*, 25 IOWA J. CORP. L. 1, 28–29 (1999).
49. Bernard Black, et al., *Liability Risk for Outside Directors: A Cross-Border Analysis* (2004).

50. Fanto, *supra*, note 47, at 50.
51. R v. Fraternity of Hostman (1702) 93 Eng. Rep. 1142.
52. Randall S. Thomas, *Improving Shareholder Monitoring of Corporate Management by Expanding Statutory Access to Information*, 38 ARIZ. L. REV. 331, 337 (1996).
53. Leslie L. Cooney, *A Modality for Accountability to Shareholders: The American Way?*, 28 OKLA. CITY U. L. REV. 717 (2003).
54. Henry Hansmann & Reinier Kraakman, *The Essential Role of Organizational Law*, 110 YALE L.J. 387, 393 (2000).
55. Blair, *supra* note 23, at 392–93.
56. Hansmann & Kraakman, *supra* note 54, at 405.
57. 30 F.Cas. 435, 1824 U.S. App. LEXIS 422 (1824).
58. Henry Hansmann & Reinier Kraakman, *The End of History for Corporate Law*, 89 GEO. L.J. 439 (2001).
59. Peter Montagnon, *A Short and Simple Regime for Corporate Europe*, FINANCIAL TIMES, September 2, 2004, at 13.
60. William J. Bernstein, THE BIRTH OF PLENTY: HOW THE PROSPERITY OF THE MODERN WORLD WAS CREATED 23 (2004).
61. Stephen Ambrose, UNDAUNTED COURAGE 52 (1996).
62. Bernstein, *supra* note 60, at 16.
63. *Id.* at 159.
64. Banner, *supra* note 20, at 1.
65. Charles P. Kindleberger, MANIAS, PANICS, AND CRASHES: A HISTORY OF FINANCIAL CRISES 109–10 (4th ed. 2000).
66. Edward Chancellor, DEVIL TAKE THE HINDMOST: A HISTORY OF FINANCIAL SPECULATION 58–95 (1999).
67. Jonathan B. Baskin & Paul J. Miranti, Jr., A HISTORY OF CORPORATE FINANCE 113 (1997).
68. Banner, *supra* note 20, at 39–40.
69. *Id.* at 29, *quoting* Journal of the House of Commons, 11:595 (Nov. 25, 1996).
70. *Id.* at 56–87.
71. *Id.* at 101–7.
72. Baskin & Miranti, *supra* note 67, at 122.
73. Paul Mahoney, *Mandatory Disclosure as a Solution to Agency Problems*, 62 U. CHI. L. REV. 1047 (1995).
74. Baskin & Miranti, *supra* note 67, at 136.
75. *Id.* at 140.
76. Micklethwait & Wooldridge, *supra* note 27, at 52.
77. Daniel Raymond, THE ELEMENTS OF CONSTITUTIONAL LAW AND POLITICAL ECONOMY 276 (4th ed. 1840), quoted in Banner, *supra* note 20, at 200.
78. Micklethwait & Wooldridge, *supra* note 27, at 70.
79. E.S. Abdy, JOURNAL OF A RESIDENCE AND TOUR IN THE UNITED STATES OF NORTH AMERICA 42–43 (1935), quoted in Banner, *supra* note 20, at 201.
80. Matthew Josephson, *Infrequent Corporation Reports Keep Investors in Dark*, 36 MAG. OF WALL ST. 302, 303 (June 20, 1925) (quoting NYSE economist Edward Meeker).
81. *Quoted in* Richard P. Brief, *Corporate Financial Reporting at the Turn of the Century*, J. ACCTCY. 144–45 (May 1987).
82. *Id.* at 147.
83. Roberta Romano, THE ADVANTAGE OF COMPETITIVE FEDERALISM FOR SECURITIES REGULATION 16 (2002).
84. Joel Seligman, THE TRANSFORMATION OF WALL STREET 47 (rev. ed. 1995).
85. John Kenneth Galbraith, THE GREAT CRASH 1929, 82–83 (1979).
86. Gary J. Previts & Barbara D. Merino, A HISTORY OF ACCOUNTANCY IN THE UNITED STATES: THE CULTURAL SIGNIFICANCE OF ACCOUNTING 267 (1998).
87. Laurence H. Sloan, CORPORATION PROFITS 333–37 (1929).
88. *Id.* at 334.

89. Thomas A. Halleran & John N. Calderwood, *Effect of Federal Regulation on Distribution of and Trading in Securities*, 28 GEO. WASH. L. REV. 86, 94 (1959).
90. *See* Ad Hoc Task Force on Corporate Governance, OECD Principles of Corporate Governance (April 16, 1999), *available at* www.oecd.org/daf/governance/principles.htm.
91. Bernstein, *supra* note 60, at 146.
92. Baskin & Miranti, *supra* note 67, at 140.
93. Mahoney, *supra* note 73, at 1088.
94. 4 App. Case 337 (HL 1889) (Halsbury opinion).
95. Baskin & Miranti, *supra* note 67, at 161.
96. Edgar v. Mite Corp., 457 U.S. 624 (1982).
97. CTS Corp. v. Dynamics Corp. of America, 481 U.S. 69 (1987).
98. Ass'n Francaise Des Entreprises Privees AFEP, Recommendations of the Committee on Corporate Governance 3–9 (1999), *available at* www.ecgi.org/codes/countrydocuments/france/vienot2 en.pdf.
99. Fanto, *supra* note 47, at 86–87.
100. Philippe Marini, *La modernisation du droit des societes, Rapport au premier ministre*, Collection des rapports officiels, La documentation francaise (1996). *See generally* Nicholas H.D. Foster, *Company Law Theory in Comparative Perspective: England and France*, 48 AM. J. COMP. L. 573 (2000).

5. Empirical analysis of the law and corporate finance

The prior chapters have presented a largely theoretical analysis of why the laws, foundational, corporate, and securities, is of economic benefit. Chapter 4 looked at their historical development in order to show how their economic value developed. This chapter undertakes a more rigorous empirical analysis of the economic effects of these laws throughout the world. The understanding that legal structures may have importance for national economic outcomes is central to the New Institutional Economics of Douglass North, as discussed in prior chapters. This understanding about the general significance of legal institutions has been confirmed by important empirical cross-country analyses, such as that of Robert Barro, who found that nations' relative devotion to the rule of law was associated with higher economic growth rates.[1]

This chapter focuses on the particularized association of foundational, corporate, and securities laws on financial development. Some of the empirical research was addressed in Chapter 2, and this chapter focuses on the international findings. We begin by reviewing the now burgeoning empirical cross-sectional analyses of this association. The existing research consistently shows a positive economic value for basic foundational law, corporate law, and securities law. We proceed to conduct our own analyses, to help measure the robustness of this association between law and the development of corporate finance.

EXISTING RESEARCH ON THE RELATIONSHIP OF LAW AND CORPORATE FINANCE

In recent years, economists have devoted considerable attention to studying the economic significance of legal structures, including capital markets. Most of this research has involved cross-country analyses, comparing different national legal structures with economic outcome variables. We begin by reviewing this existing literature.

La Porta, et al. Studies

The most significant studies on the economic effect of foundational, corporate, and securities law have been conducted by Rafael La Porta and colleagues at Harvard and elsewhere. The La Porta research has evolved in a
manner that greatly informs the understanding of the relationship of law
and corporate finance. The group's studies touch directly on the particular
aspects of basic, corporate, and securities law that we address in this book.
A key feature of these studies is their creation of independent variables to
measure various types of law. While some of these independent legal variables are rather rudimentary, they represent an important breakthrough for
the empirical study of the effects of the law.

In its earliest stage, the La Porta research considered the economic
significance of government very generally. In the late 1990s, they focused
on legal origins, comparing common law nations with countries who developed under different categories of foundational civil law traditions.[2] Their
study found that nations of the common law tradition offered more legal
protections to corporate shareholders and creditors, which in turn meant
that those nations had more minority public shareholdings. Around this
time, they also found that common law nations were significantly associated with a higher quality of government, as measured by efficiency, rights,
and the provision of public goods.[3] These studies strongly suggested the
practical importance of a nation's basic foundational law, though their
implications were somewhat murky. They left it unclear precisely what features of the common law yielded economic and government benefits, as
compared with the civil law. Nevertheless, it seemed clear that *something*
about legal administration and the courts had a substantial societal effect.

The La Porta group has produced an extensive series of articles about the
importance of the law, but the next significant article for our purposes analyzed the effect of corporate law protections on capital markets. In 2000,
they explained why legal protections for minority shareholders were critical to corporations' abilities to obtain external finance.[4] Two years later,
they conducted an empirical cross-country analysis of the effects of legal
shareholder protections.[5] This study found that companies in nations with
greater shareholder protections had higher valuations. While it is difficult
to capture the law in variables for quantitative analysis, the authors had
developed both binary variables for specific provisions and a continuous
summary variable.

The authors moved on to the study of securities laws. In another cross-
country analysis, they broke down the components of securities law, coded
national protections for these components, and tested them against measures of financial development.[6] While public enforcement of the securities

law and other variables appeared to play at best a modest role in financial markets, significant positive results were associated with mandatory disclosure requirements and with the provision for easier private enforcement of the securities laws. They found that securities law requirements might be more significant for markets than the corporate law protection of investors.

Other Studies

Numerous other authors have studied the effect of various aspects of the law on capital markets, often using La Porta's measures for the legal variables to be analyzed. This category of studies has burgeoned in the last five years, both as published articles and working papers, and they have enhanced our understanding of the role of the law, primarily through cross-sectional studies of national laws. This section highlights some of these studies.

Researchers at the World Bank have done extensive analyses of capital markets and the effects of legal institutions. Ross Levine, after studying the importance of capital markets to overall economic growth, examined the effect of the law on financial markets and economic growth.[7] His analysis considered legal variables involving the efficiency of contract enforcement, treatment of creditors and accounting standards, including the data from La Porta, et al. and other sources. Levine found that contract enforcement, legal creditor protections, and financial disclosure all contributed to greater private financial markets.

With his World Bank colleagues, Levine has also sought to measure the relative effects of legal systems, politics, and national endowments (such as geography) for national financial development.[8] To capture the law, they used the La Porta, et al. standard of national legal origin, as well as their measure for shareholder rights and property rights protection. The authors found that the legal variables dominated the alternative explanations for financial development. In particular, legal origin was the strongest determinant, even after controlling for the other possible explanations of financial development, though there was some association for the political and endowment variables. Levine has also traced the chain of connections from original legal origin to greater financial development and economic growth.[9] Another study found that countries with greater corporate shareholder rights provided higher valuations for banks.[10] Other research by this group has confirmed this finding. For example, they have found that firms in countries with French legal origin face significantly higher obstacles in accessing external finance than firms in common law countries.[11]

A separate World Bank study tackled the question from a different angle. This study took a financial organization's measure of the corporate governance quality of individual firms in emerging countries and examined the effects of the law.[12] They found that companies had weaker corporate governance in countries with less shareholder protection and judicial efficiency. They also found that the quality of corporate governance was relatively more financially important in countries with weak legal protections. This finding makes sense, as there would be more variation in governance quality in such nations, and shareholders in these companies do not have the law as a backstop protection and must rely on strong reputational signals.

Omar Azfar and others have promoted a theme they call "market-mobilized capital," which stresses the importance of free markets but also recognizes the important ways in which government can augment the market. A recent study examined the role of corporate law and creditor protections in augmenting capital markets, using the La Porta, et al. coding for particular provisions of corporate law and scores for creditor protection.[13] They found that the creditor and corporate laws had significant effects on national economic growth, operating through the growth of markets for debt and equity, even after controlling for a measure of law enforcement. The effect was a substantial one, even for the United States, in the hundreds of billions of dollars.

Other researchers affiliated with other groups have also pursued this course of study. A study associated with the Italian Centre for Studies in Economics and Finance examined the effect of legal variables, including La Porta, et al.'s origin of legal system and minority shareholder rights, as well as measures of judicial efficiency and rule of law.[14] In a series of tests of different groups of nations and different measures for financial variables, they found significant positive effects for the generalized legal variables, including legal origin and judicial efficiency but more ambiguous results for the legal protection of minority shareholder rights.

Additional research has shown that developing countries with weaker corporate governance protections tend to have thinner equity markets.[15] The combination of corporate law and rule of law variables was associated with higher levels of market capitalization.[16] A number of studies have found that greater protection of minority shareholders tends to produce more public minority shareholding, and this in turn tends to yield more investment and lower cost of capital, with lessened risk.[17] As expected, they show that such protections assure investors and reduce the private benefits of controlling a corporation (whether for opportunism or mere self-protection). Another clue as to the nature of legal benefits is the finding that there is much less firm-specific information absent shareholder rights, which undermines market efficiency.[18] A study specific to Poland found that corporate and securities laws enforced by executive regulators have stimulated rapid development of securities markets.[19] Other researchers have specifically examined laws against insider trading and found a positive economic effect, studies which will be examined in greater detail in Chapter 6.

A recent study examined the effect of laws on firms' cost of capital, as implied in contemporaneous stock price and analyst forecast data, using different valuation models.[20] After constructing national cost of capital using the La Porta, et al. legal variables for rule of law and securities regulation, the authors created a factor analysis measure for the common dimension of some legal variables. They found that both the quality of a country's basic foundational legal system and the securities laws were associated with a lower cost of capital, after using control variables for GDP, size of securities markets, and voluntary disclosures.

A separate path of research has examined the foundational law and its economic effects. A number of studies have been done on national protection of property rights and its economic effects, though most of these studies examine very broad dependent variables such as national economic growth, rather than financial markets. One published study did examine multiple measures of property rights (including survey measures), integrated with financial development, and found that higher protection for property was consistently associated with more efficient allocation of capital.[21]

The association between legal rules and financial development has generally survived the introduction of new control variables. For example, some authors hypothesized that the differences among nations might truly be a feature of religious culture. They found that religion was indeed a significant determinant of the laws involving creditor rights but that legal origin was more important than religion in explaining laws protecting equity holders.[22] The studies have employed a number of alternative control variables, such as ethnolinguistic fractionalization, settler mortality for the legal origin tests, gross domestic product, and other controls.

The cumulation of these studies strongly suggests that law plays a significant role in the growth of external finance. They have found that basic contract laws, creditor protections, corporate laws, and securities laws all contribute to the success of financial markets. Not only are the studies generally consistent, but they have used different dependent variables, different control variables, and to a lesser degree, different sets of nations, which lends greater confidence to their general findings. By its nature, such social scientific research is not totally conclusive, and the studies have some limitations. For example, they tend to be heavily dependent upon the La Porta, et al. coding of the law for independent variables. While there is no particular basis for criticism of the use of this coding, it might be affected by some other unmeasured variable, and further analyses, using different measures, would be beneficial. Moreover, some analyses over time have found little association between the law and financial measures. These findings, though, could simply reflect a failure to capture quantitatively the true influence of the law, which can be a daunting endeavor.

MEASURING THE EFFECTS OF THE LAW AND CORPORATE FINANCE

The remainder of this chapter provides some additional empirical analysis of the association of legal variables and thriving capital markets. We seek to build upon the existing literature to better inform the nature of this association. The potential breadth of this analysis is enormous, and we do not purport to deploy any particularly sophisticated empirical methods that go beyond the sound methods already employed by prior researchers. Rather, we seek to add some perspective and understanding by employing additional variables. In so doing, we provide a measure for the robustness of the relationship and information on the manner in which the law influences financial development.

This section addresses some of the complications in measuring the effects of the law on corporate finance. We discuss how existing research has operationalized the test for these effects, examining both its strengths and weaknesses. While a great degree of valuable research has been conducted, none of it has fully integrated the basic foundational law, corporate law, and securities law together in a single model. This research has also depended heavily on the La Porta, et al. variables, out of necessity, and the studies have used certain discrete financial dependent variables, with limited sensitivity testing on this end. Most of the research has also failed to trace the effects of law through the intermediate steps in the analysis, examining only the ultimate financial variables. The following analysis is not uniquely sophisticated but employs additional measures for the law, additional dependent financial variables, and the intermediate penultimate measures in order to test for the validity and reliability of the associations and help identify the particular legal rules of greatest importance for equity markets.

Legal Variables

The goal of this research is to analyze the value of the foundational law, corporate law, and securities law, which requires that they be captured in quantitative variables for statistical analyses. Unlike financial data, there are no readily accessible and accurate quantitative measures for the law. The law cannot be measured in "betterness," and it is difficult to capture any legal differences in quantitative terms. One can establish binary scores for the existence or absence of a particular legal rule and even combine them for a continuous variable, but there is no assurance that this procedure truly measures "the law," especially as it functions in courts. Absent any clear measures for the law, we will deploy a diversity of scales.

To measure the basic law, most existing studies have used "legal origin" as a variable, distinguishing between the English common law system and the various families of civil law. Although this variable has often produced significant results, it is theoretically troublesome. First, the variable largely tracks colonial heritage and might simply measure some other residual effect of the colonizing nation, rather than the source of law itself. Second, the significance of the variable today lacks some plausibility, because the differences in the common and civil law systems have been muted over time. The systems have converged, as common law nations are increasingly governed by statutory prescriptions, while civil law nations adopt common law principles such as reliance on precedent.[23] Perhaps most troubling for this association is the historic finding that in 1913, before the convergence of the systems, the common law nations did not have greater financial development than civil law nations.[24] This surely calls into question whether legal origin is truly the best measure for the foundational law and its effect on the economy.

There are some alternative measures for the nations' foundational legal systems, but these too are rather crude. There are several groups who have sought to code national property rights, such as the Heritage Foundation and Fraser Institute series.[25] International investment advisory groups, such as the Business Economic Research Intelligence and the International Country Risk Guide, have also given ratings for legal tools such as property rights, contract enforcement, and the rule of law. While helpful, these sources provide a narrow range of distinctions and typically do not directly measure legal rights. For example, a Heritage property rights scale incorporates the overall size of government as a component. While the size of government may be economically relevant, it does not truly measure protection of property from taking. Available measures for contract enforcement are even weaker. An interesting indirect measure of property rights and contract enforcement is "contract-intensive money" (CIM). Research has found this measure is significantly associated with higher levels of financial development.[26] This captures the percentage of national currency placed in contract-dependent investments, such as banks. Though not a direct measure of the law, it would seem to measure the societal functioning of the legal system.

When measuring corporate law, researchers have relied on the La Porta, et al. cross-country scaling of national legal content, with generally good results. The scale is facially valid, and the construction of any alternative measure would be a time-consuming effort. This measure, though, suffers the problems of selective incorporation of legal rules, difficulty in quantifying national embrace of those rules (thus the reliance on binary measures), and uncertain methodology for combining those rules into an overall scale. Nevertheless, it may be the best tool reasonably available.

The only real alternative to the La Porta measures is simple results of surveys of international businesspersons about the overall requirements of corporate law. For example, the World Competitiveness Report (WCR) surveys international managers on a variety of items, legal and otherwise. Use of such surveys has both advantages and disadvantages. The surveys directly measure perceptions, rather than realities, but investment decisions are made on perceptions, so this is not such a serious problem. The survey questions tend to be more general than the La Porta scaling, which has the disadvantage of vagueness of measurement but the advantage that the survey may capture aspects of the law not even measured by La Porta.

For securities laws, the La Porta, et al. measures have also dominated research, for the same reasons as explain reliance on their corporate law scaling. The authors' securities law measure is somewhat more fine-grained than their scale for corporate law, but it generally shares the values and limitations of the corporate law scale. Generalized survey data is also available on securities law. This chapter will use both types of scores in assessing the significance of the law for corporate finance. While it would be valuable to have a separate direct measure of corporate and securities laws to check on the scale of La Porta, et al., this data is unavailable. We will use different dependent and control variables, though, as a check on the conclusions of the La Porta group.

As we have observed, finding reliable measures for the law is very difficult, and any score will surely have specification shortcomings. Even when it is possible to code for the formal content of the law with some precision, such form does not inevitably translate into the operation of the law. Such errors are likely to produce an underestimate of the effect of the law, though. To capture the full effect of legal rules, one needs measures of the law in operation. The functioning of the law may be captured, to some degree, by surveys of those using national legal systems. Unfortunately, such surveys have their own shortcomings and a generalized finding about the operation of the law doesn't inform policymakers about particular policy changes that would improve that operation.

Because there is no available perfect variable to capture the effect of the law on corporate finance, the following analysis uses multiple different measures and examines their relative effects and interactions. We will consider the traditionally used La Porta, et al. variables but also employ other measures for the law, including measures of the functioning of the legal system generally and survey measures about the actual operation of the law. The breadth of variables will both enable us to assess the robustness of associations and also may allow us to disaggregate the results and identify particular laws of importance.

Legal origin is taken as a binary variable, English or civil law. This fails to capture the nuances of different civil law systems set out in La Porta, et al., but does measure the common law effect. Contract-intensive money is a quantitative financial variable that is theoretically derivative of the legal system. The other variables are all perceptual measures, though some are from surveys of international businesspersons and others are scales created by international experts. They attempt to measure the rule of law (using three different sources), the protection of property rights, judicial independence, and the relative political risk of property expropriation or failure to enforce contracts.

The variables for corporate law are primarily those of La Porta, et al. They are binary measures of whether a country's legal corporations code contains a particular provision. The one share-one vote variable is a protection of a particular interest of minority shareholders, by preventing the sale of non-voting stock. The oppressed minority standard simply recognizes some mechanism to protect these rights beyond a fraud action. Voting by proxy reduces the costs of investor control of the corporation, as does a rule that shareholders are not required to deposit their shares prior to shareholders' meetings. Cumulative voting better enables minorities to obtain board representation, and preemptive rights protect against the dilution of ownership. While La Porta, et al. consider mandatory dividend laws a form of shareholder protection, this is debatable, as it can constrain reinvestment and enhancement of corporate market capitalization. Antidirector rights are a cumulation of the individual binary variables other than the mandatory dividend requirement. The final corporate law variable that we employ is a generalized perceptual survey measure from the World Competitiveness Report that measures the effectiveness with which the nation defines and protects the rights of shareholders.

For securities law, La Porta, et al. also provide measures. These variables are not simple binary ones but scaled based on a number of criteria. For example, the measure for the disclosure requirements of a nation's securities law is based on a prospectus requirement, requirements regarding disclosure of officer compensation, equity ownership structure, insider ownership, material contracts, and transactions with insiders. Most of the securities law variables are procedural ones, though. The burden of proof variable measures the difficulties in recovering under the laws. Private enforcement incorporates the disclosure and burden of proof variables.

Other variables measure governmental enforcement in authorization of criminal liability and enforcement orders. The cumulative public enforcement variable encompasses these scores plus measures for the characteristics of the public supervisor of securities markets and the supervisor's investigatory powers. In addition to these La Porta, et al. variables, we use a general World Competitiveness Report survey response to a question about the stringency of a nation's financial regulations. The following legal variables are used in our analysis.

Legal variables

Basic foundational variables
Legal origin (La Porta) ("origin")
Rule of law (La Porta) ("rol")
Risk of expropriation (La Porta) ("riskexp")
Risk of contract repudiation (La Porta) ("riskcon")
Judicial efficiency (La Porta) ("judeff")
WB rule of law (World Bank) ("wbrol")
ICRG rule of law (ICRG) ("icrgrol")
Property rights (Fraser) ("prop")
Judicial independence (WCR) ("judindep")
Contract-intensive money (IRIS) ("cim")

Corporate law variables
One share-one vote (La Porta) ("osov")
Oppressed minority rights (La Porta) ("oppm")
Proxy by mail allowed (La Porta) ("pbm")
Shares not blocked before meeting (La Porta) ("snbbm")
Cumulative voting (La Porta) ("cumv")
Preemptive rights (La Porta) ("preem")
Mandatory dividend (La Porta) ("mand")
Anti-director rights (La Porta) ("adr")
Shareholder rights (WCR) ("shr")

Securities law variables
Disclosure requirements (La Porta) ("disc")
Burden of Proof (La Porta) ("bofp")
Private enforcement (La Porta) ("priv")
Public enforcement (La Porta) ("pub")
Enforcement orders (La Porta) ("enfo")
Criminal liability (La Porta) ("crim")
Financial regulation stringency (WCR) ("finr")

Financial Variables

The financial dependent variables of interest must also be determined. The data on such financial variables is much more available and more precise. For example, financial data on the size and trading in financial markets is regularly and reliably reported. There remains a question about which of these financial variables to use as a test for the effect of the law. Many different variables have been employed, including stock market value to GDP ratio, volatility ratings, capitalization to sales ratio, and others. Each of these measures has a legitimate claim of importance. Because there is no single variable of concern, we employ a number of different dependent financial variables from various sources.

The relatively new World Bank database adds new valuable information on the status of the world's financial markets.[27] We use several variables from the different categories of the database. The ratio variables of bank and financial institution credit and liquid liabilities to GDP measure the overall role of financial institutions in the economy. They include both banking and equity markets. The overhead costs and net interest margin variables provide measures of the efficiency by which financial intermediaries such as banks can channel funds to investors and are primarily measures of the efficiency of the banking system. The remaining variables of stock market capitalization, value traded, and turnover are measures specific to the national equity markets and their relative liquidity.

In addition to variables from the World Bank database, we use two central variables from La Porta, et al. on overall market capitalization, two purely perceptual measures of capital markets taken from surveys of businesspersons, and two more quantitative variables drawn from research by Laura Beny.[28] The first two La Porta variables are similar to those of the World Bank, as measurements of financial market capitalization relative to total sales and cash flow. The third of these variables, the ratio of Worldscope database firms to domestic firms, is meant to capture the degree of public shareholding in the market. The "cost of capital" and "adequacy of stock market capital" variables are survey measures. While they have the shortcomings of any perceptual survey measures, they have the corresponding advantage of measuring business perceptions and potentially controlling for nation-specific factors such as the need for capital. The final variables, from Beny, are cash flow to price ratio, measuring the sum of earnings and depreciation over the company's market value of common equity.

Financial variables

Market capitalization/sales (La Porta) ("mcap/s")
Market capitalization/cash (La Porta) ("mcap/c")
WLD domestic firms (La Porta) ("wldomes")
Liquid liabilities/GDP (World Bank) ("ll/gdp")
Bank and financial institution credit/GDP (World Bank) ("bvic/gdp")
Overhead costs (World Bank) ("ohc")
Net interest margin (World Bank) ("nim")
Stock market capitalization/GDP (World Bank) ("mcap/gdp")
Stock market value traded/GDP (World Bank) ("smv/gdp")
Stock market turnover/GDP (World Bank) ("smt/gdp")
Cost of capital (WCR) ("coc")
Adequacy of stock market provision of capital (WCR) ("adeqcap")
Cash flow/price ratio (Beny) ("cash/price")
Market volatility (Beny) ("mvol")

Intermediate Variables

One further general set of variables is analyzed in this chapter – the intermediate variables. The hypothesized effect of the law on markets operates
indirectly. Corporate laws, for example, are intended to overcome agency
problems, and securities laws are, *inter alia*, intended to enhance the frequency and reliability of corporate disclosures. These effects on the relative
magnitude of agency problems and relative amount of disclosure then theoretically translate into a larger or more efficiently functioning capital
market. When studies find that the law translates into thriving capital
markets, they have not tested the intermediate variables to determine that
the effect is as hypothesized. By examining certain intermediate variables,
we can better check for the possible spuriousness of the relationship and
better understand the precise nature of the effects of the law.

Unfortunately, data on the intermediate variables is only rough, like measures of the legal variables. The best source for quantitative measurement
of the intermediate variables is international surveys of businesspersons,
like that of the WCR discussed above in the context of the legal variables.
These surveys measure answers to questions such as the degree to which
managers effectively maximize shareholder value or prevent improper practices. For some other variables of interest, there are also expert rating scales,
such as accounting standards or effective corporate governance. Once
again, absent any unambiguously optimal intermediate variable measure,
we use a number of different ones.

These intermediate variables are meant to capture the processes through which the legal variables influence financial outcomes. There are two distinct types of processes at issue. The first is a measure of the quality and honesty of management in the presence of the agency problem. While this is the ultimate measure of concern, its measurement is inevitably amorphous and of uncertain reliability. The category can only be measured through survey variables. The second somewhat more reliable variable is a measure of disclosure. For the disclosure variables, the Centre for International Financial Analysis Research (CIFAR) provides several relevant measures.[29] These include financial disclosure intensity, corporate governance disclosure intensity, aggregate disclosure, and the timeliness of financial reporting. La Porta, et al. supply a national rating of accounting standards. These variables can help capture the effectiveness of corporate disclosure among the nations of the study.

Intermediate variables

Board prevention of improper practices (WCR) ("bpip")
Board management of shareholder value (WCR) ("bmsv")
Corporate ethics (WCR) ("ethic")
Accounting standards (La Porta) ("accst")
Financial disclosure (CIFAR) ("find")
Governance disclosure (CIFAR) ("govd")
Aggregate disclosure (CIFAR) ("aggd")
Timeliness of disclosure (CIFAR) ("timed")
Governance opacity (PriceWaterhouseCoopers) ("govo")
Governance quality (McKinsey) ("govq")

The legal, intermediate, and ultimate financial variables in these lists may not perfectly capture the effect of the law on corporate finance. They rely on perceptions and are undoubtedly influenced by various extralegal national considerations. However, they have the benefit of being direct measures of the behavior that the law is meant to influence, and there is good evidence that companies who score higher in these governance and disclosure rankings are valued higher in the stock market.[30] Corporate law is intended in large part to resolve agency problems and its benefits should appear in governance quality and the maximization of shareholder value. Securities law is intended in large part to ensure that corporate disclosures are comprehensive, timely, and accurate. Hence, one would expect the law's effect to appear in measures such as the intermediate variables.

Methodological Questions

Even if the independent legal variables could be perfectly measured, there would still be questions about how to test for their effects. A great number of different scales are available for measuring the financial markets, with no single scale conclusively preferable. Other questions include the directionality of the association (for example, might financial development influence the nature of the law) and the appropriate external control variables that should be incorporated in measurement. The very nature of cross-country comparisons runs the risk of producing spurious associations. Such comparisons also present a significant risk of false findings of no significant association, simply because of the great stochastic noise associated with comparing different national markets.

A very important question, often unanswered in the research, is the means by which the legal variables operate. For example, some research has found that statutory disclosure requirements are associated with greater investment in equity markets. While it seems logical that they do so by providing greater actual disclosures or reliability of disclosures to investors, this effect has gone largely untested. The failure to measure such intermediate variables leaves the logical assumption uncertain and raises a concern that some unmeasured third variable, perhaps unrelated to the law, might explain the conclusions. Testing for the intermediate variables better enables us to assess the role of the law in corporate finance.

The choice of control variables is another difficult question for this research. The outcomes might be explained by some extralegal factor that happens to be collinear with our legal variables. As noted above, the existing studies have employed various different control variables, which provides some assurance about the validity of the identified associations but leaves open the possibility that some unmeasured factor explains the results. This is especially a concern for reliance on legal origin as a measure, because it is highly collinear with the culture of the former colonial power. The failure to test for intermediate variables complicates this concern. Of course, the failure to fully capture other variables of influence could also obscure a true relationship and mean that the effect of the law on financial development is understated by this research.

Once again, we have no easy solution to these methodological problems, which must inevitably complicate cross-country analyses of the type typically employed. Since the problem cannot be precisely cured, we employ numerous different variables, independent, intermediate, and ultimate. This does not answer all the methodological concerns but can provide some degree of greater assurance about the validity of results and can expose alternative explanations for those results. With more variables and more separate tests, there is obviously some risk of spurious results, by random chance. The randomness effect can be ruled out, though, if the statistically significant associations are relatively frequent, and if they consistently operate in one direction, we can be confident in the nature of the association. Random effects are just as likely to show a negative effect for the law as a positive one.

Not only will we use a large number of variables, we will run a large number of correlations and regression analyses. We do not follow a precise path, testing particularized hypotheses, but instead cast a wide net to find significant associations. We have a generalized theory; that legal rules including restrictive legal rules can serve to strengthen financial markets in various ways. They can reduce investment risk, particularly risks that cannot be effectively cured through diversification, and facilitate efficient trading markets by reducing the transaction costs associated with investing. Our null hypothesis is that the laws do *not* have this effect, so that measures of statistical significance can be used to reject that null hypothesis.

Before reporting results, some additional explanation is required. For simple space reasons, reporting of the results will be brief. The number of observations in the regressions is generally around 50, and we will note when this is not the case. We will also explain when the R^2 term is significantly large or small. When reading the results of these studies, it is important to keep in mind that the scales are not normalized. The independent variable scales run the gamut from binary to quite precise (out to three decimal places). Hence, one cannot simply seize on the significant variable with the largest correlation coefficient as the most substantively important determinant. The important results are the existence of statistically significant relationships and the strength of those relationships, as can be measured by a R^2 term. With these background principles and caveats in mind, we now turn to statistical analysis.

SIMPLE ANALYSIS OF BASIC FOUNDATIONAL LAW ASSOCIATIONS

The empirical analysis of this chapter begins with simple, one variable regressions of the legal measures against the ultimate financial variables of concern. Given the very large numbers of variables in the analysis and enormous numbers of permutations of independent variables, we start by looking for some basic associations. While this study includes no intersecting relationships or control variables, that mere fact has some value. The law is constitutive of much in society and is likewise somewhat endogenous to societal preferences, and legal variables surely have a cybernetic association with one another and with potential independent control variables. To the extent that additional variables are endogenous of the law (or vice versa), they will not be truly independent checks on the effects of the law. Hence a simple regression is of some value.

We begin the simple regression with a consideration of the basic foundational legal variables. Because the basic law and its enforcement governs and theoretically facilitates all business transactions, one might expect that the recognition and enforcement of property rights and contracts would associate with richer financial markets. Similarly, one would expect that the actual operation of the rule of law, with consideration for judicial efficiency and judicial independence, might also yield stronger financial markets, because they presumably mean that the law on the books is better translated into practice. And regardless of the substantive content of the law on the books, the rule of law should provide economic benefits by creating some stability and avoiding costs associated with corruption.

The first analysis involves the correlation among the basic foundational legal variables themselves. Different studies have used different combinations of these variables, but collinearity between the scaling of the variables may obscure the truly significant determinants. Intercorrelations among the variables should be identified as a threshold matter. Bivariate Pearson correlations were taken for the paired foundational legal variables, and Table 5.1 reports their statistical significance. Those positive correlations significant at 0.01 are marked with ++, those significant at 0.05 were marked with +, and insignificant associations were marked with −. In this analysis, none of the correlations were significant in a negative direction.

Plainly there is a high intercorrelation among the foundational legal variables, with most significant at the 0.01 level. The procedural legal variables (such as judicial independence, judicial efficiency, and rule of law) not only significantly correlate with one another, they also significantly correlate with the more substantive legal variables (such as property rights and enforcement of contracts). The one foundational legal variable that is not significantly associated with the others is English origin, which, ironically, is the variable

Table 5.1   Associations among legal foundational variables

	origin	riskprop	riskcon	prop	cim	rol	wbrol	icrgrol	judeff	judindep
origin	—									
riskprop	−	—								
riskcon	−	++	—							
prop	−	++	++	—						
cim	−	++	++	++	—					
rol	−	++	++	++	+	—				
wbrol	−	++	++	++	++	++	—			
icrgrol	−	++	++	++	++	++	++	—		
judeff	−	++	++	++	+	++	++	++	—	
judindep	++	++	++	++	++	++	++	++	++	—

Table 5.2   Legal foundational variables and World Bank financial variables

	ll/gdp	bvic/gdp	ohc	nim	mcap/gdp	smv/gdp	smt/gdp
origin	−	−	−	−	−	−	−
riskprop	+ +	+ +	+ +	+ +	+ +	+ +	−
riskcon	+ +	+ +	+ +	+ +	+ +	+ +	−
prop	+ +	+ +	+ +	+ +	+ +	+ +	−
cim	+ +	+ +	+ +	+ +	+ +	+	−
rol	+ +	+ +	+ +	+ +	+ +	+ +	−
wbrol	−	+ +	+ +	+ +	+ +	+ +	−
icrgrol	+ +	+ +	+ +	+ +	+ +	+ +	−
judeff	+ +	+ +	+	+ +	+	+ +	−
judindep	+ +	+ +	+ +	+ +	+ +	+ +	−

that has been most widely used in the cross-country studies of the effect of the law. This gives some reason to question whether legal origin best captures the role of the foundational law but also gives some confidence that its significance can indeed be isolated from other measures of the law, so that the true practical importance of legal origin can be assessed.

The next analysis continues the simple regressions of the foundational basic legal variables but introduces financial measures as independent variables. Each of the foundational legal variables is regressed as an independent variable against the World Bank's measures for financial markets as dependent variables. These variables are all traditional quantitative measures of financial markets. Again, statistically significant bivariate correlations are reported with + + or +. For each result, a better performance (that is, lower overhead costs) merits a +.

The table demonstrates a consistent and strong statistical association between most of the basic foundational legal variables and sundry measures of financial markets. The associations were highly significant and consistently positive in direction. The only independent legal variable lacking in consistent positive significance was English legal origin. None of the variables explained the relative degree of stock market turnover, though. Both the substantive legal measures and the purely procedural assessments of the legal system showed a significant association with larger and more efficient financial markets, as measured by the World Bank variables. This finding is especially significant, because the foundational law would also be expected to affect the overall GDP, which is the denominator in many of these ratios. It appears the law has a positive effect on financial markets that surpasses its general economic value to GDP. The next analysis considers the effect of the same basic foundational variables on other non-World Bank financial variables from a variety of sources, reported in Table 5.3. These sources

Table 5.3   Legal foundational variables and other financial variables

	mcap/s	mcap/c	wldomes	coc	adeqcap	cash/price	mvol
origin	−	−	−	−	+	−	−
riskprop	−	−	+ +	+ +	+ +	−	+ +
riskcon	−	−	+ +	+ +	+ +	−	+ +
prop	−	−	+ +	+ +	+ +	−	+ +
cim	−	−	−	−	−	−	−
rol	−	−	+ +	+ +	+ +	−	+ +
wbrol	−	−	+ +	+ +	+ +	−	+ +
icrgrol	−	−	+ +	+ +	+ +	−	+ +
judeff	−	−	+	+ +	+ +	−	+ +
judindep	−	−	+	+ +	+ +	−	+ +

include both the La Porta, et al. measures and international business survey responses on the cost of capital and adequacy of national capital markets.

The effect of the basic foundational legal variables on these measures is not as strong as was the case with the World Bank variables, but the results are typically positive and relatively consistent in their pattern. The vast majority of the variables had a strong positive association with perceptions of lower cost of capital and adequate supply of capital, with lessened market volatility and with the increased proportion of Worldscope firms to domestic firms. None of the variables were significantly associated with the measures of market capitalization to sales or cash flow or cash flow to price. The latter absence of an association is rendered much less troubling, though, by the consistent significant positive associations of these variables with the quantitative World Bank measures of markets in Table 5.2. While the reason for the lack of association in this table is not perfectly clear, it might be that the foundational variables are affecting both the numerator and the denominator in the same positive direction and similar amount, so that they do not show up as a significant determinant of the ratio.

Because these are simple regressions, and because the independent legal variables are highly intercorrelated, one should be cautious about drawing any significant conclusions at this point. A significant association with one legal variable might be attributable to another collinear legal variable or to some yet unmeasured third factor. In addition, the absence of an association of the basic foundational law with some measures of financial markets leaves some doubt about the nature of the positive effect from this law.

On balance, though, the evidence on the financial value of the basic foundational law is strong. None show any significant negative association, and all but legal origin and contract-intensive money have a pattern of highly significant positive associations for a majority of the financial variables of interest. For these variables, we reach some preliminary tentative conclusions. First, we find that legal origin is not a fruitful test for legal systems' effect on financial markets, at least given the available alternative measures. Second, we find that both the substantive and procedural basic foundational legal rules strengthen national financial markets, though the high association between procedural protection and substantive protection leaves the independent importance of each in some doubt.

SIMPLE ANALYSIS OF CORPORATE LAW ASSOCIATIONS

Having assessed the association of some basic legal variables with financial markets, we turn to simple regressions of the corporate law measures on these same financial variables. The independent variables for corporate law are more limited and highly dependent upon the coding effort of La Porta, et al. They code for particular features of a nation's corporate law and also provide a cumulative score for antidirector rights generally. Previous research has demonstrated that the intercorrelation among the individual corporate law measures is not high. We supplement this with the survey measure of generalized legal "shareholder rights" taken from the World Competitiveness Report.

As in the prior section, we begin with simple regressions of our corporate law variables against various quantitative measures of national financial markets taken from the World Bank database. Some of the World Bank measures (such as ohc and nim) are banking measures. While banks have their corporate governance issues, one would not expect as great an association between the corporate law independent variables and these measures, and the theoretical association with ll/bdp and bvic/gdp is somewhat attenuated. One would particularly expect an association to show up in the final three variables that measure equity markets. Table 5.4 reports the associations. Once again, we designate statistically significant associations with a + or + +, depending upon the level of significance.

The associations for corporate law variables with World Bank financial variables are much weaker than those for our basic foundational legal variables. Nevertheless, there is some clear evidence of a positive association for corporate law, especially for the cumulative measure of antidirector rights, which is significant for the three variables for which an association is hypothesized but not for the two variables for which an association seemed less likely. The survey measure of shareholder rights also showed some meaningful positive associations with strong financial markets. In addition, a few more of the individual corporate law variables would have shown a

Table 5.4   Corporate law variables and World Bank financial variables

	ll/gdp	bvic/gdp	ohc	nim	mcap/gdp	smv/gdp	smt/gdp
osov	−	−	−	−	−	−	−
oppm	−	−	−	−	−	−	−
pbm	−	+	−	−	+	−	−
snbbm	−	−	−	−	−	+	−
cumv	−	−	−	−	−	−	+ +
preem	−	−	−	−	+	−	−
mand	−	−	−	−	−	−	−
adr	−	−	−	−	+	+	+
shr	−	+ +	−	−	+ +	+	−

Table 5.5   Corporate law variables and other financial variables

	mcap/s	mcap/c	wldomes	coc	adeqcap	cash/price	mvol
osov	−	+	−	−	−	+ +	−
oppm	+ +	+ +	+ +	−	−	+	−
pbm	−	−	−	−	+	−	+
snbbm	−	−	−	−	−	−	−
cumv	+ +	+ +	−	−	−	−	−
preem	−	−	−	−	−	−	−
mand	−	−	−	+	+	−	−
adr	+	+	−	−	−	+	−
shr	−	−	−	+ +	+ +	−	+ +

positive association at a less rigorous (0.10) standard of statistical significance. In the absence of any significant negative correlations, there is reason to believe that corporate law aimed at agency problems has a positive effect on financial markets. To examine this relationship further, Table 5.5 reports the results of bivariate correlations between the corporate law variables and the other financial variables.

The corporate law variables appear to have a positive effect on these measures of financial markets, if a variable one. Some intermittently strong associations appear in the table, with no significant negative associations. We see a significant correlation between some corporate law variables and the ratios of market capitalization to sales and cash flow, which was missing from the analysis of the basic foundational legal variables, suggesting an additional effect for corporate law on these financial measures.

These results enable some preliminary conclusions. As one might logically expect, different aspects of corporate law have an effect on different financial variables. Consequently, a cumulative index, such as the antidirector rights measure, might obscure some of the effects of corporate law, by muting the differentiation in the aspect of corporate law that matters for a particular financial measure. When one combines all the financial dependent variables, however, the cumulative measures for antidirector rights and protection of defined shareholder rights show somewhat more power than does any single individual independent corporate law variable. This feature illustrates the complexity of measuring the effects of the laws.

There is evidence of the financial value of corporate law in these preliminary correlations. Its overall economic effect is not so great as that of the basic foundational law, which would be expected. Corporate law builds upon and elaborates on the basic foundational law and cannot be as effective where that foundation is missing.

SIMPLE ANALYSIS OF SECURITIES LAW ASSOCIATIONS

The final set of legal regulations to be analyzed are those of securities law. Our analysis of securities laws parallels the preceding analysis of basic foundational laws and corporate law. Again, we are highly dependent on the coding efforts of La Porta, et al. for our independent measures of securities law. We supplement these measures with a survey from the World Competitiveness Report assessing the overall stringency of national regulation of securities law. Table 5.6 reports the results of our simple bivariate correlations, using the same approach as for basic foundational law and corporate law variables.

The results reflect an extremely strong effect for some of the independent securities law variables on the World Bank financial variables. Disclosure requirements and private enforcement authority show very strong associations. This essentially confirms the results of La Porta, et al. with an entirely

Table 5.6   Securities law variables and World Bank financial variables

	ll/gdp	bvic/gdp	ohc	nim	mcap/gdp	smv/gdp	smt/gdp
disc	+ +	+ +	+ +	+ +	+ +	+ +	−
bofp	−	+	+	−	+ +	+ +	−
priv	+ +	+ +	+ +	+ +	+ +	+ +	−
pub	−	−	−	−	−	−	−
enfo	−	−	−	−	−	−	−
crim	−	−	−	−	−	−	−
finr	−	+ +	+ +	+ +	+ +	+ +	−

different set of dependent financial variables, giving greater credibility to the findings. They also found that disclosure requirements and private enforcement were the key determinants of securities law. The variables for public enforcement, though, show no significant associations with the World Bank variables, demonstrating the importance of private securities law enforcement. While it would be premature to dismiss all importance of public enforcement, it seems clear that private enforcement is the more critical attribute of securities law. The cumulative variable of perceived stringency of financial regulation also shows a very strong association for many of the World Bank financial variables. The significant associations for net interest margin and overhead costs are somewhat surprising, however, and suggest that possibly some other factor, such as basic foundational law, might be the determinant of these results.

As in the preceding discussions, we turn next to measure in simple bivariate correlations the securities law variables against financial dependent variables other than those of the World Bank database. Table 5.7 reports the results in the same format as the prior tables.

Many positive associations in these results help confirm the economic value of the securities laws. The variables of disclosure, burden of proof, and private enforcement are associated with many measures of market development, and the public regulation and enforcement variables show some effect on these dependent variables as well. The preliminary analysis at this point suggests that the securities laws increase market valuation as compared with GDP, sales, or cash flow, they allow investors to better capture the cash flow as capital value, they help ensure that the cost of capital is low and adequate capital is supplied, and they may reduce market volatility. These simple regression results confirm the La Porta, et al. findings, with different sets of dependent variables. The results support the findings that private monitoring is especially valuable but provide some additional support for public regulatory enforcement that the previous research did not find.

Table 5.7   Securities law variables and other financial variables

	mcap/s	mcap/c	wldomes	coc	adeqcap	cash/price	mvol
disc	+ +	+ +	−	−	+	+ +	−
bofp	+ +	+ +	−	+	+ +	+ +	−
priv	+ +	+	−	+	+ +	+ +	+
pub	+	−	−	−	−	−	−
enfo	+	+ +	−	−	−	+ +	+
crim	+	−	−	−	−	−	−
finr	−	−	−	+ +	+ +	−	+ +

The simple correlations between legal protections and strong financial markets are strongly suggestive but leave many uncertainties. It is unclear if each of these laws has an independent effect on the markets or if collinearities among the variables are producing spurious results for some variables. Potentially, an omitted variable may explain the results that appear associated with certain legal requirements. The rest of the chapter elaborates the analysis to get closer to understanding the true effects of the law and of particular legal requirements.

ANALYZING THE LEGAL VARIABLES

To proceed further with our analysis of the effects of the law on corporate finance, the effects of the basic foundational legal variables need to be better understood. Virtually all of these variables were significantly correlated with positive economic consequences. Yet these variables are highly intercorrelated, so the effect of one particular variable is difficult to discern with confidence. In addition, it is important to reduce the number of variables to be used for purposes of multiple regressions that integrate the basic foundational variables with others.

Theoretically, the relative effect of particular variables might be discerned from multiple regression analyses of all the basic foundational legal variables on our dependent financial variables of interest. Unfortunately, the high degree of multicollinearity obscures this process. For example, six of the eight variables were associated with the wldomes variable in the simple regression, but in a multiple regression *none* of the variables had statistical significance. The same was true for the cash/price variable. For the coc variable, only the World Bank rule of law variable was significant at the 0.05 level. For adeqcap, none of the variables had statistical significance in the multiple regression. These findings indicate that virtually all of the positive financial results of these variables derive from their common variance, so that the specific variance unique to each particular variable is not a significant determinant of our measures of financial outcomes. The positive results come primarily from something that is common to all of our basic foundational variables.

One approach for dealing with this multicollinearity problem is factor analysis. This is a statistical technique designed to identify the variables with the greatest common variance among a set of collinear variables and extract some common dimension from the many variables, enabling a reduction of their number. One obvious possible mutual dimension would be English legal origin, but this seems unlikely, because it had the lowest intercorrelation of the basic foundational legal variables. Absent a clear theory about the common dimension of these variables, our factor analysis is essentially exploratory.

The descriptive intercorrelation matrix among the basic foundational legal variables has already been presented in Table 5.1. The next step is to identify the "communality" which measures the proportion of the variance in the particular legal factor that can be explained by the common factors. All initial communalities are one, and Table 5.8 reports the extraction communalities of the factor analysis for the basic foundational legal variables.

From this table, we can see that the common dimension appears to be closely related to our measures of "rule of law." This might be expected, as "rule of law" is not an input into the legal system but instead a measure of its general effectiveness. Of the other variables, only contract-intensive money is relatively unrelated to the common dimension. While use of one of the rule of law variables might successfully capture the commonality of all the basic foundational legal variables, the factor analysis procedure enables the creation of a separate factor variable or variables that better capture the common dimension.

There are a variety of ways in which to develop this variable, and we employ principal component analysis, though the results are extremely similar under principal factor analysis. For results, the analysis gives "eigenvalues," which measure the dispersion of data points around a given access and try to determine the pattern of least dispersion. The factor analysis yields one component with an eigenvalue of 6.683, explaining over 66 percent of the common variance, as opposed to other components. The second-best component has an eigenvalue of only 1.173, which is not materially different from the third component at 0.859. Examination of the associated scree plot shows that the "elbow of the curve" occurs at the second component, so we use only the initial clearly superior factor in our

Table 5.8   Factor analysis communalities

	initial	extraction
origin	1.000	0.831
riskprop	1.000	0.909
riskcon	1.000	0.875
prop	1.000	0.748
cim	1.000	0.321
rol	1.000	0.923
wbrol	1.000	0.867
icrgrol	1.000	0.923
judeff	1.000	0.692
judindep	1.000	0.766

analyses. This yields a factor variable that tries to capture the common dimension of the basic legal foundational variables. The factor variable captures both the substantive and procedural aspects of the foundational law and serves as a good measure for the overall effect of this law.

For a corporate law variable, the statistically significant results were somewhat spotty and concentrated around the variables of protection against oppression of minority shareholders, the cumulative La Porta, et al. index of antidirector rights, and the survey variable of defined and pro- tected shareholder rights. The antidirector rights measure includes the oppressed minority scale, so our initial reduction of independent variables will be the La Porta, et al. scale of antidirector rights (adr) as a proxy for the strength of corporate law.

For securities law, the basic regressions showed more consistent positive statistical significance, but most of the associations came from disclosure requirements, the burden of proof in enforcement actions, private enforce- ment, and the survey variable of stringency of financial regulation, though there were some important associations with public enforcement. The measure for private enforcement combines the scores for disclosure and burden of proof, so use of those variables becomes unnecessary. The ini- tially reduced independent variables used for securities law are private enforcement (priv) as a proxy for the strength of securities law. Significantly neither adr nor priv is closely correlated with the factor score measure for basic foundational law. The data reduction gives us one variable as a proxy for each of the three main families of law.

We considered using the survey variables of shr and finr as measures of the strength of corporate and securities law in practice. Clearly, the measures for adr and priv capture only a portion of the effect of corporate and securities law, by their own formulae. The survey measures might better capture the entirety of a nation's corporate and securities law. However, both shr and finr are significantly correlated, at the 0.01 level, with our factor variable for basic law. Thus, it appears possible that the executives responding to the survey asking about the protection of shareholder rights and stringency of financial regulation were implicitly factoring in the effect of the basic law in their esti- mates. Consequently, these variables hold little promise for our next endeavor — identifying the discrete effects of the different categories of law.

SEPARATING THE FINANCIAL EFFECTS OF LEGAL VARIABLES

Now that we have a manageable set of legal variables, with a proxy for the basic foundational law (factor), corporate law (adr), and securities law (priv), it is possible to try to separate their unique effects on financial market development. We can examine whether the basic foundational law is all that is required or whether securities law might be counterproductive, given a nation's functioning basic and corporate law. The first step is a multiple regression that uses these three legal values as independent variables. The dependent variables are seven of the financial variables used above, with a focus on measures for equity markets and attention diversification among the World Bank financial measures (mcap/gdp and smv/gdp), the La Porta, et al. financial measures (mcap/s), the WCR survey measures (coc and adeqcap) and other financial measures (cash/price and mvol). In Table 5.9, we report the results with correlation coefficient and statistical significance level in parentheses. As our analysis becomes more refined, we also report the R^2 level and the number of countries in the analysis. In the following tables, we boldface all correlations significant at the 0.10 level. Bear in mind that for the final two measures, a negative sign is preferable (lower ratio of cash flow to share price and lower market volatility).

Each of the full equations was statistically significant at the 0.01 level, and the R^2 levels are relatively high for such cross-country analyses, which inevitably have a high degree of random noise. The financial variables, coming from different sources and slightly different samples, give some confidence in the robustness of the consistent results.

The results in Table 5.9 are not entirely consistent and do not tell a perfectly clear story. In general, the factor measure for basic foundational law is statistically significant and shows a typically positive effect, though it is significant and negative for the La Porta, et al. measure of mcap/s, a quite curious outcome. The corporate law measure of adr, by contrast is typically insignificant and frequently shows a negative sign, except for mcap/s. The securities law measure of priv, by contrast, shows the expected positive sign for the variables generally and demonstrates statistical significance for a majority of the independent financial variables.

Table 5.9   Regression of groups of legal variables on stock markets

	mcap/gdp	smv/gdp	mcap/s	coc	adeqcap	cash/price	mvol
factor	**0.453**	**0.394**	**−0.352**	**0.842**	**0.663**	0.237	**−0.592**
	(0.002)	**(0.009)**	**(0.018)**	**(0.000)**	**(0.000)**	(0.193)	**(0.000)**
adr	−0.066	−0.028	**0.409**	−0.107	−0.094	−0.168	0.086
	(0.698)	(0.875)	**(0.026)**	(0.349)	(0.521)	(0.482)	(0.603)
priv	**0.380**	**0.357**	0.234	0.163	**0.325**	**0.560**	0.236
	(0.034)	**(0.056)**	(0.185)	(0.161)	**(0.032)**	**(0.021)**	(0.159)
R^2	0.409	0.348	0.419	0.754	0.577	0.434	0.431
n	38	38	33	34	35	24	37

Before drawing our preliminary conclusions, it is important to introduce a caveat on statistical significance, which should not be worshipped as a standard for validity. Every single securities law measure was significant at the 0.2 level or better, which means that there is a better than 80 percent probability that there exists an authentic relationship between priv and the dependent variable of interest. Moreover, every full equation was significant at the 0.01 level, so one should not place undue emphasis on the statistical significance for each individual independent variable in each individual equation.

At this point, the data suggest that there is a strong positive relationship between the factor variable for basic foundational law and equity market development and efficiency, save for the single anomalous significant negative association. There is a comparably strong positive relationship between securities law and equity markets, with more consistency than even that of basic foundational law. The evidence for the positive value of the antidirector rights measure of corporate law, though, is quite frail. The only positive association of any strength was with mcap/s, a regression that seems a little dubious given the significant negative association with the factor variable for basic foundational law.

Table 5.9 above included no control variables. Given the multitude of differences among the nations and their potential effects on securities markets, consideration of some third factor control variables is necessary. The choice of appropriate control variables, though, is a difficult one. For example, GDP is a commonly used control variable in many cross-country analyses but would be inappropriate here. Ample empirical research demonstrates that GDP is significantly affected by our independent variable of basic foundational law and significantly affected by the dependent financial market variables as well. With this high level of endogeneity, GDP is not helpful as a control variable, although it has sometimes been used. Another potential control variable, the degree of corruption in the nation, suffers the same problem of endogeneity to the law.

Because the very nature of the law, especially the basic foundational law, affects all of society, endogeneity is pervasive and some studies have used relatively few or no control variables. Some of the control variables that have been used are inapplicable to our research. For example, settler mortality has been used as a control variable when studies have sought to measure the significance of a nation's legal origin, but the origin variable has not been an important one in our analyses.

Given the relatively limited size of the sample, the number of control variables should be limited as well. One good control variable is ethnolinguistic fractionalization (ethn), which measures the ethnic and linguistic heterogeneity of a nation's people.[31] This variable is largely exogenous of the legal and financial variables, yet has a plausible effect on the study;

as noted in Chapter 2, greater ethnic homogeneity tends to yield greater trust, which may yield greater investment in equity markets. Another variable that could have an important economic effect on markets is education, or human capital. Such human capital is commonly used in cross-country analyses and produces positive economic outcomes for a nation. Human capital is commonly operationalized as the percentage of the eligible populace enrolled in secondary education (secon).[32] For both these variables, data is available for the relevant nations. Table 5.10 reports the same multiple regressions as those of the prior table, but with these two control variables added to the equations. Once again, each of the full equations was statistically significant at the 0.01 level, and the R^2 levels are good.

The introduction of control variables do not dramatically alter our results though they tend to reduce the associations with the legal variables. The statistical significance of our legal variables in some equations slips somewhat, typically from the 0.05 level to the 0.10 level. The latter findings are still salient ones, because of the statistical noise associated with cross-country comparisons and the high significance of the full model. The introduction of the control variables does not substantially alter or change the directionality of any of the coefficients or patterns of results for the legal variables, and these variables have a very modest effect on the resulting R^2 measures. The control variables were generally not significant (or even close to significant) independently.

While there was strong theoretical reason to believe that these control variables would be significant determinants of our financial variables, they

Table 5.10 Regression of groups of legal variables and control variables on stock markets

	mcap/gdp	smv/gdp	mcap/s	coc	adeqcap	cash/price	mvol
factor	**0.450**	0.423	−0.202	**0.700**	**0.528**	0.773	−0.681
	(0.053)	(0.084)	(0.351)	**(0.000)**	**(0.006)**	(0.449)	(0.501)
adr	−0.053	−0.021	**0.363**	−0.087	−0.080	−0.179	0.032
	(0.762)	(0.911)	**(0.050)**	(0.446)	(0.593)	(0.475)	(0.827)
priv	**0.341**	**0.334**	**0.323**	0.136	**0.301**	**0.564**	0.113
	(0.069)	**(0.091)**	**(0.089)**	(0.252)	**(0.057)**	**(0.031)**	(0.459)
ethn	0.133	0.086	−0.216	−0.002	0.016	0.084	−0.201
	(0.436)	(0.634)	(0.233)	(0.985)	(0.914)	(0.671)	(0.168)
secon	0.096	0.023	−0.311	0.199	0.194	0.778	**−0.720**
	(0.693)	(0.928)	(0.208)	(0.173)	(0.335)	(0.440)	**(0.002)**
R^2	0.420	0.353	0.460	0.773	0.592	0.452	0.586
n	38	38	33	34	35	24	37

proved significant in only one of the 14 possible instances. This illustrates the great statistical noise associated with any cross-country comparisons and the difficulty in finding significant associations at the more rigorous levels of statistical significance. It is noteworthy that securities law (priv) was a relatively more important determinant of financial outcomes than was secondary education, in five of the seven equations. Securities law was significant at the relaxed 0.10 level for five of the financial dependent variables (more than even for the basic foundational law). This finding of the relative importance of securities law is consistent with the results of a study of transition economies, which found that of different indexes for shareholder protection, the securities regulation scale was the only one to show significance.[33]

The association for securities law, and only securities law, on the cash/price variable is important. The prior studies showing that the basic foundational law increased the valuation of firms and equity markets may be due to the effect of legal systems on cash flow. For example, the greater valuation could be due to reduced risk of expropriation or greater opportunities for sales. This effect is independent of that of the risk premium demanded by investors, to account for agency problems. Our results for this variable suggest that the latter concern is directly addressed by securities law, rather than basic or corporate law.

At this point in our analyses, it appears clear that the basic foundational law and securities law have an important, if not entirely consistent, effect in strengthening equity markets. The association for corporate law, at least the antidirector rights measure, is much less clear. The lack of positive effect for corporate law is somewhat surprising, given the theory and some of the past empirical findings on antidirector rights measures of corporate law. The prior empirical research has not combined corporate law and securities law, though. It may be that extensive securities law envelops the effects of corporate law, that the positive effect of corporate law disappears when broader antifraud protections of securities law are adopted. To consider this possibility, the next analysis considers only those nations whose securities laws are below the median for the private enforcement variable of significance, to test for the effect of corporate law when securities laws are relatively weak. Table 5.11 reports the results of the multiple regression with control variables and absent the effect of securities laws.

The antidirector rights measure does relatively worse as a determinant of stock market size and efficiency in nations with weaker private enforcement of securities laws. Only the continued anomalous results for mcap/s are significantly positive, as they were for the full sample of nations.

Table 5.11 contains one other suggestive, potentially very significant finding. The correlations for our factor variable of basic foundational law lose much of their significance in nations with weak securities laws. This at

Table 5.11   Regression of groups of legal variables and control variables on stock markets in nations with weak securities laws

	mcap/gdp	smv/gdp	mcap/s	coc	adeqcap	cash/price	mvol
factor	−0.005	−0.029	−0.309	**0.560**	0.227	0.681	0.350
	(0.989)	(0.936)	(0.457)	**(0.001)**	(0.500)	(0.140)	(0.336)
adr	0.060	−0.164	**0.891**	0.057	−0.136	**−1.029**	−0.024
	(0.806)	(0.497)	**(0.028)**	(0.519)	(0.557)	**(0.050)**	(0.910)
ethn	−0.155	**−0.689**	0.430	0.012	−0.356	−0.608	−0.260
	(0.664)	**(0.065)**	(0.354)	(0.925)	(0.302)	(0.243)	(0.404)
secon	0.507	0.028	0.369	**0.478**	0.309	−0.407	**−1.192**
	(0.212)	(0.943)	(0.507)	**(0.004)**	(0.379)	(0.395)	**(0.005)**
R²	0.400	0.416	0.541	0.945	0.620	0.659	0.610
n	18	18	12	14	14	9	16

least hints at the prospect that it is the substance of securities laws that is most important for securities markets, rather than the substance of basic property and contract law. However, with substantive securities laws in place, it appears that the procedural attributes of the basic law (for example, judicial independence and efficiency), show a greater effect. Those legal procedural variables would be of relatively little value to markets, absent some effective substantive law to implement. However, the significance of the foundational variables assumes importance in the presence of securities regulation, which demonstrates their contribution under those circumstances. With the limitation to nations with below average securities law, the sample size in this regression grows small, so one should be cautious about drawing any conclusions from the results. The findings certainly do not support the hypothesis that corporate law is more important in the absence of strong securities law. Indeed, our results show that it is securities law that has particular value, comparable to that of basic foundational law.

The next analysis focuses on public enforcement of the securities laws. As noted above, the strong associations for securities law are associated with private, not public, enforcement of these laws. Theoretically, public enforcement should show some positive effect, though, if the securities laws themselves contribute to efficient capital markets. To consider this effect in a multiple regression with control variables, we repeat in Table 5.12 the analyses reported in Table 5.10 above, but use public enforcement (pub) rather than private enforcement for our securities law variable.

Public enforcement of securities laws is not a significant determinant of any of our financial dependent variables. However, it is noteworthy that the direction of the association is beneficial in every one of the measures of the public enforcement variable, which hints at some positive effect.

Law and corporate finance

Table 5.12   Regression of groups of legal variables with public securities law enforcement and control variables on stock markets

	mcap/gdp	smv/gdp	mcap/s	coc	adeqcap	cash/price	mvol
factor	**0.485**	**0.454**	−0.269	**0.518**	**0.697**	0.668	−0.638
	(0.047)	**(0.072)**	(0.214)	**(0.007)**	**(0.000)**	(0.512)	(0.534)
adr	0.115	0.101	**0.429**	−0.028	−0.075	**0.514**	0.199
	(0.493)	(0.562)	**(0.015)**	(0.844)	(0.480)	**(0.059)**	(0.844)
pub	0.062	0.146	0.255	0.237	0.133	−0.074	−0.119
	(0.712)	(0.406)	(0.153)	(0.114)	(0.230)	(0.768)	(0.390)
ethn	0.211	0.155	−0.135	0.070	0.017	−0.017	−0.216
	(0.228)	(0.392)	(0.441)	(0.635)	(0.870)	(0.939)	(0.129)
secon	0.196	0.138	−0.114	0.356	**0.278**	0.167	**−0.794**
	(0.469)	(0.605)	(0.640)	(0.089)	**(0.061)**	(0.511)	**(0.001)**
R^2	0.264	0.309	0.443	0.505	0.774	0.298	0.588
n	38	38	33	35	34	24	37

Moreover, it is important to recognize that the public enforcement variable does not truly capture the value of the regulatory actions of the Securities and Exchange Commission. A central part of the SEC's role is the establishment of regulations for disclosure and otherwise, which are enforceable through private actions. These regulations considerably facilitate private enforcement and their value would be expressed through the private enforcement variable as well. The public enforcement variable captures just that, enforcement, and not the rule creation function of the SEC. It does seem fair to conclude that in the securities law enforcement context, it is the private right of action and not government prosecution which has the greatest financial value. This is unsurprising, because the remedy for private violations can be many billions of dollars of damages to the harmed investors, while public enforcement actions typically result in lesser sanctions, and because private enforcers may be more efficient in their choices of the actions to be pursued.

INTERMEDIATE VARIABLES

The studies reported above, as well as a considerable body of other research, indicate that legal variables are important to the size and efficiency of equity markets and the cost of capital in a nation. It is important to investigate empirically how this effect takes place. The primary theoretical justification for corporate law is its attempted correction of managerial agency problems. The primary theoretical justification for securities law is its regime of compelled disclosure, and associated protection against fraud and other agency problems. The basic foundational law should serve to address these same problems, though less directly, and the basic foundational law is also relevant to the enforcement of all legal rules, including those of corporate and securities law.

One check on the broad financial market results is to examine the effect of the laws on measures of the intermediate agency problem and control variable processes. If an effect shows up on these measures, we can have greater confidence in our overall findings. Absent such an effect, the broader findings might be questioned as reflecting the effect of some omitted variable. If disclosure requirements, for example, do not in fact produce better quality disclosures, it is difficult to imagine how they would have a positive effect on the markets. Of course, our test of effect on intermediate variables can only be as good as those variables themselves. There can be no precise quantitative measure for the accuracy of corporate disclosures or the degree to which managers selflessly represent the interest of their shareholders.

While the effect of legal rules on the intermediate steps necessary for building strong equity markets is not as extensively studied as for the ultimate market variables, there is some existing research on the matter. One published article examined accounting standards, the enforcement of accounting standards (measured by a factor analysis variable including both securities law and basic foundational law measures), and the accuracy of earnings forecasts.[34] The study found that strong enforcement was associated with higher forecast accuracy, which should imply more efficient markets and relatively less risk for investors. Other research has found that higher forecast accuracy is indeed associated with higher firm valuations.[35]

A variety of rough measures are available for our intervening intermediate variables. We begin with measures of corporate agency problems. Here, we are heavily dependent on WCR survey measures for board prevention of improper practices (bpip), board management of shareholder value (bmsv), and corporate ethics (ethic). In addition, we have scales of simple corporate governance quality prepared by the international consulting firm of McKinsey & Co. (govq) and of governance opacity prepared by the international accounting firm of PriceWaterhouseCoopers (govo). For govq and govo, lower numbers are better, so a negative sign would be a beneficial association. One would hypothesize that there would be a positive significant association between these variables and basic foundational law and corporate law, with less likelihood for securities law. The governance opacity index does involve corporate disclosures, though, so a higher association with securities law might be expected for this variable. Table 5.13 reports the results of our standard multiple regression model on these intermediate dependent variables, with the standard control variables.

Table 5.13 *Regression of groups of legal variables and control variables on intermediate agency problem variables*

	bpip	bmsv	ethic	govq	govo
factor	**0.854**	**0.736**	**0.917**	**−0.534**	**−0.961**
	(0.000)	**(0.001)**	**(0.000)**	**(0.022)**	**(0.019)**
adr	0.174	0.140	0.121	−0.002	0.020
	(0.271)	(0.386)	(0.384)	(0.992)	(0.947)
priv	−0.143	0.003	−0.069	0.075	**−0.725**
	(0.379)	(0.987)	(0.625)	(0.728)	**(0.067)**
ethn	0.127	**0.330**	**0.240**	−0.264	−0.400
	(0.419)	**(0.047)**	**(0.089)**	(0.168)	(0.219)
secon	−0.128	0.035	−0.077	−0.401	−0.162
	(0.542)	(0.871)	(0.676)	(0.112)	(0.219)
R^2	0.549	0.524	0.650	0.468	0.142
n	35	35	35	24	19

Here we see a very favorable association between the basic foundational law and measures of higher quality corporate governance. Once again, the corporate law variables do not show much effect. The securities law variable is significant for the opacity variable, which is as expected. One surprising finding is the apparent association between higher levels of ethnic fractionalization and better corporate governance. Perhaps companies in these countries voluntarily adopt stronger corporate governance to overcome the somewhat lower levels of basic trust associated with ethnic heterogeneity, though this is speculative. These corporate governance quality scales are highly subjective, but they do reflect the perceptions of market participants and therefore have real world significance.

The next set of intermediate variables to be tested involve disclosure. For this measure, we expect the securities law variables to be more important than corporate law variables, though the corporate law duty of disclosure might produce some effect. In this analysis, we rely heavily on several measures by the Centre for International Financial Analysis Research (CIFAR), which analyzes national corporate disclosure on several dimensions. These include financial disclosure intensity (find), corporate governance disclosure intensity (govd), aggregate disclosure intensity (aggd), and timeliness of disclosure (timed). We also use the La Porta, et al. variable for a rating of accounting standards as a dependent disclosure variable. The independent variables are taken from the basic model except, for securities law, we use the direct disclosure requirement variable. Table 5.14 reports the result in the same manner as the preceding tables.

Table 5.14   Regression of groups of legal variables and control variables on intermediate disclosure variables

	find	govd	aggd	timed	accst
factor	**0.413**	**0.586**	**0.501**	**0.500**	**0.504**
	(0.061)	**(0.013)**	**(0.011)**	**(0.037)**	**(0.007)**
adr	0.093	0.301	0.187	0.252	0.033
	(0.591)	(0.102)	(0.219)	(0.171)	(0.828)
disc	**0.339**	0.050	**0.324**	0.080	**0.461**
	(0.064)	(0.786)	**(0.044)**	(0.666)	**(0.005)**
ethn	−0.028	−0.125	0.032	0.196	0.122
	(0.869)	(0.489)	(0.835)	(0.294)	(0.407)
secon	0.028	−0.267	0.074	−0.005	0.046
	(0.903)	(0.271)	(0.714)	(0.986)	(0.809)
R^2	0.408	0.362	0.540	0.373	0.582
n	35	35	34	34	34

The results are roughly as might be expected. The factor measure for basic foundational law is highly associated with the disclosure variables, and the securities law disclosure requirement shows a significant association for at least the financial disclosure measures. Corporate law is not significant, though it approaches significance for disclosures about corporate governance measures, which might be anticipated.

The analyses of the intermediate corporate governance and disclosure variables generally confirm our broader findings on the ultimate measure of effects on financial markets overall. The basic foundational law is consistently correlated with better quality corporate governance and better quality corporate disclosures. Securities law shows some association with disclosure quality, and these are the two variables that also demonstrated the strongest association with larger and more efficient financial markets. Corporate law shows very little effect on the intermediate variables of interest and likewise shows very little effect on the broader ultimate financial market variables.

CONCLUSION

The empirical evidence confirms that the law matters, in a beneficial way, for financial markets. We examined many dependent variables of financial significance, both ultimate and intermediate, and the law frequently was associated with better economic results. Table 5.15 summarizes the results of the four multiple regressions (Tables 5.9, 5.10, 5.13 and 5.14) that used

Table 5.15   Summary of statistically significant associations from multiple regressions

basic foundational law	18 positive, 1 negative
corporate law	2 positive, 0 negative
securities law	12 positive, 0 negative

the three basic independent legal variables (factor, adr, priv, or disc). Twenty four separate dependent variables were tested in these regressions.

These results are powerful, given the complicated context of cross-country regressions. Despite the noisy nature of our dependent variables, the basic law was significant in the multiple regressions at the 0.10 level three-quarters of the time, and securities law was significant half of the time. The simple regressions had an even greater frequency of statistical significance for the legal variables. Nearly all of the significant associations were in a beneficial direction, with the prominent exception of the odd regression on mcap/s, which was negative for the basic law but positive for corporate law. The positive effect for the law was confirmed by the studies of intermediate variables, which display the pathways through which the law provides economic benefits. The real world significance of this frequency of positive statistical significance is shown by the fact that ethnic fractionalization and secondary education, two widely used cross-country variables of obvious societal importance, were statistically significant determinants in only four of 24 regressions in which they were used. This fact is ample evidence of the clarity of law's effect.

The basic foundational law appears to be especially important, as might be surmised. Without this law, deals become unreliable and trust becomes riskier. The foundational legal system creates rules protecting property and enforcing contracts and establishes an adjudicatory structure to implement those rules. As the rules and structure improve, the risk of investment and other transactions decline, and the quantity and efficiency of such transactions increase as theory projects.

Securities law is also very important to the success of financial markets. It is associated significantly with larger and more efficient markets, at least as captured by the private enforcement measure, which incorporates the disclosure requirements of securities law. This finding provides support for the theoretical hypotheses of Chapter 2, about the ability of even restrictive laws to reduce transaction costs and create external economic information benefits, and the hypotheses of Chapter 3, about the systematic biases of behavioralism and the economic efficiency values of addressing them through the legal system. The substantiality of this benefit can be roughly calculated.

We now estimate a very rudimentary calculation of the value of securities laws. Chapter 2 showed that the cost of going public for NYSE-listed companies was around US$12.2 billion. This probably overstates the costs of securities law itself by a considerable degree, but we use it for our measure of costs for such laws. For benefits, we employ the results of Table 5.9 above for the ratio of market capitalization to GDP, for which the best point estimate for a unit change of priv was 0.341, and for which the 2000 ratio for the United States is 1.4344. If we apply these numbers to the contemporary capitalization of the NYSE, it suggests that the value of the Exchange would be US$2.28 trillion lower, absent the securities laws, giving a positive cost/valuation ratio for those laws of nearly 2000:1 for listed companies. This is only a rough estimate, of course, and it calculates the overall value of the private enforcement of those laws, not marginal changes in the requirements of the securities laws. This finding and our other results do counter the claim that restrictive securities laws cause economic harm and should at least put the onus on those who criticize securities law to justify their position with something more than a generalized defense of private ordering and criticism of government intervention in financial markets.

Corporate law showed relatively little effect on financial markets or the intermediate variables. This is not a basis for dismissing the value of corporate law, as only the most dramatic effects will appear significant in such cross-national studies. Perhaps the variables used to measure corporate law do not capture the essence of corporate law as well as for the other variables. The economic value of corporate law is apparent from firms' consistent choice to incorporate themselves in Delaware and take advantage of its legal system. If corporate law were trivial, there is no reason for such concentration of locus of incorporation. However, the results suggest that the corporate law variables are not a primary determinant of our financial variables.

While the reason that corporate law shows little significant market effect cannot be proved, it is possible to speculate. Possibly, corporate law is too strong and overly empowers minority shareholders in corporate governance, thereby undermining good management by directors. Given the generally permissive nature of corporate law, though, this seems likely. Corporate law may instead be overly permissive, and insufficiently mandatory, thereby failing to reduce transaction costs and inefficient behavioral tendencies of managers and shareholders and leaving serious agency problems unaddressed. The greater positive results for the much more restrictive securities law measures lends some credence to this theory that corporate law may be insufficiently restrictive. Mark Roe provides an alternative explanation, that corporate law may fail because of "opaque businesses" or social mistrust that "impedes professionalization of management," and

suggests that the failure of corporate law in some nations is in its inability
to prevent mismanagement, even as it successfully prevents self-dealing.[36]

As the earlier theoretical chapters have discussed, there is a relatively
common economic presumption in favor of private ordering, without governmental restraint. This theory favors governmental action insofar as it
enforces private deals, thereby empowering such transactions, but disfavors
any governmental constraints on such deals. While there is little doubt that
the empowering functions of law, as reflected in basic foundational law,
have considerable economic benefit, restrictive securities law rules may also
produce significant economic benefits, measured in the trillions of dollars.
The pure private ordering paradigm is not optimal for securities markets.

NOTES

1. Robert J. Barro, DETERMINANTS OF ECONOMIC GROWTH (1997).
2. Rafael La Porta, Florencio Lopez-de-Silanes, Andrei Shleifer, & Robert W. Vishny, *Law and Finance*, 106 J. POL. ECON. 1113 (1998).
3. Rafael La Porta, Florencio Lopez-de-Silanes, Andrei Shleifer, & Robert W. Vishny, *The Quality of Government*, 15 J. LAW ECON. ORG. 222 (1999).
4. Rafael La Porta, Florencio Lopez-de-Silanes, Andrei Shleifer, & Robert W. Vishny, *Investor Protection and Corporate Governance*, 58 J. FIN. ECON. 3 (2000).
5. Rafael La Porta, Florencio Lopez-de-Silanes, Andrei Shleifer, & Robert W. Vishny, *Investor Protection and Corporate Valuation*, 57 J. FIN. 1147 (2002).
6. Rafael La Porta, Florencio Lopez-de-Silanes, & Andrei Shleifer, *What Works in Securities Laws?*, NBER Working Paper No. 9882 (July 2003).
7. Ross Levine, *Law, Finance, and Economic Growth*, 8 J. FIN. INTERMEDIATION 8 (1999).
8. Thorsten Beck, Asli Demirguc-Kent, & Ross Levine, *Law, Politics, and Finance*, World Bank Working Paper No. 2585 (2001).
9. Ross Levine, Norman Loayza, & Thorsten Beck, *Financial Intermediation and Growth: Causality and Causes*, 46 J. MON. ECON. 31 (2000).
10. Gerard Caprio, Luc Laeven, & Ross Levine, *Governance and Bank Valuation*, NBER Working Paper No. W10158 (December 2003).
11. Thorsten Beck, Asli Demirguc-Kent, & Ross Levine, *Law and Firms' Access to Finance*, World Bank Working Paper No. 3194 (2004).
12. Leora F. Klapper & Inessa Love, *Corporate Governance, Investor Protection, and Performance in Emerging Markets*, World Bank Working Paper No. 2818 (April 2002).
13. Omar Azfar & Thornton Matheson, *Market-Mobilized Capital*, 117 PUB. CHOICE 357 (2003).
14. Davide Lombardo & Marco Pagano, *Legal Determinants of the Return on Equity*, CESF Working Paper No. 24 (October 1999).
15. Klaus Gugler, Dennis C. Mueller, & B. Burcin Yurtoglu, *The Impact of Corporate Governance on Investment Returns in Developed and Developing Countries*, 113 ECON. J. F511 (2003).
16. Frank H. Stephen & Stefan van Hemmen, *Legal Rules and the Development of Financial Systems*, presented at the Conference of the European Association of Law and Economics, September 2003.
17. Charles P. Himmelberg, R. Glenn Hubbard, & Inessa Love, *Investor Protection, Ownership, and the Cost of Capital*, World Bank Policy Research Working Paper No. 2834 (2002).

18. Randall Morck, Bernard Yin Yeung, & Wayne Yu, *The Information Content of Stock Markets: Why Do Emerging Markets have Synchronous Stock Price Movements*, 58 J. FIN. ECON. 215 (2000).
19. Edward Glaeser, Simon Johnson, & Andrei Shleifer, *Coase versus The Coasians*, 116 Q. J. ECON. 853 (2001).
20. Luzi Hail & Christian Leuz, *International Differences in the Cost of Equity Capital: Do Legal Institutions and Securities Regulation Matter*, Wharton Financial Institutions Center Working Paper 04–06 (November 2003).
21. Stijn Claessens & Luc Laeven, *Financial Development, Property Rights, and Growth*, 58 J. FIN. 2401 (2003).
22. Stulz & Williamson, *Culture, Openness and Finance*, NBER Working Paper No. 222 (2001).
23. *See* Ugo Mattei, COMPARATIVE LAW AND ECONOMICS (1997).
24. *See* Raghuram G. Rajan & Luigi Zingales, *The Great Reversals: The Politics of Financial Development in the 20th Century*, NBER Working Paper No. 8178 (July 2002).
25. *See* James Gwartney, Robert Lawson, & Walter Block, ECONOMIC FREEDOM OF THE WORLD 1975–1995 (1996); Gerald P. O'Driscoll, Jr., Kim Holmes, & Melanie Kirkpatrick, INDEX OF ECONOMIC FREEDOM (2000).
26. *See* Christopher Clague, et al., *Contract-Intensive Money: Contract Enforcement, Property Rights, and Economic Performance*, 4 J. ECON. GROWTH 185 (1999).
27. *See* Thorsten Beck, Asli Demirguc-Kunt, & Ross Levine, *A New Database on the Structure and Development of the Financial Sector*, 14 WORLD BANK ECON. REV. 597 (2000).
28. *See* Laura Nyantung Beny, *Do Shareholders Value Insider Trading Laws? International Evidence*, Harvard John M. Olin Series Discussion Paper No. 345 (December 2001).
29. Robert Bushman, Joseph Piotrosi, & Abbie Smith, *What Determines Corporate Transparency?*, 42 J. ACCTG. RES. 207 (2004).
30. Art Durnev & E. Han Kim, *To Steal or Not to Steal: Firm Attributes, Legal Environment, and Valuation* (March 2004).
31. Data for this variable come from Albert Alesina, et al., FRACTIONALIZATION (2003).
32. Data for this variable come from World Economic Forum, THE GLOBAL COMPETITIVENESS REPORT 312 (1999).
33. Katharina Pistor, Martin Raiser, & Stanislav Gelfer, *Law and Finance in Transition Economies*, European Bank for Reconstruction and Development Working Paper No. 48 (February 2000).
34. Ole-Kristian Hope, *Disclosure Practices, Enforcement of Accounting Standards, and Analysts' Forecast Accuracy: An International Study*, 41 J. ACCTG. RES. 235 (2003).
35. Mark H. Lang, Karl V. Lins, & Darius P. Miller, *ADRs, Analysts, and Accuracy: Does Cross Listing in the United States Improve a Firm's Information Environment and Increase Market Value?*, 41 J. ACCTG. RES. 317 (2003).
36. Mark J. Roe, *Corporate Law's Limits*, 31 J. LEGAL STUD. 233 (2002).

6. Current controversies in law and corporate finance

This book has heretofore made a case for the value of law in general and securities law in particular in promoting the development of a nation's capital markets and economy. The new empirical evidence presented in Chapter 5, in tandem with that produced by other scholars, confirms the theory and clearly demonstrates that at least some aspects of securities laws produce great economic benefit for a nation. The prior chapters present theoretical support that supplies the basis for these results. On a gross overall basis, securities law is beneficial, but this finding does not necessarily mean that any particular securities regulation is necessarily valuable. Some regulations may "go too far." Others may fail to implement the types of practices that produce benefits for corporate finance. Concern about the effectiveness and efficiency of securities regulation by the SEC has prompted a series of major reform proposals in recent years.

This chapter applies our background understanding to several current academic and political controversies surrounding US securities law and regulation. Most recent reform proposals by academics embody a serious deregulatory approach. These proposals include (a) deregulating insider trading, (b) authorizing companies to contract out of liability for securities fraud, (c) deregulating issuers in favor of registering investors, (d) creating a competitive system of differential state securities regulation, and (e) modifying or repealing much of the recently enacted Sarbanes-Oxley Act. All of these proposals would minimize government regulation in favor of private contracting to control fraud. This chapter applies the theory and evidence set out in the preceding chapters to these controversies, supplemented by empirical evidence that is available on the specific issues.

This chapter emphasizes that although securities regulation in this country certainly has room for improvement, its basic structure must be maintained. Although even the authors of this text have specific ideas for reforming and paring back some SEC rules and regulations, critiques of specific provisions of Sarbanes-Oxley, for example, do not justify any proposal that would lead to substantial replacement of federal regulation by private ordering.

INSIDER TRADING

The 1934 Exchange Act prohibitions on securities fraud and other securities law provisions outlaw insider trading in securities. Such insider trading centrally involves prohibitions on "corporate insiders," such as officers and directors and others privy to secret internal information, from selling or buying stock based upon their private information gleaned from their positions. For example, these insiders usually have access to financial information, such as quarterly profit reports, before the information is made public. If such information is negative (worse than the market expects), an insider could sell shares in his or her company before the market incorporates this information in the company's value and profit from specialized nonpublic knowledge. Of course, the law does not effectively prohibit all insider trading, but it surely reduces the practice. The SEC cannot catch all wrongdoers, but by outlawing insider trading the law actually changes people's minds regarding the morality of insider trading and in that way, among others, reduces its incidence.[1] Research suggests that the legal prohibitions prevent more blatant insider trading on advance knowledge of financial reports but do not prevent trading on more subjective inside information, such as the future value of corporate research and development activities.

Intuitively, such insider trading seems unfair to most market investors. It is unethical because it allows insiders to profit at the expense of outsiders who cannot trade on equal footing no matter how diligently they follow the market.[2] It allows managers to appropriate for their own purposes information that rightfully belongs to their principals. Beyond these equitable instincts, economic analysis suggests that insider trading puts outside investors at greater risk and thereby discourages equity investments and undermines capital markets.

Some, however, have suggested that parties be allowed to trade on inside information. The legalization of insider trading is generally associated with arguments initially made some time ago by a leading law and economics scholar, Henry Manne.[3] His theory was that because corporate insiders were generating the inside information, they might therefore be given some sort of property right in it. This would supposedly encourage insiders to generate more useful information and, in the process, make the market more informative and efficient. Manne even suggested that "profits from insider trading constitute the only effective compensation scheme for entrepreneurial services in large corporations."[4] Manne argued that this efficiency can benefit other traders. For example, by driving down the price of shares of a failing company through insider trading, insiders may protect other investors from buying the shares at an inflated price. Some economists and others have agreed with Manne and argued that efficiency considerations counsel for legalizing insider trading in stock.[5] Insider trading, it has been argued, can also compensate controlling shareholders for their status and eliminate their need to diversify their portfolios.[6]

In a similar vein, others have argued that insider trading can be restrained, if need be, without government statutory intervention.[7] Under this plan, companies could contractually prohibit their insiders from trading in corporate stock, or allow insider trading on certain terms. Allowing such trading could serve as a form of compensation to the insiders and thereby replace other compensation, such as salaries and bonuses, to some degree. In the process, allowing corporate insiders to trade on nonpublic information could benefit the company, by saving it money it would otherwise have to pay in compensation.

Assuming that these contractual relationships are not secret, investors can decide whether to trade in the shares of a company that allows insider trading. They can make their own assessment of the tradeoff between the negative of dealing with others who have superior knowledge and the possible benefit of more accurate market prices using the inside information. The fact that few companies prohibited insider trading before the federal government stepped in may be viewed as evidence that this is an efficient form of compensation. Such private decisions are generally regarded by economists as efficient. When insider trading is bad for a company, the company presumably would prohibit it.

On its face this theory of beneficial insider trading suffers from some substantial theoretical challenges. First, the assumption that inside information will be more quickly translated into market prices is not at all clear. The extent that insiders can profit from nonpublic information by trading is proportional to the degree to which the market price is otherwise inaccurate. Insiders thus have an incentive to make the actual market price as inaccurate as possible, in order to profit from its correction. There is relatively little incentive for insiders to correct marginal mispricing by promptly supplying information to the market. Rather, they benefit from waiting until the market price is far from the mark. They even have some incentive to first make the market price erroneous, so that they can profit from its correction. Indeed, this was the reality in the famous early insider trading case, *SEC v. Texas Gulf Sulphur Co.*[8] In that case, a company with a major mineral find first misleadingly downplayed its significance while insiders traded and only later announced the full scope of the discovery, enabling insider profits.

Thus, insider trading enables insiders to profit even from inaccurate information that is of no efficiency benefit. The ideal strategy for insider profit might be first to release inaccurate, disappointing information about the company's financial results. This would have the effect of driving the price to a low level. Then, the insider could buy up large numbers of shares at low prices and release the accurate, positive information about the company, which would produce a rise in share price from which the insider would profit. The key to such a scheme's success is purposeful dissemination of inaccurate information that is only later corrected. Insiders can reap the most profits when a share price is very volatile, and they can manipulate and benefit from the volatility by the selective release of accurate or inaccurate positive or negative information. Because the information in question is nonpublic, outside investors have no idea whether the original negative or later positive information represents the true and accurate report of the company's situation. This creates inefficient markets and obviously makes outsiders reluctant to invest in capital markets. More rigorous theoretical analyses have shown the inefficiency of allowing insider trading, for it can drive capital out of the market, increase the costs of funds and thereby damage overall economic welfare.[9]

The prevailing rules of insider trading encourage management to promptly supply relevant information to the market. The basic rule of insider trading is "disclose or abstain,"[10] that is, insiders must either refrain from buying or selling stock in their company or disclose all material information to the market. Insiders have a considerable incentive to trade shares in their company. Many have large shareholdings resulting from options or other incentive compensation and need to sell those shares to diversify their portfolios. This encourages insiders to fully release all material nonpublic information in order to be able to legally trade in their company's stock. To allow insider trading would reverse the incentives and discourage such public disclosures. One study confirmed this intuition, finding that more trading by insiders was linked to lesser information content in quarterly earnings reports.[11]

Insider trading is also a poor method of compensating officers. Shareholders want to pay officers for doing a good job and making the company thrive. Thus, companies provide stock or options that will profit the insider if share prices increase or bonuses based on corporate performance. Insider trading compensation, by contrast, would allow an officer to profit greatly from corporate failure. The insider could sell short the company's shareholdings while running the company into the ground and then disclose the company's collapse and profit from plummeting share prices. Because it is no doubt easier to make a corporation fail than succeed in a competitive market, this corporate destruction scheme might be the most profitable strategy for insiders.

Insider trading is also an ineffective method of encouraging employees to do their jobs well. Professor Manne only assumes that allowing insider trading encourages the production of beneficial information. A perusal of litigated insider trading cases makes it clear that most insider trading is done by people other than those who actually produce the information, and that insider trading is just as profitable when the news created is bad as when it is good.

Allowing insider trading could also significantly disrupt corporate management.[12] Officers might profit from trading on inside information, absent prohibitions. The potential magnitude of their profits will be greater if they are the only ones trading on the information. This creates an incentive for officers not to share information internally, at least not promptly, in an internal competitive drive to profit from the information. Alternatively, they might manipulate information submitted to coworkers in order to advance their personal investment objectives.

The considerations raised in our prior chapters also counsel against the legalization of insider trading. Given the well-established agency problems associated with shareholder control of officers, the fact that a company may voluntarily permit insider trading does not establish that the authorization is an efficient one in the interest of shareholders. Because there is substantial evidence that current compensation schemes in major public companies are anything but efficient,[13] there is no reason to believe that insider trading compensation schemes would be either. Again, while one might hope that insiders would not sacrifice the company's interests to advance their own in so naked a fashion, during the dot.com boom more stock option compensation for officers tended to create more earnings management[14] and more financial restatements.[15]

There is reason to believe that true arm's length bargaining, absent agency problems, would privately prohibit insider trading. One study found that insider trading profits for officers were smaller in companies with institutional shareholders and where the board chairman was not the chief executive officer.[16] Because the latter features are closely associated with better corporate control over officers, the finding suggests that insider trading does represent a manifestation of agency problems, with officers taking advantage of the shareholders they are supposed to be serving.

Allowing insider trading also increases transaction costs for investors. Investors might reasonably have varying views of the value of allowing insider trading and prefer to invest in firms that prohibit, or don't prohibit, the practice. Before investing in a company, parties would have to identify the corporation's practices. If this were simply a binary (allow/disallow) matter, this investigation would be simple, but companies are likely to adopt more refined rules that permit insider trading by some insiders but not by others, and under some circumstances but not in others. The need to identify particular corporate practices would add cost (or risk) to investing. Even if Manne were correct that insider trading carries some benefits, they might not outweigh these increased transaction costs.

Behavioral considerations further justify insider trading restrictions. Emotions can play a significant role in people's decisionmaking. One feature of this is the "level playing field" or fairness criterion. People are generally unwilling to participate in a game that they believe to be unfairly rigged to benefit others. Insider trading is just the sort of "rigging" of the investment game that can cause people to avoid it. Even in the unlikely event that insider trading did improve market efficiency, some people might avoid markets for fear that they would be the ones taken advantage of by insiders with non-public information. As discussed in Chapter 3, humans intrinsically value fairness. Indeed, one of the strongest human desires is not to be made a sucker. People are so concerned with fairness that they will punish those who act unfairly, even at economic cost to themselves.[17] Therefore, many potential investors will reject participating in markets that seem structurally unfair. This will undermine trust in equity markets generally. Insofar as insider trading will increase and inevitably be sometimes publicized, investors may even overestimate and overreact to its occurrence (due to the availability heuristic) and shy away from markets (due to their loss aversion). Thus, behavioral research also suggests that a company's internal decision to allow insider trading as compensation will not in fact be an efficient one.

Regret theory finds that people have negative emotional responses not just to a loss but to feeling responsible for the loss. Individuals who suffer after taking a risk, say on others' honesty, feel shamed and blameworthy. This psychological feature also shows up in anticipated regret; people will avoid circumstances where they fear they are likely to suffer regret.[18] Trading in a market where some can use inside information is just the situation to produce such anticipated regret. People tend to avoid the risk of regret "by preferring inaction to action."[19] Allowing insider trading surely increases the risk of regret by other investors and therefore reduces the number of people willing to "play the game."

Although the theoretical case for allowing insider trading is thus weak, the debate over regulatory prohibitions must be informed by empirical research. Laura Beny has conducted analyses of the strength of insider trading laws in around 30 countries.[20] Her variables included the scope of the law, the nature of sanctions, whether there was liability for tipping, and other measures, as well as measures of the enforcement of these laws. She found that countries with stronger insider trading laws had greater dispersion of ownership, had more informative pricing of shares, and had more liquid stock markets. In contrast to the more general findings on securities laws and disclosures, she found that public enforcement of insider trading laws was especially important to reap their benefits.

Other research has generally confirmed Beny's basic findings about the value of banning insider trading. Bhattacharya and Daouk studied a broad sample of more than one hundred nations and found that most had some formal prohibition on insider trading but that only a minority had actually enforced those prohibitions.[21] They compared these nations on various measures, including the mean returns and liquidity of firms, the value of the companies, the cost of equity, and country risk measures. They found that the mere presence of a prohibition had little effect on the cost of capital but that the active enforcement of the prohibition had a substantial positive effect in decreasing the cost of equity. Another study combined the LaPorta measures for securities law with the Bhattacharya and Daouk insider trading enforcement measures and found that the combined variable was associated with statistically significant benefits.[22] After insider trading is restricted, analyst following of companies increases.[23]

Other research also seems to contradict the claimed benefits of insider trading. A study using a different measure found that countries with more insider trading had more volatile stock markets.[24] A study of the Polish stock market found that insider trading did not make the market quantitatively more efficient by reducing earnings surprises, as Manne assumed would occur. Two reasons for this result were that outsiders misinterpreted the meaning of insiders' trading and that independent analysts showed less interest in following firms with substantial insider trading.[25]

While Manne and others have made a purely theoretical case for eliminating insider trading prohibitions, the theory assumes optimal private efficiency in decisionmaking. That assumption is dubious given the presence of agency problems and transaction costs, added to the behavioral finance considerations. The empirical evidence now consistently affirms the economic benefit of insider trading prohibitions. The proposal to legalize insider trading is not in the best interest of capital markets. When Manne made his original argument in favor of insider trading 40 years ago, the United States was virtually alone in outlawing the practice. Over this period, virtually every developed nation in the world has rejected Manne's arguments and outlawed insider trading. Not a single nation's experience with these laws has led it to reconsider and reauthorize insider trading.

CONTRACTING AROUND FRAUD

Central to the laws generally and securities law in particular are proscriptions against fraud, especially misrepresentations made prior to stock purchases. Parties have sought to escape the commands of those laws in their private contracts and proponents of private contracting as an alternative to governmental securities regulation believe that they should be able to do so. Consider a situation where an investor and potential plaintiff agrees to provisions in an investment contract that he or she will not be able to sue for certain statements that may be misrepresentations. Typically, this involves a written contract that functionally exonerates any false oral representations that the potential defendant had made to the investor. In *Carr* v. *CIGNA Securities*,[26] an unsophisticated investor was orally told that certain investments were safe and conservative, an assurance that was contradicted by certain disclosures buried in 427 pages of documents delivered to the plaintiff. The court found that even if the plaintiff could prove that he had been lied to, the written disclaimer was effective to prevent plaintiff from suing.

When adopting the 1933 Securities Act, Congress enacted an explicit provision in section 29(a) that prevented waivers of its provisions, even if they were express and knowing on the part of the investors. The 1934 Exchange Act carries a comparable savings provision. Although these provisions generally prevent courts from giving effect to simple waivers of coverage, issuer companies and securities industry professionals have designed strategies to achieve the same effect. As in *Carr*, this could be through use of a written contract with an integration clause that disclaims the effect of prior oral representations. Other companies have written nonreliance clauses, where investors declare that they did not rely on earlier misstatements, which tends to defeat any securities fraud action (because reliance is an essential element of any such claim). Courts have divided over the effect of these provisions. Some courts have held that the contract provisions are an impermissible circumvention of the antiwaiver provision and perhaps part of a broader scheme to defraud, but others have given effect to contractual provisions disclaiming liability for misstatements or other fraud.

Contractual modifications of liability present the transaction costs problem associated with private ordering in the absence of securities fraud regulation. An investor must scrutinize the contract closely and ascertain what rights it retains in the event of fraud. Judge Posner, who has allowed contracting around fraud, acknowledged this fact, writing that contracts are "costly to make" and that such added costs can outweigh the investment benefits.[27] These investment losses could be economically efficient if society could count on the parties' wisdom in contracting around fraud, but this decision is infected by the agency problems that make sensible observers dubious of managerial fraud insulation generally. Sometimes, the contract may be quite clear in disclaiming fraud actions, and the investor would be aware of what it was sacrificing without high transaction costs. Of course, these lower transaction cost contracts are precisely the sorts of blanket waivers that Congress explicitly prohibited.

In addition to the transaction costs of examining the contract itself, the potential plaintiff must also assume additional transaction costs in assessing the desirability of the investment in light of the contractual limitations. An investor must also engage in a more searching *ex ante* investigation into the risk of fraud (an investigation made less necessary by the availability of a subsequent liability action). These additional costs are not ameliorated by the clarity and consciousness of the scope of the contract, and some reduction in investments will occur due to the added costs of investing imposed by the contract, in addition to the economic costs associated with the fraud itself.

The behavioral case against contracting around fraud is even stronger. When investors are presented with lengthy written contracts, many will simply sign the contracts without examining them in detail. The terms are usually contracts of adhesion that cannot be altered by negotiation in any event. Certainly the employee whom the investor deals with typically will not have the authority to alter the provision. It is not worth the time and other transaction costs associated with contractual detail—investors will either make a leap of faith or not invest. Those who suffer the overoptimism or overconfidence biases will tend to make the leap of faith, though it may not be an economically efficient decision. Those with more cautious biases will avoid investing in equity securities. Chapter 3 explained how traditional efficiency theories of contracting omit behavioral considerations that prevent optimum results and artificially favor the party proposing the contract. Investors will either agree to inefficient form contracts intended to evade fraud proscriptions or decline to trade at all. Eventually, this will create norms that undermine trust in the system overall.

Investment decisions are also colored by the false consensus effect, which causes people to believe that others see the world as they do.[28] Thus, honest people expect others to be honest, while those who are less trustworthy tend to be less trusting. This creates an arbitrary system in which investors assume (or refuse to assume) risks without regard to the true probability or magnitude of those risks. The flaw is compounded by the general inability of people to detect deception by others. Numerous studies have shown that the average person is not a good detector of others' dishonesty.[29]

In addition, people tend to be influenced by the salience of oral communications, which are more vivid, when the written contract disclaimers provide that the oral communications made in association with the investment are meaningless. Legal rules against fraud create a framework that promotes trust in these deals (by deterring brokers or others from committing fraud). Eliminating those legal rules sends a message to securities professionals and issuing companies that it is permitted (and therefore arguably ethical) to mislead investors. Ultimately, such a regime must result in an atmosphere of less trust and fewer transactions.

The prospect of contracting around fraud is not as threatening to the economic benefits of the securities laws as are many other proposed changes.

Most transactions in securities are executed in an anonymous marketplace. Governed by the Exchange Act, these transactions have no written contract between buyer and seller by which fraudulent misrepresentations may be evaded. Thus, this approach does not strike at the foundation of securities law, as do other proposals. Its primary effect is in protecting brokers or private issuers from fraud actions. However, allowing contracting around fraud raises precisely the same concerns, just on a smaller scale. Enforcing contracts that preclude fraud claims simply shifts some securities transactions from the regulatory scheme to a market-based scheme. The theoretical concerns about market costs and the empirical evidence amply confirm that this is an inefficient shift. It benefits individual potential defendants but inevitably undermines the capital markets generally.

ISSUER DEREGULATION

The US securities law system is primarily built around the regulation of issuers, the companies whose stock is traded. These are the entities that must make periodic filings with the SEC, reporting such information as revenues and profits. The public disclosure requirements tested in Chapter 5 involve disclosures by issuers. A recent article by Stephen Choi has called for a major restructuring in this system, which deregulates issuers in favor of investor regulation.[30]

Choi argues that the current model of regulating issuers is an inefficient, indirect regulation of investors that prevents them from making certain investments that they wish to make. He suggests that many rational investors inevitably lose out on desirable opportunities but recognizes that investors have various degrees of sophistication. He would recognize four different categories of investors, based on their level of knowledge. Then he would impose a sliding scale of restrictions on their investment choice, depending on the degree of their knowledge and sophistication. Well-informed investors would face relatively little regulation of their investment choices. They could freely bargain for just the level of disclosure and fraud protection that they desired, presumably paying more for their securities if they desired more protection and less if they were willing to take their chances. Unsophisticated investors would not be permitted to invest in any instruments other than passive mutual funds.

The underlying basis of Choi's creative proposal is that government rules inevitably interfere with efficient free markets. However, Choi largely ignores the ability of uniform rules to minimize transaction costs and create valuable network effects, or perhaps he just too casually assumes it away. Choi acknowledges that too many separate private fraud protection rules could produce mass confusion among investors. He suggests that such uncertainty and associated transaction costs might be reduced if regulators publicized the contents of the private rules selected by issuers on the Internet. Of course, any multiplication of choices involves greater transaction costs, and publicizing the mere content of contractual rules does little to reduce costs. The relevant issue is how those rules will be applied to a given investor's case, which would require ongoing monitoring of the judicial implementation of each of the rules, in all relevant jurisdictions. Basically, the proposal rests on an entirely unsupported assumption that sophisticated investors are better off with more risky options and much greater uncertainty and transaction costs associated with choosing among those options. Choi has no evidence for this claim.

Even assuming away the transaction costs problem, the issuer deregulation proposal has a significant agency problem. The individuals who would choose the menu of fraud protection options to be offered investors are the very corporate officers who are most likely to be sued under those options. They have every incentive to adopt a self-protective rule rather than the most economically efficient standard. Shareholder voting rights and other protections under corporate law are too weak to provide protection against this self-serving behavior. While such laws are important and produce benefits, the empirical evidence, such as that discussed in Chapter 5, demonstrates that corporate law is insufficient and inferior to securities law in producing economic benefits. In addition, allowing management to select a securities fraud regime adds yet another level of transaction costs for shareholders, monitoring management's actions in this regard. Intermediary monitors have proved ineffective at correcting this problem. Given the undeniable agency problems, there is no reason to believe that corporate managers will select economically optimum fraud protection, as opposed to self-interested decisions. Consider that during the dot.com boom, managers were happy to exaggerate earnings so that they could personally benefit by hitting stock option targets, even though their firms were then saddled with paying real income taxes on the imaginary earnings.[31]

Research in behavioral economics also counsels against Choi's proposal. Some overconfident investors will leap into markets without fraud protection, and while they will provide some capital, they will encourage fraudulent and inefficient use of those resources. Other more risk-averse investors and those who require assurances of fairness will stay out of the equity markets altogether, depriving them of capital. A program of investor education and regulation will not overcome these problems. The research shows that even educated professionals often employ inefficient behavioral heuristics in decisionmaking.[32] For example, studies have shown that professionals, including securities analysts, suffer biases such as overconfidence.[33]

Even proponents of greater investor education concede that it cannot effectively protect against fraud.[34] Other biases, such as the false consensus effect and other psychological susceptibilities noted in the previous section, also prevent Choi's efficient negotiation from occurring.[35] While these *ex ante* behavioral features also affect the current system, the status quo offers investors an effective remedy in the event of fraud, while the issuer deregulation plan could eliminate that remedy, by taking advantage of behavioral characteristics.

The clearest evidence against the issuer deregulation proposals lies in the empirical evidence. While no nation has regulated investors, the central part of Choi's proposal, from which its alleged merits emanate, is the deregulation of issuers. Many nations have limited regulation of issuers, with no public disclosure rules or other requirements. As detailed in Chapters 2 and 5, these nations have suffered from the lack of compulsory national issuer regulation for fraud. Nations with stronger issuer regulation have larger and more efficient stock markets. Natural experiments such as the developing markets of post-communist Eastern Europe show the same benefits of issuer regulation.

US history further confirms the value of issuer regulation. Prior to the creation of such regulation, there was little disclosure. The initial adoption of the 1933 and 1934 Acts had some positive effect on the stock market. Choi contends that investors will be able to bargain for contractual fraud protection, but this did not occur prior to federal intervention in the market. Observers of corporate disclosure practices at the time noted "the atmosphere of secrecy which prevails so widely in corporate circles."[36] The positive effect of securities regulation has grown over time, and again revealed its benefits when regulation is extended to new internal markets. The value provided foreign companies that voluntarily cross-list and assume US regulatory burdens (rather than contractually doing so) further establishes the economic virtues of uniform government securities regulation. The fact that other companies do not cross-list may simply be testimony to their inability or unwillingness to provide protections against fraud generally beneficial to investors.

Choi's plan of issuer deregulation and investor regulation is functionally little different from simply allowing an unregulated free market in securities. Its structure relies on the efficient market negotiation and implementation of contractual fraud protection schemes for investors. For the economic reasons set forth in Chapter 2 and the behavioral considerations of Chapter 3, this structure is an inferior one that will undermine capital markets. The theoretical response to this proposal is amply confirmed by the historical evidence described in Chapter 4 and the quantitative empirical analyses of Chapter 5. Bernie Black has concluded that the essential prerequisites for strong securities markets are laws that "give minority shareholders (1) good information about the value of a company's business; and (2) confidence that the company's insiders . . . won't cheat investors out of most of the value of their investment."[37] Issuer deregulation undermines both objections and thus would be an unwise modification to the current system of securities law. As Black stated elsewhere, "[i]t's magical, in a way. People pay enormous amounts of money for completely intangible rights. Internationally, this magic is pretty rare. It does not appear in unregulated markets."[38]

COMPETITIVE REGULATION

A relatively new reform proposal contends that competition among regulators can produce superior securities law. Competition could arise from various sources, but the primary proposal has involved creating competitive state securities regulation regimes. Securities regulation began at the state level with legislation commonly known as "blue sky laws" that were discussed in Chapter 4. The national securities laws and regulations were adopted precisely because this existing competitive state law regime was sorely inadequate. Some wish to restore states to primacy, though.

Roberta Romano has argued that securities regulation should be returned to the states in order to create competitive regulatory systems.[39] This approach would parallel current corporate law, in which companies may choose in which state to incorporate and thereby choose the rules that govern them. While Romano has suggested that states are "closer" to the affected bodies, the focus of her proposal stresses the benefits of competition among the producers of securities law.

Competition among states, Romano argues, gives regulators an incentive to be accountable and responsive to the demands of the regulated. By creating better securities regulations, the theory suggests that states will attract more companies and capital that adopt their rules. This would also act to spur innovative regulatory improvements. Attracting more companies could in turn attract more revenue through fee payments to the states. The states would engage in a competitive "race to the top" in pursuit of the best rules. The spur of competition would make the state actions preferable to those of the federal government.

One fundamental theoretical problem with this approach is its presumption that states will behave in an economically efficient manner in structuring their governing rules. Gillian Hadfield and Eric Talley have challenged this premise that states "behave like profit-maximizing firms, choosing laws and regulations that maximize state profits."[40] State legislators gain some benefit from creating efficient laws, and regulated parties have an opportunity to affect their decisions. Agency problems certainly infect governmental responses to public interest, as collective interests and lobbyists are certainly influential.

The operationalization of this competitive regime is also somewhat unclear, even if state governments did operate efficiently. A state's incentive to produce optimal securities law supposedly involves the receipt of fees. Yet there is no obvious reason why a company would be required to pay a fee to use a state's law. A company need not be located in a state, or even have any connection to a state, to use that law. "Choice of law" clauses in contracts are commonplace, and could adopt any state's law in connection with their share issuances. Such clauses would not necessarily extend to private secondary market sales of shareholders, but there is no obvious way that a state could profit from use of its law in such transactions. Indeed, the use of law in these sales would presumably raise choice of law issues beyond the control of the corporations that are supposedly selecting the laws, a problem discussed further below.

Even if the state governments did not engage in effective competition for optimal securities laws, competitive state regulation could theoretically still yield benefits by enabling companies to "vote with their feet" and choose the states with the best laws. They would have a menu of 50 laws from which to select. Assuming at least one of the state laws provided a better system than the current federal law, the ability of businesses to choose that better system could provide better regulation. Or perhaps different regimes better fit different types of companies, so the flexibility would be efficient.

The most obvious problem with this theory of state competition is that it allows the regulated entity to choose its regulator, which is akin to allowing the fox to guard the henhouse. The purpose of the securities laws is to protect investors, but they will not be choosing the state regulatory regime. Rather, this choice will inevitably be made by corporate management, which is the entity to be constrained by securities regulation. A management that wishes to defraud investors or simply wishes to preserve its flexibility would not choose the optimal system of securities regulation, it would choose the least constraining system. Rather than a "race to the top," we could have a "race to the bottom," with inefficient laws that fail to protect against fraud.[41] The adoption of anti-takeover statutes, provisions protecting directors from liability for their managerial shortcomings, and other recent changes in state corporate law are more consistent with a race to the bottom than one to the top.

Of course, management decisions are constrained to some degree by investors, as officers need to attract capital. Investors might prevent a true race to the absolute bottom, with management choosing the weakest securities regulations, but this does not eliminate the basic agency problem discussed in Chapter 2. For investors to constrain management in the choice of regulatory regime, they would have to familiarize themselves with the functioning of 50 state regimes. Managers are likely to forgo some investment and share price gain, in order to be able to immunize themselves (and their lucrative salaries) from oversight. This is another of the greatest shortcomings of the competitive state regulation approach, the transaction costs that it imposes.

Competitive state regulation would lose the foremost font of the benefits of securities regulation, which derive from reduced transaction costs and network effects. Investors would have significantly increased transaction costs under a competition program. They would have to familiarize themselves with the laws of 50 states. The laws could vary in innumerable ways, such as accounting standards, substantive fraud rules, procedural enforcement rules, and others. The investor effort would involve not only investigation of the legislation itself but also implementing administrative rules (which may change over time) and judicial interpretations of the law. Not only may these judicial interpretations change, but they also depend on the nature of the state's judicial system, the investigation into which represents yet another transaction cost. Moreover, investors would have to discern which state's law governs their potential lawsuit, a determination that could be quite complicated in practice. In the process, all the efficient simplifying network effects of a single fraud governance system are lost.

The choice of state laws that apply to a given case is an extraordinarily complex field of law. The general standards for such choice of law involve the state where the underlying events took place and the state with the greatest interest in its resolution. The underlying events in a securities fraud action would be the actual purchase or sale (which might be the location of the stock exchange on which the shares were traded) or the fraudulent actions complained of. The latter might well be the corporate headquarters where the primary officers were located but not necessarily, as the fraud might involve revenue recognition by lower level officers at various locales about the country or the state in which the company was incorporated (the source of its corporate governance law rules). This creates a substantial problem insofar as the applicable securities law will neither be clear to investors nor within the control of the corporation purportedly seeking the optimally efficient law to govern transactions in its securities. This problem substantially enhances both the transaction costs and risks for investors and undermines the claimed benefits of the competitive law selection system. The problem might be overcome by an arbitrary choice of law rule based on the company's adoption of particular securities laws but this would be a substantial departure from prevailing rules, losing their established benefits, and would also be difficult to enforce (as any given state would have the right to reject this standard).

The competitive system is also questionable in the light of behavioral decisionmaking analysis. The managers who make the decisions about choice of securities law will make self-serving decisions. If they did not do so, there would be no agency problem and no need for law whatsoever, and we could count on voluntary disclosure. Unfortunately, the reality is that even honest managers will be influenced by unconscious self-serving biases that infect their decisionmaking.

Behavioral considerations also affect the ability of investors to respond to managerial choices to use the securities laws of a particular state. Putting a market price on the difference between two state laws would be extremely difficult, especially when those laws may change and are substantially influenced by unknown future administrative interpretations and judicial rulings. It is "difficult to imagine how an investor would be able to judge the effectiveness of different regulatory regimes, much less quantify that knowledge in a manner allowing the investor to change the purchasing or selling price of a particular security."[42] Without this ability, investors are necessarily economically at sea, forced to make investment judgments they cannot accurately value or, if they are risk averse, avoid many investments due to the valuation uncertainty.

There is no empirical experience with competitive state securities laws by which this competitive regulation proposal may be tested, but there are some slightly analogous contexts to examine. Corporate law, for example, is largely left to state governance. In corporate law, Delaware has become the overwhelmingly preponderant source of law for major national corporations. This state primacy might be due to the fact that Delaware law is optimal, but this seems unlikely. More likely, the decision is attributable to network effects. Reincorporation to change the law of corporate governance is an extremely rare event, suggesting that the market is not truly competitive, and the predominance of Delaware law refutes suggestions that different firms could benefit from different laws. Moreover, other states have generally not even sought to compete with Delaware, because the tax receipts from being the locus of incorporation are quite small.[43] Instead, they have typically piggybacked upon such law, with limited exceptions such as anti-takeover laws, which are a dubious defense for state choice.

Additionally, the corporate law context is unaffected by the substantial choice of law problems, as the widespread "internal affairs doctrine" provides that corporate law cases are governed by the state of incorporation. When state corporate laws do change, state legislators appear to act to satisfy local constituencies, such as the demands of major employers, rather than in an effort to attract more corporations.[44] Delaware has become dominant, and network effects ensure that it preserves this position. Other states have largely adopted Delaware's law, rather than competing with it, and Romano concedes that the substantive content of the 50 state corporation laws is "substantially uniform."[45] Ninety-seven percent of new incorporations choose either Delaware or their home state, which does not suggest the presence of any meaningful competition.[46] In short, competition among states to provide corporate law is largely a myth and therefore provides no reasonable basis for arguing that a similar regime of competition to provide securities law could succeed. If there is no meaningful competition to provide corporate law, a realm where the states have been the primary providers for decades, how much less likely is it that there will be meaningful competition to provide securities law where the states have played only a supporting role (and have no obvious means of profiting)?

Europe has provided something of a natural experiment for such choice. While the continent has some coordinated governance, individual nations persist and historically established their own securities laws. This was a competitive system, though evidence indicates that it was not working efficiently.[47] This system recently changed as the European Union adopted uniform securities disclosure requirements in order to bring more consistency to regulation, as different standards were inhibiting cross-border trading. Inconsistent international standards were limiting the number of investors willing to purchase ownership from corporations governed by different laws. The continent harmonized its laws in order to provide stronger capital markets.[48] The mere fact that European governments are moving toward a centralized system and coordinated standards resembling the US model refutes competitive regulatory proposals, because those proposals rely on the assumption that governments will make efficient decisions.

In some respects, the competitive state regulation approach appears to offer the worst of both worlds. While the purported benefits of such competition arise from market-based checks on regulatory systems, it is inferior to a purely private system. In a private system, companies could design any investor protection scheme and implement it via contract. Regulatory competition loses much of this assumed competitive benefit, because it limits corporate choices to those offered by the states and requires formal government approval, legislative or bureaucratic, before any new systems could be implemented. The disadvantage of the purely private system lies in transaction costs and network effects (addressed in Chapter 2) and inefficient behavioral decisionmaking heuristics (addressed in Chapter 3). Regulatory competition suffers these same disadvantages. While transaction costs might be slightly reduced by the limit of regulations to 50 state systems, they would not be much reduced, given the need to understand and monitor

50 different systems, not to mention the interpretation of those systems by 50 different state court systems. State regulatory competition proposals thus offer nearly all the disadvantages of private systems with only a fraction of their benefits. Given the demonstrated empirical superiority of federal securities regulation over private systems, the competitive state system seems to offer a poor alternative.

A related proposal would not rely on state government regulation but instead on regulation by the private securities exchanges, on which stocks are listed for purchase and sale.[49] Unlike the states, stock markets do have a meaningful financial incentive to compete for listings and they do currently compete for this purpose. Although the New York Stock Exchange has long been predominant, it has increasingly faced competitors. Thus, actual competition among these groups has somewhat more potential.

Any competition plan, including one that uses the exchanges, suffers the same basic problems as state competition, however. The listing decisions remain under the control of management, which has a self-interest in suboptimal disclosure and suboptimal fraud protection. The exchanges existed before the Securities Act, but they displayed little sign of competing efficiently. As discussed in Chapter 4, before 1933, disclosures were minimal and fraud enforcement was spotty. When the great crooks of the 1920s, such as Ivar "The Match King" Krueger and Samuel Insull, needed to do so, they simply defied the exchange rules without any serious consequence. Exchanges will always be hard-pressed to enforce their rules against the very people who make the decision where to list. Former SEC chairman, Harvey Pitt, whose outlook was generally antiregulatory, noted that in such a system exchanges would not raise listing standards out of a fear "that to do so would give the other a competitive advantage."[50] Historically, competitive pressures have caused the exchanges to jettison stringent listing requirements whenever they threatened the exchanges' prosperity. In 2006, the Securities Industry Association proposed overhauling the separate regulatory rules of the exchanges in favor of a uniform set of self-regulatory standards for all, an action that does not suggest the promise of exchange competition.[51]

Even if exchanges had the will to enforce their rules, they lack the mechanism. They lack the force of law. Romano has observed that government regulation "does . . . offer some decided benefits over stock exchange regulation: a more effective mechanism of private dispute resolution for securities suits against issuers, and a public enforcement system, should the deterrent effect of criminal prosecution for securities law violations be a necessary complement to civil liability."[52] Exchanges have only a few remedies and enforcement tools at their disposal even if they wanted to punish disclosure violations or stop fraud by listing companies.[53] Lacking a mechanism for shareholder class actions, exchange-based regulation would be a poor mechanism for resolving disputes.[54]

Exchange competition also has transaction cost problems. Investors might readily familiarize themselves with the protections offered by a given exchange but would have to confine their investments to companies listed on that exchange. If the investors desired to invest in companies on another exchange, that would require additional transaction costs. If companies could readily swap exchanges, investors would be forced either to sell or undertake those costs. Indeed, a truly competitive exchange market would probably involve a great deal of company switching and thus investors would have to choose between a known fraud protection system or the companies in which they wish to invest. If companies could not readily switch exchanges, then if exchanges really did compete by changing legal regimes any benefit to shareholders would be minimal because they would be locked into the jurisdiction their firm first chose even if it were not the most efficient. Finally, all of the behavioral issues involving state competitive regulation apply to exchange regulation as well. For all these reasons, competitive regulation by exchanges would produce less disclosure and less effective fraud protection at a higher cost.

A third version of regulatory competition in securities law counts not on states or stock exchanges, but upon other nations to provide securities law regimes. Under such a plan, a Delaware corporation headquartered in California could choose to have transactions in its securities governed by the laws of France, Thailand, or Bolivia. Needless to say, all the complications noted above in terms of transaction costs and behavioral considerations would be multiplied under such a system. Furthermore, the best evidence indicates that the fees that might be generated by providing securities law would be so minimal that they would not interest the governments of the world's nations that could realistically provide the machinery for meaningful securities regulation.[55] For these reasons and many others,[56] regulatory competition to provide securities law has not been taken seriously and should not be.

SARBANES-OXLEY ACT

Perhaps the greatest current controversy in securities law (and corporate law) involves the Sarbanes-Oxley Act (known colloquially as "SOX"). In response to several huge corporate scandals (Enron, WorldCom, Tyco, Adelphia, and so on) Congress passed SOX in 2002. While America has a rich history of corporate scandals, the spate of corporate disasters that prompted the Act's passage was remarkable for its magnitude. This law made several significant changes in US securities regulation. Perhaps the best known of the new rules was a requirement in section 302 that corporate executives certify their financial statements as accurate. The requirement was designed to prevent officers from disclaiming awareness of false disclosures, which often was a central element in their defense, most notoriously in the case of Bernard Ebbers, the WorldCom chief executive officer. The law also required some additional disclosure requirements, such as faster disclosures of material changes in corporate financial condition (a change, by the way, that empirical studies indicate seems to have worked).[57]

Another important aspect of SOX involved the section 404 requirements for internal financial controls, the procedures used by corporations to ensure the accuracy of financial data reported to outside auditors and to protect against fraudulent reports. Officers were also required to certify that they had designed internal controls to ensure the accuracy of this information and produce an "internal control report" as part of each annual filing with the SEC.

The law created the Public Company Accounting Oversight Board (PCAOB) to establish rules governing auditing and to regulate firms auditing public companies in America. The law also strengthened insider trading regulation and increased the penalties imposed for legal violations. Although it is conceivable that the costs will outweigh the benefits, all these provisions should serve to strengthen the disclosure requirements of securities law, and should therefore benefit the securities markets which thrive when bountiful, accurate information flows. In addition, Chapter 3 explained how behavioral psychology shows that such requirements are vital to optimal corporate monitoring.

In addition to these modifications of federal securities law, the new statute placed restrictions on substantive corporate governance that went well beyond existing state law requirements. The most significant of these requires that board audit committees be comprised entirely of outside independent directors,[58] expands the powers of board audit committees, prohibits corporations from purchasing most nonauditing services from their outside auditors,[59] forces certain officers to disgorge their bonus compensation in the event of a material restatement of the company's financial reports,[60] and prohibits corporate loans to officers.[61]

Although the main purpose of these provisions was to improve the reliability of information reported under federal securities laws, some complained that they represented a partial nationalization of certain corporate law principles. The federal securities laws have historically focused on corporate disclosure and securities fraud. The SEC has generally ceded to the states jurisdiction over matters of corporate structure or internal obligations. However, the line between corporate law on the one hand and securities law on the other hand is exceedingly murky. Various aspects of federal securities law, such as those dealing with the proxy system and insider trading, have long directly impacted corporate governance.

In passing SOX, Congress determined that the existing state corporate rules enabled the cheating of investors (the agency problem) and that disclosure of corporate practices was insufficient to provide protection for them. Thus, the new law was actually a blend of securities law and corporate law. During the last 70 years or so an equilibrium has evolved such that "[w]hen a problem with national market implications arises, all parties expect the national system to address it."[62] Just as Hurricane Katrina demanded primarily a federal response, so did the Enron-era scandals. For Congress to sit on the sidelines because corporate board composition has traditionally been a concern of state law would have been comparable to FEMA turning its back on the survivors in the Superdome.

Law and economics scholars have harshly criticized much of Sarbanes-Oxley, claiming that the Act imposed inefficient requirements upon business. Much of the criticism of the Act has gone to the costs of compliance, which can be quite high. The primary source of these costs has been the new internal controls requirements. Some companies already had modern and efficient internal financial controls and their costs of compliance with SOX section 404 have been minimal. For other companies, though, compliance costs have been substantial.

SOX has clearly necessitated additional corporate spending on auditing, especially through its internal controls provision. A survey by Financial Executives International found that the cost of the internal controls compliance alone averaged US$4.36 million per company. Another study estimated average cost of US$3.5 million per company.[63] Another report estimated initial annual compliance costs of SOX at US$6.1 billion.[64] Litigation costs have also increased, as reflected in insurance premiums, but this might actually reflect a net benefit of the Act, given the evidence on the economic effects of private enforcement of securities law.[65] Where there is greater litigation risk, firms tend to release both good news and bad news earlier and with more precision.[66]

Some of the greater cost estimates for SOX compliance may prove exaggerated, because they involve one-time, rather than annualized, expenses. The Association of Finance Professionals estimated that costs would decline by 40 percent in just the second year of compliance.[67] A recent survey of practicing internal auditors found significant benefits stemming from improved internal financial controls and an expectation that costs would decrease as soon as effective controls are in place.[68] Once companies have brought their internal controls up to par, continuing costs will be much lower. Nonetheless, it is clear that SOX compliance costs have been high, much higher than the SEC had predicted. Current Commission efforts have sent a message that they will take a reasonable approach to assessing compliance to hold down costs.

Perhaps the greatest concern about SOX is the indirect cost associated with regulatory direction of business decisionmaking and associated inefficiencies. One widely publicized study examined the market reactions to legislative events during the passage of the statute and concluded that SOX resulted in a loss of US$1.4 trillion in total market value.[69] While this would be a profound negative effect, it reflected only the market's anticipation of SOX regulations and their effects, not the actual practice under the law. In addition, a different study used the same methodology of examining market reactions to SOX and reached exactly opposite conclusions. It found negative market effects while the application of the law was uncertain but significantly positive market effects once the precise obligations of those terms reached their final form, indicating that investors expected the Act to have a net beneficial effect on the market.[70] Another study found that SOX had a positive and statistically significant effect on the value of large companies, but not small ones,[71] while yet another indicated that its benefits exceeded its compliance costs.[72]

The contradictory event studies associated with enactment and implementation do not provide definitive guidance on the economic effect of SOX but suggest that its effect may well have been beneficial. The performance of the American stock market in the wake of the statute's passage indicates that it was successful in restoring the confidence of American investors, which had been at a post-9/11 low. Empirical research indicates that SOX restored investor confidence in the markets and restored liquidity that had been greatly reduced by Enron-era scandals.[73] Another post-SOX study found that investors value information about internal controls and that small investors benefited the most from disclosure of the information.[74] A survey of public company directors found that more than 60 percent believed that SOX had been positive for their companies.[75]

A major concern about SOX has been the fear that its costly requirements may promote "going private" or "going dark" (reducing the number of public shareholders below a certain threshold). If the costs of compliance were great, some companies might be expected to give up their publicly traded status and avoid those costs. There is evidence that this occurred, with an increase in going-private transactions following SOX. The increase was especially pronounced among smaller companies with relatively higher compliance costs.[76] This going private trend would be evidence of a negative effect of SOX, though other research suggests that the immediate increase in going-private transactions was unrelated to the statute.[77]

Other relevant research involves the effect of SOX on cross-listing behavior of foreign companies. A decrease in cross-listing would suggest that the additional compliance costs outweighed the bonding effects of this practice. Again, the evidence is conflicting. One study found that passage of the Act had a significant positive value on cross-listing companies, in nations with effective judiciaries.[78] A more recent study of the effects of the Act after a short time found that stocks of cross-listed companies declined significantly as compared to comparable companies in response to SOX.[79] This is probably the best evidence questioning SOX as a whole, but it did not address the effect of individual changes made by the statute. There is thus some evidence of a negative effect of SOX in the going-private and cross-listing evidence, but the case is not yet a conclusive one.

The evidence regarding SOX's most controversial provisions, those dealing with internal financial controls, especially section 404, is at this stage quite mixed. The debate over whether the benefits of these provisions outweigh the costs cannot currently be settled. Indeed, it may never be settled for the simple reason that although the costs of SOX in this regard are largely measurable, measuring the benefits is somewhat more elusive. The primary benefits of more effective internal financial controls will relate to the mismanagement, earnings management, frauds, and other crimes that will not occur. It is easy to measure the cost of installing a metal detector in an airport, but it is impossible to determine how many attempted hijackings or bombings its installation averted. The same is true with Sarbanes-Oxley's internal control provisions.

It is worth remembering that shareholder losses in Enron-era scandals totaled well over US$200 billion. The US$25 billion loss involving Enron alone will substantially outweigh even the most exaggerated estimates of total SOX implementation costs.[80] If SOX could indeed prevent or minimize the financial consequences of such scandals, it would have considerable benefit. The internal control rules were a sensible approach to preventing a reoccurrence of the Enron-era scandals, for empirical evidence indicates that before SOX was passed, firms with poor internal controls tended to have more restatements of their financial statements and other disclosure problems than did other firms.[81] Firms with weak internal controls also tend to engage in more earnings management.[82]

Studies of the actual impact of SOX's internal control provisions are somewhat encouraging. One study indicates that SOX's internal control provisions are leading managers to report financial results more conservatively.[83] Another study found that since SOX was passed firms discovering problems with their internal controls have tended to have poorer quality disclosures than other firms, indicating that sections 302 and 404 of SOX are appropriately helping identify the drivers of poor quality financial reporting and that overall financial reporting quality should improve as SOX kicks in.[84] An examination of market responses to internal control reports demonstrated that they provided valuable information to investors.[85] Another study found that investors value information about internal controls and that small investors have benefited most from the disclosure of this information.[86]

Professor Romano reviewed the empirical studies on the effect of the corporate certification requirement. These studies were inconsistent, with one showing no market effect from an untimely certification and the other showing that for some issuers (bank holding companies), the certification "provided new, and positive, information to the market."[87] In addition to the inconsistent results, the information available to conduct these studies was quite limited, and she appropriately cautioned against drawing any generalizations from their findings.

Recent research on the certification requirement is also somewhat more positive than portrayed previously by Romano. A study on the certification requirements of SOX not discussed by Romano found that investors responded favorably to certification events, to a degree that was both statistically and substantively significant.[88] Another found that certification narrowed bid-ask spreads and added valuable information and liquidity to capital markets.[89] Still a third additional study confirmed that certifications provided assurance to investors in certifying companies, as reflected in a higher share price for the certifying company.[90] Certification of controls under section 302, combined with the audits of internal controls required under section 404, combined to provide investors with much more timely information about internal control systems than had previously been available and market reaction to the information indicated that investors found it useful.[91] The available financial empirical evidence appears to provide strong support for the benefits of the SOX certification requirement.

The internal control requirements of SOX may also have some spinoff effects. For example, they are leading to the uncovering of more corporate violations of the Foreign Corrupt Practices Act (FCPA), which prohibits overseas bribes to gain business. FCPA prosecutions are up significantly, in substantial part due to corporations voluntarily self-reporting their newly discovered violations.[92] While there is no legal obligation to so report, companies are doing so out of a sense of responsibility instilled by SOX's demanding standards or, perhaps, in hopes of ensuring that they receive lighter punishment.

Professor Romano's discussion of the new requirements was part of perhaps the most comprehensive critical analysis of SOX that has been published. Romano's primary focus, however, was on the corporate governance requirements rather than the securities law changes.[93] She began by examining the political economy of the adoption of SOX. This included an intricate study of the procedure by which the law was passed and noted the Congressional disregard of evidence questioning the value of the new statutory mandates. She concluded that the law was a frantic overreaction to a perceived crisis, driven in significant part by entities that stood to benefit from enactment.

In addition to her procedural objections to how the Sarbanes-Oxley Act was enacted, Romano addressed empirical research regarding some of the corporate governance problems that SOX addresses. She began with director independence requirements and was able to reference a substantial research literature on the effect of independent directors in corporate governance and some research on the effect of independent directors on audit committees. She identified 16 studies that considered the latter question, a majority of which found no effect of this independence.[94] On the provision of nonaudit services, 19 of the 25 studies she reviewed found no connection between such acts and audit quality, while the other studies were not conclusive.[95] There was a general absence of empirical research on the officer loan prohibitions of SOX. This review, though, relied on the effect on corporate performance as reported by the company, not on the accuracy of financial reporting.

Considerable research shows that director independence improves financial reporting. Firms with more independent directors tend to have less earnings management,[96] fewer financial restatements,[97] and less corporate fraud.[98] Firms with a higher percentage of independent directors on their audit committees also tend to have less earnings management,[99] fewer financial restatements,[100] and less corporate fraud.[101] SOX's provisions are consistent with a large body of empirical literature to this effect.

Of course, SOX required that *all* members of the audit committee should be independent, and there is also evidence supporting the efficacy of that requirement. Goodwin and Yeo found that audit committees made up of all independent directors were more active in monitoring than were audit committees with some inside directors.[102] Bedard and colleagues found that audit committees composed solely of independent directors were correlated with less earnings management.[103] McMullen and Raghundun found that audit committees with all independent directors were less likely to restate their earnings and less likely to get into trouble with the SEC.[104]

Finally, SOX's requirement of at least one financial expert on the audit committee is also strongly supported in the empirical literature. Felo and colleagues found that having a financial expert on the audit committee was correlated to higher quality financial reporting.[105] Chtourou and colleagues found that having a financial expert on the audit committee reduced earnings management.[106] Abbott and colleagues found that audit committees without financial experts as members were more likely to be associated with restatements of financial statements.[107] And Krishnan found that audit committees with financial experts as members were less likely to have internal control problems.[108]

Most of the research referenced by Romano involved studies of relevant corporate practices *before* SOX was passed. On the other hand, research on the actual effect of the law has been somewhat more positive. Some of this research pertaining specifically to internal financial controls and officer certification was referenced above. Additionally, one study of earnings report manipulation (earnings management) found that managers had engaged in opportunistic behavior to increase their stock option values prior to SOX's passage and that there was a significant decline in earnings management after the passage of SOX.[109] This enhanced disclosure accuracy was surely of important benefit to markets. While it is still soon after passage, the preliminary research on the market effects of SOX demonstrates some clear benefits from reducing officer manipulation of the agency problem and better informing investors about corporate value.

The potential virtue of the Sarbanes-Oxley requirements is further confirmed by an interesting survey of corporate directors that took place in early 2002, before SOX was passed. The directors consistently favored more monitoring than was their practice. For example, 71 percent of the directors concluded that boards should hold executive sessions without the presence of the chief executive officer, but only 45 percent of the board actually did so.[110] Since SOX was passed, most of these desirable practices have increased. For example, the percentage of boards holding sessions without the CEO present has skyrocketed.[111] The Conference Board, an association of major US companies, also proposed reforms at about the time SOX was being implemented, and it basically supported the SOX legislation. This information surely provides more evidence of the agency problems that require substantial government regulation. Other indirect support for the value of Sarbanes-Oxley comes from the tendency of other developed nations to adopt similar requirements.[112]

Our theoretical defense of securities law can be used to justify only a portion of SOX. The theoretical and empirical analysis of law and corporate finance demonstrates the substantial merit of traditional securities disclosure requirements but is much weaker in showing a benefit from regulation of corporate governance practices (the focus of Romano's critique). There is certainly reason to question the value of the latter category of requirements. The main focus of criticism of SOX has involved the internal controls provisions, which should be beneficial to markets in the long term. The costs of these provisions may be excessive for small companies, though, and regulators are currently considering ameliorating the burden for smaller companies. SOX undoubtedly could benefit from some tailoring that may relax some requirements, but such adjustments should be grounded in the empirical evidence about the effects of the law and account for the demonstrated benefits of securities regulation for markets.

CONCLUSION

While the verdict is surely out for any particular change in US securities law, including the particular changes of the Sarbanes-Oxley Act, this analysis suggests that we should be wary of making deregulatory changes as to any basic matters. The case for many proposed deregulatory reforms fails to appreciate the value of the law. The reform proposals are all animated by a devotion to private ordering—allowing issuers and investors to define the scope of their obligations. Such private ordering is fundamental to the value of free markets but should not be worshipped so religiously. Proper legal structures not only do not hinder such private ordering, they are necessary for it to work efficiently.

Among the legal structures that facilitate markets is uniform, mandatory disclosure, and meaningful protection against securities fraud. Such a system has classical economic benefits by sparing investors the need to undertake extensive transaction costs or substantial risks. It has behavioral economic benefits by giving investors some comfort that they will not readily be defrauded and lack any remedy. By penalizing disclosure failures and fraud, the system deters their commission, to some degree, making the markets more welcoming and economically efficient. These claims are amply confirmed by the empirical evidence, in various contexts such as cross-country research and historical analyses. The empirical studies show that, whatever the benefits of the privatizing reforms, their costs to equity markets are greater.

The general benefits of securities regulation do not justify any and every new requirement. But the prevailing system of US securities regulation is working very well and has produced thriving markets. The corporate scandals that inspired SOX demonstrate that our system is flawed but suggest that past regulation may have been too weak rather than too strong. Moreover, despite that fraud, "the US economy and stock market have performed well both on an absolute basis and relative to other countries" over recent decades.[113] The success story of US securities law has made it a model for regulatory reforms in virtually all other developed nations.[114]

Given the demonstrable benefits of securities regulation, reformers therefore should bear the burden of proving the value of any major proposed modifications to that system. This proof must at minimum involve grappling with the transaction cost/network effect benefits of uniform fraud protection rules, as well as some consideration of the behavioral factors influencing human decisionmaking. It should also draw on empirical evidence about the actual effect of the proposed reform. The advocates of fundamental reform in US securities laws have not even come close to meeting those logical burdens for most of their proposed changes.

NOTES

1. Richard H. McAdams, *An Attitudinal Theory of Expressive Law*, 79 OR. L. REV. 339, 389 (2000).
2. *See* Alan Strudler & Eric W. Orts, *Moral Principle in the Law of Insider Trading*, 78 TEX. L. REV. 375 (1999).
3. Henry G. Manne, INSIDER TRADING AND THE STOCK MARKET (1966).
4. *Id.* at 116.
5. *See* Dennis W. Carlton & Daniel R. Fischel, *The Regulation of Insider Trading*, 35 STAN. L. REV. 857 (1983).
6. *See* Harold Demsetz, *Corporate Control, Insider Trading and Rates of Return*, 76 AM. ECON. REV. 313 (1986).
7. Kimberly D. Krawiec, *Privatizing "Outsider Trading,"* 41 VA. J. INT'L L. 693 (2001).
8. 401 F.2d 833 (2d Cir. 1968).
9. *See* Lawrence M. Ausubel, *Insider Trading in a Rational Expectations Economy*, 80 AM. ECON. REV. 1022 (1990).
10. United States v. O'Hagan, 521 U.S. 642 (1997).
11. S.C. Udpa, *Insider Trading and the Information Content of Earnings*, 23 J. BUS. FIN. & ACCOUNTING 1069 (1996).
12. *See* Robert J. Haft, *The Effect of Insider Trading Rules on the Internal Efficiency of the Large Corporation*, 80 MICH. L. REV. 1051 (1982).
13. Lucian Bebchuk & Jesse Fried, PAY WITHOUT PERFORMANCE THE UNFULFILLED PROMISE OF EXECUTIVE COMPENSATION (2004).
14. Qiang Cheng & Terry D. Warfield, *Equity Incentives and Earnings Management* (November 2004), *available at* http://ssrn.com/abstract=457840.
15. Jap Efendi, Anup Srivastava, & Edward P. Swanson, *Why Do Corporate Managers Misstate Financial Statements? The Role of In-the-Money Options and Other Incentives* (September 4, 2005), *available at* http://ssrn.com/abstract=547922.
16. James S. Ang. & Don. R. Cox, *Controlling the Agency Cost of Insider Trading*, 10 J. FIN. & STRATEGIC DECISIONS 15 (1997).
17. *See* Herbert Gintis, *et al.*, *Moral Sentiments and Material Interests: Origins, Evidence, and Consequences*, in MORAL SENTIMENTS AND MATERIAL INTERESTS: THE FOUNDATIONS OF COOPERATION IN ECONOMIC LIFE 8 (Herbert Gintis, et al eds. 2005).
18. *See* Robert A. Prentice & Jonathan J. Koehler, *A Normality Bias in Legal Decision Making*, 88 CORNELL L. REV. 583, 606–12 (2003).
19. Robert A. Prentice, *Contract-Based Defenses in Securities Fraud Litigation: A Behavioral Analysis*, U. ILL. L. REV. 337, 376 (2003).
20. Laura Nyantung Beny, *Do Insider Trading Laws Matter? Some Preliminary Comparative Evidence*, 7 AM. LAW & ECON REV. 144 (2005).
21. Utpal Bhattacharya & Hazem Daouk, *The World Price of Insider Trading*, 57 J. FIN. 75 (2002).
22. Pankav Jain, *Institutional Design and Liquidity at Stock Exchanges Around the World* (January 2002).

23. Robert M. Bushman, Joseph D. Piotroski, & Abbie J. Smith, *Insider Trading Restrictions and Analysts' Incentives to Follow Firms*, 60 J. FIN. 35 (2005).
24. Julan Du & Shang-Jin Wei, *Does Insider Trading Raise Market Volatility*, 114 ECON. J. 916 (2004).
25. Tomasz P. Wisniewski, *Reexamination of the Link Between Insider Trading and Price Efficiency*, 28 ECON. SYSTEMS 209 (2004), *available at* www.sciencedirect.com/science/article/B6W8Y-4CVX0YT-1/2/01c276b6edf476dfba6fe0ec26f321e9.
26. Carr v. CIGNA Securities, Inc., 95 F.3d 544 (7th Cir. 1996).
27. William N. Landes & Richard A. Posner, THE ECONOMIC STRUCTURE OF TORT LAW 280–81 (1987).
28. Lee Ross, et al., *The "False Consensus Effect": An Egocentric Bias in Social Perception and Attribution Processes*, 17 J. EXPERIMENTAL SOC. PSYCHOL. 279 (1977).
29. Joseph W. Rand, *The Demeanor Gap: Race, Lie Detection, and the Jury*, 33 CONN. L.REV. 1, 3 (2000).
30. Stephen Choi, *Regulating Investors Not Issuers: A Market-Based Proposal*, 88 CAL. L. REV. 279 (2000).
31. *See* Merle Erickson, Michelle Hanlon, Michelle, & Edward L. Maydew, *Is There a Link Between Executive Compensation and Accounting Fraud?* (February 24, 2004), *available at* http://ssrn.com/abstract=509505.
32. Robert A. Prentice, *Chicago Man, K-T Man, and the Future of Behavioral Law and Economics*, 56 VAND. L. REV. 1663 (2003).
33. *See* Gary Belsky & Thomas Gilovich, WHY SMART PEOPLE MAKE BIG MONEY MISTAKES—AND HOW TO CORRECT THEM 152 (1999).
34. James A. Fanto, *We're All Capitalists Now: The Importance, Nature, Provision and Regulation of Investor Education*, 49 CASE W. RES. L. REV. 105, 135 (1998).
35. Robert A. Prentice, *Whither Securities Regulation? Some Behavioral Observations Regarding Proposals for its Future*, 51 DUKE L.J. 1397 (2002).
36. Matthew Josephson, *Infrequent Corporation Reports Keep Investors in Dark*, 36 MAG. OF WALL ST. 302, 374 (June 20, 1925).
37. Bernard Black, *The Legal and Institutional Preconditions for Strong Securities Markets*, 48 UCLA L. REV. 781, 783 (2001).
38. Bernard S. Black, *Information Asymmetry, the Internet, and Securities Offerings*, 2 J. SMALL & EMERGING BUS. L. 91, 92–93 (1998).
39. Roberta Romano, THE ADVANTAGE OF COMPETITIVE FEDERALISM FOR SECURITIES REGULATION (2002).
40. Gillian K. Hadfield & Eric L. Talley, *On Public Versus Private Provision of Corporate Law 11*, University of Southern California Law & Economics Research Paper No. 04–118 (2004).
41. *See e.g.*, William L. Cary, *Federalism and Corporate Law: Reflections upon Delaware*, 83 YALE L.J. 663 (1974).
42. David S. Ruder, *Reconciling U.S. Disclosure Policy with International Accounting and Disclosure Standards*, 17 NW. J. INT'L L. & BUS. 1, 10 (1996).
43. *See* Marcel Kahan & Ehud Kamar, *The Myth of State Competition in Corporate Law*, 55 STAN. L. REV. 679, 687–88 (2002).
44. *Id*. at 701–24.
45. Romano, *supra* note 39, at 21.
46. Robert Daines, *The Incorporation Choices of IPO Firms*, 77 N.Y.U. L. REV. 1559, 1562 (2002).
47. Klause Heine & Wolfgang Kerber, *European Corporate Laws, Regulatory Competition and Path Dependence*, 13 EUROPEAN J. LAW ECON. 47 (2002).
48. Eric Pan, *Harmonization of U.S.–EU Securities Regulation: The Case for a Single European Securities Regulator*, LAW & POLICY IN INT'L BUS (Winter 2003).
49. Mahoney and Pritchard have made the most persuasive cases for an increased role for securities exchanges in securities. Paul G. Mahoney, *The Exchange as Regulator*, 83 VA. L. REV. 1453 (1997); Adam C. Pritchard, *Markets as Monitors: A Proposal to Replace Class Actions with Exchanges as Securities Fraud Enforcers*, 85 VA. L. REV. 925 (1999).

50. Albert B. Crenshaw, *SEC to Toughen Rule on Option Plans*, WASHINGTON POST, December 20, 2001, at E1.
51. Jenny Anderson, *Should the Securities Industry Have Just One Set of Rules?*, N.Y. TIMES, January 25, 2006, at C3.
52. Romano, *supra* note 39, at 145.
53. Edward Rock, *Securities Regulation as Lobster Trap: A Credible Commitment Theory of Mandatory Disclosure*, 23 CARDOZO L. REV. 695, 697 (2002) (noting numerous limitations of the NYSE and other exchanges, especially an inability to impose criminal sentences).
54. Roberta Romano, *Empowering Investors: A Market Approach to Securities Regulation*, 107 YALE L.J. 2359 (1998).
55. Frederick Tung, *Lost in Translation: From U.S. Corporate Charter Competition to Issuer Choice in International Securities Regulation*, 39 GA. L. REV. 525, 590–91 (2005).
56. One of the authors has addressed these matters in some detail. Robert A. Prentice, *Regulatory Competition in Securities Law: A Dream (that Should Be) Deferred*, 66 OHIO ST. L.J. 1155 (2005).
57. Lisa Bryant-Kutcher, Emma Yan Peng, & Kristina Zvinakis, *Timeliness and Quality of 10-K Filings: The Impact of the Accelerated Filing Deadline* (June 3, 2005). These authors found that the quality of filings did not diminish after the SEC shortened the deadline for filing 10-Ks from 90 days to 75 days, as critics had predicted. Therefore, under the new rules, investors were receiving just as reliable information in a timelier fashion.
58. Independent directors are those who are not officers, nor controlled by officers or controlling corporate shareholders.
59. Much of the blame in the major corporate scandals provoking SOX was placed at the feet of outside auditors, who approved fraudulent financial statements. The argument was that the auditors did so in order to preserve their more lucrative income received from providing consulting and other services to the very companies that they were auditing.
60. Sarbanes-Oxley Act, S. 304.
61. *Id* S. 402.
62. *See* William W. Bratton & Joseph A. McCahery, *The Equilibrium Content of Corporate Federalism* 12 (October 2004), ECGI – Law Working Paper 23/2004, *available at* http//ssrn.com/abstract=606481.
63. William J. Carney, *The Costs of Being Public After Sarbanes-Oxley: The Irony of Going Private* 55 EMORY L.J. 141 (2006).
64. Larry E. Ribstein, *Sarbanes-Oxley after Three Years*, University of Illinois Law & Economics Research Papter No. LE05–016, 378 (2005).
65. *Id.* at 6.
66. Stephen Brown, et al., *Management Forecasts and Litigation Risk* (April 2005), *available at* http://ssrn.com/abstract=709161.
67. *See* www.afponline.org/pub/res/news/ns_20051229_cs.html.
68. Larry E. Rittenberg & Patricia K. Miller, *Sarbanes-Oxley Section 404 Work: Looking at the Benefits*, Institute of Internal Auditors. Research Foundation (November 9, 2005), *available at* www.theiia.org/?doc_id=5161.
69. Ivy Xiying Zhang, *Economic Consequences of the Sarbanes-Oxley Act of 2002* (February 2005).
70. Haidan Li, Morton Pincus, & Sonja O. Rego, *Market Reaction to Events Surrounding the Sarbanes-Oxley Act of 2002* (January 11, 2006).
71. Vidhi Chhaochharia & Yaniv Grinstein, *Corporate Governance and Firm Value : The Impact of the 2002 Governance Rules* (June 2004).
72. Zabihollah Rezaee & Pankaj K. Jain, *The Sarbanes-Oxley Act of 2002 and Security Market Behavior: Early Evidence* (May 2005).
73. Pankaj K. Jain, Jang-Chul Kim, & Zabihollah Rezaee, *The Effect of the Sarbanes-Oxley Act of 2002 on Market Liquidity* (March 2004), *available at* http://ssrn.com/abstract=488142.

74. Gus De Franco, Yuyan Guan, & Hai Lu, *The Wealth Change and Redistribution Effects of Sarbanes-Oxley Internal Control Disclosures* (April 17, 2005), *available at* http://ssrn.com/abstract=706701.
75. Cynthia Harrington, *The Value Proposition*, J. ACCOUNTANCY, 77 (September 2005).
76. Stanley B. Block, *The Latest Movement to Going Private: An Empirical Study*, 14 J. APPLIED FIN. 36 (2004).
77. Peter C. Hsu, *Going Private : A Response to an Increased Regulatory Burden?*, UCLA School of Law-Econ. Research Paper No. 04–16 (May 2004).
78. Philip G. Berger, Feng Li, & M.H. Franco Wong, *The Impact of Sarbanes-Oxley on Foreign Private Issuers* (October 21, 2004).
79. Kate Litvak, *The Effect of the Sarbanes-Oxley Act on Non-US Companies Cross-Listed in the U.S.*, U. of Texas Law and Econ. Research Paper No. 55 (December 22, 2005).
80. Pamela MacLean, *"SOX" inspires Backlash—and Benefits*, NAT'L L.J. (April 22, 2005).
81. Hollis Ashbaugh-Skaife, Daniel W. Collins, & William R. Kinney, Jr., *The Discovery and Consequences of Internal Control Deficiencies Prior to SOX-Mandated Audits*, McCombs Working Paper No. ACC-02–05 (September 15, 2005), *available at* http://ssrn.com/abstract=694681.
82. Kam C. Chan, Barbara R. Farrell, & Picheng Lee, *Earnings Management and Return-Earnings Association of Firms Reporting Material Internal Control Weaknesses Under Section 404 of the Sarbanes-Oxley Act* (June 2005), *available at* http://papers.ssrn.com/sol3/papers.cfm?abstract_id=744806.
83. Gerald J. Lobo & Jian Zhou, *Did Conservatism in Financial Reporting Increase after the Sarbanes-Oxley Act? Initial Evidence*, 20 ACCT. HORIZONS 57 (2006).
84. Jeffrey T. Doyle, Ge Weili, Ge, & Sarah E. McVay, Accruals Quality and Internal Control over Financial Reporting, AAA 2006 Financial Accounting and Reporting Section (FARS) Meeting Paper (August 2005), *available at* http://ssrn.com/abstract=789985.
85. Jacqueline S. Hammersley, Linda A. Myers, & Catherine Shakespeare, *Market Reactions to the Disclosure of Internal Control Weaknesses and to the Characteristics of those Weaknesses under Section 302 of the Sarbanes Oxley Act of 2002* (October 2005).
86. Gus De Franco, Yuyan Guan, and Hai Lu, *The Wealth Change and Redistribution Effects of Sarbanes-Oxley Internal Control Disclosures* (April 17, 2005) *available at* http://ssrn.com/abstract=706701.
87. *See* Roberta Romano, *The Sarbanes-Oxley Act and the Making of Quack Corporate Governance*, 114 YALE L.J. 1521, 1542 (2005).
88. *See* Paul A. Griffin & David H. Lont, *Taking the Oath: Investor Response to SEC Certification Under Sarbanes-Oxley* (April 30, 2004).
89. Pankav K. Jain, Jang-Chul Kim, & Zabihollah Rezaee, *Have the Sarbanes-Oxley Act of 2002 and the CEO Certifications Made the Market Participants More Informed* (January 2003).
90. Hsihui Chang, Jeng-Fang Chen, & Woody M. Liao, *CEO's/CFO's Swearing by the Numbers: Does It Impact Share Price of the Firm?* (October 2003).
91. Hammersley, Myers, & Shakespeare, *supra* note 85.
92. Michael T. Burr, *Corporations Caught in Rising Tide of FCPA Enforcement*, CORPORATE LEGAL TIMES, November 2005, at 22.
93. *See* Romano, *supra* note 87.
94. *Id*. at 1530–32.
95. *Id*. at 1535–36.
96. April Klein, *Audit Committee, Board of Director Characteristics, and Earnings Management*, 33 J. ACCT. & ECON. 375 (2002).
97. Anup Agrawal & Sahiba Chadha, *Corporate Governance and Accounting Scandals*, 48 J. L. & ECON. 371 (October. 2005).
98. Mark S. Beasley, *An Empirical Analysis of the Relations Between the Board of Director Composition and Financial Statement Fraud*, 71 ACCT. REV. 443 (1996).
99. Sonda M.Chtourou, Jean Bedard, & Lucie Courteau, *Corporate Governance and Earnings Management* (April 21, 2001) *available at* http://ssrn.com.abstract=275053.

100. Lawrence J. Abbott, Susan Parker, & Gary F. Peters, *Audit Committee Characteristics and Financial Misstatement: A Study of the Efficacy of Certain Blue Ribbon Committee Recommendations*, 23 AUDITING: A J. OF PRAC. & THEORY 69 (March 2004).
101. Mark S. Beasley, et al., *Fraudulent Financial Reporting: Consideration of Industry Traits and Corporate Governance Mechanisms*, 14 ACCT. REV. 441 (2000).
102. Jennie Goodwin & Tech Yeow Yeo, *Two Factors Affecting Internal Audit Independence and Objectivity: Evidence from Singapore*, 5 INT'L J. AUDIT. 107, 116 (2001).
103. Jean Bedard, et al., *The Effect of Audit Committee Expertise, Independence, and Activity on Aggressive Earnings Management*, 23 AUDITING: A J. OF PRAC. & THEORY 13 (September 2004).
104. Dorothy A. McMullen & K. Raghundan, *Enhancing Audit Committee Effectiveness*, 182 J. ACCTCY. 79 (August 1996).
105. Andrew J. Felo, et al., *Audit Committee Characteristics and the Perceived Quality of Financial Reporting: An Empirical Analysis* (April 2003), *available at* http://ssrn.com/abstract=401240.
106. Sonda M.Chtourou, Jean Bedard, & Lucie Courteau, *Corporate Governance and Earnings Management* (April 21, 2001), *available at* http://ssrn.com/abstract=275053.
107. Lawrence J. Abbot, et al., *Audit Committee Characteristics and Financial Misstatement: A Study of the Efficacy of Certain Blue Ribbon Committee Recommendations*, 23 AUDITING: A J. OF PRAC. & THEORY 69 (March 2004).
108. Jayanthi Krishnan, *Audit Committee Quality and Internal Control: An Empirical Analysis*, 80 ACCT. REV. 649 (2005).
109. Daniel A. Cohen, Aiyesha Dey, & Thomas Z. Lys, *Trends in Earnings Management and Informativeness of Earnings Announcements in the Pre- and Post-Sarbanes Oxley Periods* (February 2005).
110. *See* Bengt Holmstrom & Steven N. Kaplan, *The State of U.S. Corporate Governance: What's Right and What's Wrong*, NBER Working Paper No. 9613, 18 (April 2003).
111. *See* Lina Saigol, *Fewer Willing to Take Director Risk*, FIN. ANCIAL TIMES, November 24, 2004, at 22.
112. *See* Robert A. Prentice, *The Inevitability of a Strong SEC*, 91 CORNELL L. REV. 775 (forthcoming) (describing the popularity of American-style securities regulation in Asian and European nations).
113. Bengt Holmstrom & Steven N. Kaplan, *The State of U.S. Corporate Governance: What's Right and What's Wrong*, NBER Working Paper No. 9613 (April 2003) at Table 1.
114. *See* Gerard Hertig, *Convergence of Substantive Law and Enforcement*, in CONVERGENCE AND PERSISTENCE IN CORPORATE GOVERNANCE 33, 53 (Jeffrey N. Gordon & Mark J. Roe eds. 2004).

Index

Titles of publications and legal cases are in *italics*.

Index 229

Roe, M. 187–8
Romano, R. 202, 207, 213–14
rule of law, factor analysis 175

Sale, H.A. 100
salience of oral communication, and
    fraud 100
Sarbanes-Oxley Act (SOX) 18–19, 59,
    92, 128, 136–7, 208–16
SEC, *see* Securities Exchange
    Commission
SEC v. *Texas Gulf Sulphur Co.* 192
Securities Act 15–16, 136
    fraud provisions 140, 197
    and return on investment 59–60
Securities Exchange Act 16–18, 136–7
    fraud provisions 140, 197
    and insider trading 142
    and mandatory disclosure 60
Securities Exchange Commission
    (SEC) 2, 16, 102–3, 182
securities law 8, 15–19
    America, *see* America, securities law
    analysis of variables 172–4
    and acquisitions 61
    and behavioral decision theory
        93–101
    benefits 59–63
    costs 64–5
    development 129–47
    economics of 51–63
    effect of public enforcement 181–2
    factor analysis 176, 180
    and financial development 153–4,
        176, 180–82, 186
    fraud provisions 20, 54–6
    government role 101–3
    and network externalities 57
    studies 59–63, 153–4
    valuation 187
    variables 160–61
Securities Litigation Uniform
    Standards Act (SLUSA) 15,
    16–17
self-serving bias 72
    and auditor failure 88
separate legal identity, corporations
    118–19
shareholder protection 125–7
    effect on company value 153

Shavell, S. 4
Shleifer, A. 81
Simon, H. 72
Sloan, L. 136
Smith, A. 123
social norms and corporate disclosure
    96
social welfare, effect of financial
    markets 6
South Sea Bubble 132
SOX, *see* Sarbanes-Oxley Act
state law 9–10
    securities regulation 60–61, 202–7
status quo bias
    and contract law 83–4
    and corporate disclosure 95–6
    and decisionmaking 78
    and fraud protection 100
stock issuers, opportunism 40
stockbrokers and behavioral decision
    theory 93–4
Stout, L.A. 90, 90–91, 118
sunk cost effects and decisionmaking
    78
sunk costs, private intermediaries
    42–3

takeovers, regulation 143–7
Talley, E. 202
Taylor, M. 29–30
tender offer regulation, Williams Act
    17
Thaler, R.H. 80
time delay traps and decisionmaking
    78–9
tort law development 114–16
transaction costs
    and exchange competition 208
    and insider trading 194
    and law 22
transactions
    effect of law 37–9
    monitoring, private intermediaries
        39–44
    and trust 28–9
trust
    and basic law 29–31
    and commercial transactions 28–9,
        84–5
    and corporate governance 90